PSYCHOTHERAPY THROUGH IMAGERY

———————————— Joseph E. Shorr, Ph. D.

To Mary Anne & Joe with love — Joe

INTERCONTINENTAL MEDICAL BOOK CORPORATION
New York

Contents

Copyright © 1974
Intercontinental Medical Book Corporation
381 Park Avenue South
New York, N. Y. 10016

LC 74-4114
ISBN 0-913258-19-9
Printed in U. S. A.

Introduction

Most books on psychotherapy are hackneyed retreads with very little new or valuable for the practicing psychotherapist to sink his teeth into. I am very pleased to say that *Psychotherapy through Imagery* is a rare exception to this trend. Dr. Shorr is advancing the state of the art by creating new concepts and psychotechnologies.

His most singular contribution, in my opinion, is his own original emphasis upon imagery. Psychodrama, for example, uses the protagonist's imagination to set the stage and plot for action — which is the main element, not the imager. Gestalt therapy employs a multitude of vehicles, including action, abreaction or fantasy, with one or the other superordinate at the therapist's discretion. Behavior therapy, particularly implosive therapy and counterconditioning (desensitization), uses fantasy as only one method among others to promote extinction of undersirable responses. While psychoanalysis relies heavily upon fantasy in dream analysis, many classical analysts still tend to see imagery as defensive — a thing to work through or around rather than to produce as a means of reaching deeper into the primitive recesses of the unconscious. Jungian analysis and psychosynthesis stress the symbolic use of imagery for conflict identification and resolution, whereas Dr. Shorr stresses the greater impact and generalization to real life situations of concrete, personified imagery. However, Psychosynthesis probably comes closest to rivaling Dr. Shorr's great attention to fantasy, but restricts it to standard, fantasy-inducing procedures. In contrast, Dr. Shorr's Psycho-Imagination Therapy provides the means to generate an infintely possible variation of techniques. Psychosynthesis also lacks a defined theoretical backbone and is more of a general movement, contrasted to the specificity of Psycho-Imagination Therapy's existential and phenomenological frameworks. Nevertheless, both therapies share the common assumption that imagination is the direct pathway to the unconscious, unlike psychoanalysis.

The content of Psycho-Imagination Therapy realizes an old ideal of clinical psychologists to use psychodiagnostic testing therapeutically. Psycho-Imagination Therapy is a verbal and imagistic analog of popular projective tests. For example, Imaginary Situations (IS), e.g., "Imagine taking a journey through someone's body!", resembles the somewhat realistic though structured projective stimuli of the T.A.T. The more abstract the imaginary situation, the more like a Rorschach the stimuli become. Dr. Shorr's Finish the Sentence (FTS) statements, e.g., "never refer to me as ————," directly simulate the Incomplete Sentence Blank. In the therapy process, a multitude of such fantasy-inducing vehicles is employed consecutively with such variety that neurotic conflicts begin to emerge clearly from this heterogeneous background with striking poignancy for both patient and therapist. Thus, Psycho-Imagination Therapy becomes, in effect, what the classical Rorschach was always supposed to be, an X-ray of the personality.

By no menas are Dr. Shorr's techniques applied randomly. "Psychotherapy through Imagery" vividly shows Dr. Shorr's incisive intentionality in using these methods to help patients become more acutely aware of their neurotic conflicts, of their "alien" versus "true and emerging" identities, of how they were defined falsely by significant others, of their self-defeating reactions to their "alien" internalized self-attributes, of their need and lack of self-confirmation by others and of their inability to make a significant difference to someone.

As conflict awareness increases, Dr. Shorr encourages patients to confront their "false definers'" fantasized presence. Dr. Shorr frequently lends his ego to the patient by entering the fantasy situation in a supportive role.

Through a rich assortment of case illustrations, Dr. Shorr's very active, emphathetic, warm approach to patients comes through strongly, along with a willingness to help the patient venture into very primitive areas of conflict. So many ingenious techniques, with lucid rationales and methodologic instructions, flow from each page that after awhile the reader may feel somewhat inundated by examples. However, the serious practitioner with the patience to pore through the book carefully will certainly absorb the quintessence of Psycho-Imagination Therapy.

I would also strongly recommend Dr. Shorr's first book, *Psycho-Imagination Therapy*, as a preamble to this one, since it provides an excellent overview of the whole therapeutic process. In contract, this work puts Psycho-Imagination Therapy in historical perspective, describes more sophisticated and comprehensive procedures and demonstrates group therapy applications.

In brief, the uniqueness of Dr. Shorr's contributions rests not only in his pervasive commitment to imagination as a therapeutic mechanism but also in his singular projective process, his simplication and practical application of complex existential and phenomenologic concepts and his psychotechnologic innovations, e.g., bipolarization, Dual Imagery and Task Imagery. For example, in Dual Imagery, he will have a patient imagine two animals walking down a road and having a dialogue together. The two animals often become the clear representations of the bipolarized sides of a neurotic conflict. When he has the patient imagine the animals fighting, the nature of the conflict often becomes clearer. In Task Imagery, he places the patient in an imaginary situation in which the patient has to "work through" a problem, e.g., building a bridge across a gorge or hacking a road through thick jungle brush. Often in imagining these situations, the patient vividly reveals resistances. One has to see the process in action in order to truly appreciate the uniqueness of Psycho-Imagination Therapy.

As an interested colleague and friend of the writer, I feel strongly that the therapeutic community will benefit greatly by becoming more acquainted with "Psycho-Therapy through Imagery." I feel that Psycho-Imagination Therapy is now ready for a complete case study to be presented in book form that would reveal the intricacies of the process over time and in depth. As the patient becomes healthier, it would be fascinating to observe the transformation from pathologic to constructive imagery. In view of Dr. Shorr's extremely prolific activity in recent years, I wouldn't be surprised if such a work or comparable offering appeared in the near future.

Dr. Shorr silences those critics who have decried the lack of imagination in therapeutic procedures. The range of patient imagery and therapist ingenuity is comprehensively presented in such an original manner that one can only wonder what exciting vistas are ahead. This book is impressively rich in clinical material and fulfills the demands of creative therapy.

Dr. Peter Wolson

President, Los Angeles, Society of Clinical Psychologists

Preface

It seems ordinary to say one owes it all to one's patients. Not with me. For without their imagery productions, difficulties, tendencies, unique styles and feelings, the explorations would be severely limited. The infinite range and variety of visual imagery in psychotherapeutic experience are oftentimes dazzling. Added to this are some spectacular individual variations, ubiquitously unfolding and providing fresh challenges to meanings. The imagery can have the quality of mystery that each newborn child possesses. What will it look like? What will it grow into? What will it be?

As a result, most of the formulations about imagery come from reported and observable experiences, including my own imagery.

How a person changes in psychotherapy is a fascinating process. But, fascinating as it may be, it is also multifaceted, complex, sometimes inexplicable, sometimes dramatic. In this book I emphasize the use of imagery in the process of psychotherapy, but I do not believe imagery in and of itself is all of what makes people change in the course of therapy. To my way of thinking it is one of the most important dimensions that can be utilized in therapy, but we have only opened the doors. There is more to learn and do. A few years ago I never imagined what new dimensions imagery had in store for me. I cannot exactly imagine what lies ahead. When I close my eyes I see a beautiful field of flowers with the purple mountains in the distance. What does it mean? Time will tell.

In human experience when men spoke of the "five senses," vision was considered the noblest. Today the special status or significance of vision has lost none of its importance. Most of us can experience much more of the world visually than through any other sense modality. We can perceive visually events and objects distant and near and otherwise not available to our senses. Visual memory, moreover, seems to be especially vivid and permanent; we are more likely to forget or mistake someone's voice than his face, and it is easier to summon up a visual image than a tactile or olfactory one.

I refer to "imagery" essentially as visual imagery. On occassion, I might ask a person to imagine listening to some other person speaking to him; or how he or she might feel touching others or solid substances or how certain imagined substances might taste. The auditory, olfactory and tactile images are not omitted, but the visual predominates.

vi

Imagery seems to play a part in nearly all of the proliferating new psychotherapeutic techniques. When solid theoretical constructs as the source of these techniques are not incorporated, we are on shaky ground. Spectacular use of imagery is no substitute for experience in the solid use of imagery. That is why I have tried to connect theoretical bases for the specific uses of imagery. Otherwise, transfer of skill is technique-centered and can leave the therapist bereft of genuine resource and theory.

Apart from therapy, human curiosity and imagination appears mired in contemporary man beset by an alienated, sometimes meaningless, sometimes absurd world. To free one's imagination and to stir curiosity is for me a desired goal in an age of reduction.

I have been asked many times how I became interested in imagery and the concept of Psycho-Imagination Therapy. It came from many directions. I cannot name them all. The two more important influences are as follows. Foremost was the book *The Self and Others* in 1962 and the *Divided Self* shortly thereafter in 1963. These helped me formulate and concretize what I had already learned from Rollo May. (Surprisingly few psychotherapists I met were specifically aware of Laing's work until 1967, with his *Politics of Experience.*) Second, about the same time I came across the works of Desoille, Ven Den Berg (Caslant) and a little later Hanscarl Leuner and Roberto Assajioli and their studies in imagery. It seemed that the phenomenology of Laing and May et al. needed to be integrated with the developing work in imagery through a natural bridge – psychotherapeutic imagery productions. Out of this (plus other influences) emerged Psycho-Imagination Therapy, which then assimilated its own experiences and directions.

The "other influences" upon my work refer to those investigators who are not directly involved in psychotherapy but who nevertheless have helped expand the importance of the role of imagination and imagery in human living. Imagination and fantasy is now recognized as an indispensable resource in human life. Full accessibility to their own private imagery are the hallmarks of creative persons (Dellas and Gaier, 1970). It is known that vivid imagery does not obfuscate the accurate viewing of the real world (Sheehan, 1966). Contrary to previous thought, Jerome L. Singer has shown that the better able one is to make images, the better one is capable of fun, able to live more imaginatively, to discriminate between fantasy and reality better, and to be less disconcerted by unexpected thoughts and images (Singer, 1966).

It has been my observation that the intensive use of imagery in psychotherapy heightens therapist motivation and involvement because of the interesting and dramatic nature of the material that is elicited. The probability is great that the vividness and intensity of the patient's imagery productions serves as a catalyst to his or her own therapeutic motivations.

Some of the developments in the book came from a class I gave in "Identity and Imagination" at UCLA. Other material was developed from the many workshops given in Wurzburg, Tokyo, Hawaii, Montreal and in Los Angeles. As consultant to the California School of Professional Psychology, I helped participate in research projects involving imagery.

I wish to acknowledge those persons who read portions of the manuscrip and who offered encouragement, criticism and suggestions. They are Dr. Jerome L. Singer of Yale; Dr. David L. Shapiro of the Center for Forensic Psychiatry, Ann Arbor, Michigan; Dr. Lili Wolf, N.Y.U. School of Social Work; Dr. Peter Wolson, President of Los Angeles Society of Clinical Psychologists; Dr. Hans Rosenwald of the Albert Schweitzer Colleges; Raymond J. Vespe of Palo Alto; and Jess Millman, Milton Shapiro, Dr. Ernest L. Rossi, Dr. Karl Pottharst and Dr. David Bilovsky of Los Angeles.

CHAPTER I

Imagination and Psychotherapy

Man's imagination is as infinite as the universe: it knows no bounds, has no known limitations. The awareness of discovered imagination is awesome; even more awesome are those discoveries which have yet to be revealed beyond existing frontiers.

Man has always been intrigued by his imagination. Throughout the history of human thought it has variously been granted great prominence or relegated to virtual insignificance. The concept of imagination has been utilized as an explanation of human behavior, as an agent of casualty. Montaigne felt that it was responsible for the contagious effects of human emotion; it was the source of physical, emotional and mental disease — even death; it produced manifestations which other men might have attributed to magic; it was the cause of conspicuous physical phenomena, capable even of transforming the one sex to the other. In the history of psychotherapy, imagination has played many roles with diverse implications. As early as 1784, as a result of the enormous conflict surrounding the veracity of Anton Mesmer and his concept of "animal magnetism," the king appointed a commission of inquiry enlisting members of the Academic Sciences and the Academie de Medecine; another commission was formed among the Society Royale. Benjamin Franklin, at that time the American Ambassador and a foremost scientist of his time, deliberated the matter and concluded that no evidence could be found for the physical existence of any "magnetic fluid" at all — and finally the effects of Mesmer's hypnotic technique were ascribed to imagination.

In the same century, an Italian, named Muratori, wrote a treatise called "On the Power of Human Imagination," which gained wide currency. Muratori's concept of imagination comprised dreams, visions, delusions, *idées fixes,* phobias, and somnambulism. This last subject became the central focus of all contemporary discussions dealing with imagination; stories were often told of people who while apparently asleep would write, swim rivers, walk over rooftops — people whose lives would be critically endangered if they were suddenly awakened. These stories were widely believed at the time and, remarkably, persist to this day. Somnambulism became the purest example of imagination's marvelous workings, and it was inevitable that interest in this phenomenon should spread to other fields, including the arts. An early sample and a classic one is Shakespeare's unforgettable portrait of Lady Macbeth as she walks Dunsinane Castle by night, recounting scenes of her murderous role and giving herself confessional.

During the nineteenth century, actions once attributed to imagination were deemed the products of suggestion or autosuggestion, and it was not until the twentieth century that imagination and imagery were redefined and revitalized by Freud, Jung and Forenczi. In America, the use of imagination and imagery as psychotherapeutic tools followed a difficult path, however; and we are fortunate that in recent time, the concept of imagination has gained respectability.

Prior to the twenties, Titchener of Cornell worked for a time with problems related to imagination, such as introspection. Later, J. B. Watson, America's first star of behaviorism, turned the direction of human psychological investigation away from a concern with man's inner images — his daydreams, his dreams, his fanciful ruminations — and toward concepts of conditioning. It was only the psychoanalysts of the period who viewed the fantasies and dreams of their patients as relevant areas of imagery investigation. These dreams and fantasies were personalized between the patient and the analyst, and it was primarily the dream which was of interest. "Free Association," the technique of reporting everything one thought, neglected the full range of imagination itself in that it required the patient to turn his flow of thought into verbal reporting. The free use of imagination was not encouraged since, to many analysts, it reeked of resistance; the patient was usually guided back to his verbalization. Slips of the tongue which were undoubtedly related to the unconscious were considered merely as slips in the verbal reporting. A patient's imaginings of feelings for the analyst were viewed as transference reactions and usually not explored beyond that point. Freud, however, as early as 1892, attempted a "concentration technique" in which the patient reclined on a couch and Freud placed his hand on the patient's forehead, pressing firmly.

Freud described his technique in the following manner:

"I inform the patient that, a moment later, I shall apply pressure to his forehead, and I assure him that, all the time the pressure lasts, he will see before him a recollection in the form occurring to him; and I pledge him to communicate this picture or ideal to me, whatever it may be. He is not to keep it to himself because he may happen to think it is not what is wanted, nor the right thing, or because it would be too disagreeable for him to say it. There is to be no criticism of it, no reticence, either for emotional reasons or because it is judged unimportant . . . Having said this, I press for a few seconds on the forehead of the patient as he lies in front of me; I then leave go and ask quietly, as though there were no questions of a disappointment: "What did you see?" or, "What occurred to you?"

This procedure has taught me much and has also invariably achieved its aim. Today I can no longer do without it." (Breuer, J. and Freud, S., 1953, p. 270.)

Freud was enthusiastic about his technique: "My expectations were fulfilled; I was set free from hypnotism. . . . Hypnosis had screened from view an interplay of force which now came in sight and the understanding of which gave a solid formation to my theory." (Freud, S., 1959, p. 29.) This was in the year 1892.

"Freud's emphasis on the visual elements may clearly be seen in the precedence of terms: '... he will see before him ... a picture or will have it in his thought ...' and, 'What did you see?' or 'What occurred to you?' and again, 'Things that are brought to light from the deeper strata are also recognized and acknowledged, but only after considerable hesitations and doubts. Visual memory-images are of course more difficult to disavow than the memory-traces of mere trains of thought." (Breuer, J. and Freud, S., 1953, p. 299.)

After a while, Freud abandoned the technique: While initially an expedient, it could lead to increased resistance and difficult transference reactions later in treatment. In an article titled, "The Relation of the Poet to Daydreaming," published in 1908, Freud showed an embarrassing intransigence in declaring, "We can begin by saying that happy people never make fantasies, only unsatisfied ones. Unsatisfied wishes are the driving power behind fantasies; every separate fantasy contains the fulfillment of a wish, and improves on unsatisfactory reality." (Freud, S., 1963, p. 37.)

Freud notwithstanding, imagination is not the compensatory obverse of reality but man's way of organizing reality from his imaginings of the past and into the future. The simplest demonstration of this is to ask a person how many doors there were in the house he lived in as a child. I think you will see, if you ask yourself that question, that you will begin to visualize the image of the house itself, the stairs, the rooms, etc., as you begin your count. In this way, you are organizing the reality of the past into the present. If you are asked to imagine a house you have never seen, it is still the imagination of houses seen in the past that is brought to bear in your visual representation of the house, whatever you may imagine. Even if you were to imagine a house without any doors at all, you bring to such a visual image imagined feelings of your past. It goes without saying, then, that one cannot engage in imagination – or even disallow imagination – without involving experience from the past. Imagination is a way of organizing one's world, utilizing the past to assist in making sense of the present. Rollo May stated it as clearly as one could possibly imagine when he said, "... you can live without a father who accepts you, but you cannot live without a world that makes sense to you." (1967, p. 8.)

Dr. Jerome L. Singer, who has devoted a great deal of investigation to the role of imagery and cognition, has made a statement about Freud which warrants full examination. "... Freud may have errored in not insisting on imagery alone rather than allowing patients to shift to free verbal association. He might have gotten more powerful uncovering more rapidly from his earlier technique. Undoubtedly individual practitioners have sensed the importance of fostering greater emphasis on concrete imagery by patient and have found themselves impatient with the apparent glibness or defensiveness that often characterizes verbal free association." (Singer, 1971, p. 9.)

One can only imagine what enormous changes would have occurred in the field of psychotherapy if Freud had proceeded with "Free Imagery." This is not to deny credit to the concept of "Active Imagination" and Carl Jung who fostered it; throughout his life, Jung investigated the most subtle recesses of imagination and had important influences on European intellectual life.

On December 12, 1913, Jung began his own self-analysis, resorting to the technique of provoking the upsurge of unconscious imagery and its overflowing into consciousness. He recorded his dreams daily; he also wrote down stories, forcing himself to take them in any direction his imagination went. He imagined himself digging into the earth and into underground galleries and caves where he encountered many kinds of strange figures. Then, according to Ellenberger, " . . . he had to examine carefully each image from the unconscious and to translate it, insofar as this was possible, into the language of the consciousness." (Ellenberger, 1972, p. 67.) This led Jung to this technique of "Active Imagination."

Jung suggested that the contents of the unconscious are presented in conscious form as images. Since the unconscious is divided into its personal and collective aspects, so are its images. Those that are based on the remnants of the innumerably repeated, universal experiences of primitive man are referred to as "primordial images" to distinguish them from the "personal images" which are peculiar to each individual. These primordial images, or inherited patterns of thought, correspond closely to universal symbolisms. They are identical or similar among all people and are easily to be found in the unconscious of the present day human being. A half century ago, Forenczi, the most innovative of the Freudians, asked his patients to "fabricate" a fantasy if they could not readily imagine one; that is, tell " . . . all that comes into their mind without regard for objective reality." He sometimes offered fantasies which he felt the patients *should* have been experiencing until the process took over within them.

Forenczi claimed his "forced fantasies" to have an unquestionable analytical value because they brought about the production or reproduction of scenes quite unexpected by either patient or analyst (" . . . which leave an indelible impression on the mind of the patient") that aided perceptibly in advancing the analytical work; important also because " . . . they furnish a proof that the patient is, generally speaking, capable of such psychical productions of which he thought himself free, so that they give us a grasp of deeper research into the unconscious." (Healy, Bronner and Bowers, 1930, p. 476.)

Historically, the psychoanalysts have not been kind to the function of "images" which may spontaneously emerge in the course of psychoanalysis.

They have labeled such imagery as manifestations of regression or resistance; images, like symbols, they say, are defenses and pose an alternative to the verbalization and ideation of the ego. At best — according to this line of reasoning — images are screens memories (i.e., what a memory conceals); in short, they defend against revealing the unconscious conflicts and lead to decreased communication. Recently, however, Horowitz (1970) has indicated that some psychoanalysts are now paying more attention to the images created by the patient.

In 1955, Fromm wrote a little publicized paper in which he voices a plea for moving beyond the conventional, free association procedure into the therapist-initiated situations. This is to be experienced by the patient in a vivid, alive way. His advice to analysts is for them to make fullest use of their own imagination, and suggest active imagery methods to improve the flow of the patient's free associations. Alberta Szalita in her fine article "Reanalysis," dealing with the reanalysis of unsuccessful psychoanalysis of persons, strongly suggests "a daring" is needed to reach a patient and elicit a response. "I don't seen any discrepancy in this kind of activity on the part of the analyst with the psychoanalytical tenets. It does not differ from the analysis of a dream. Perhaps that is why dream analysis is so useful in that it gives a legitimate opportunity for the analyst *to use, his imagination.*" (Szalita, 1968, p. 98-99.)

Freud believed fantasy and imagination to be related to the person's defenses. Even Anna Freud (1946) considered fantasy a defense mechanism. That the imagination might have an adaptive function was not stressed by psychoanalysts until Hartman in 1958 and then only with minimal knowledge of his publications. By and large, American psychologists have tended to regard reverie and imagination as unproductive, impractical, and completely unempirical.

The return of the *image* in American psychology in the last half decade has oddly enough been given great impetus by the same theoretical framework which delayed its emergence, namely, the present day behaviorists, heirs to the tradition of J. B. Watson. The emphasis is on visualization during systematic desensitization of the patient to "bad" images related to disturbing symptoms. The patient's production of vivid imagery is a critical feature of desensitization therapy as he learns to respond to increasingly difficult images to which he has phobic feelings. Aversive conditioning for persons with so-called deviant sexual fantasies is also accomplished by shocking the person in a painful manner, as he responds to images or pictures of unacceptable sex partners or objects and rewarded for imagery involving acceptable sexual fantasies.

Still another variation with more powerful negative imagery is the "Implosive Therapy" of Stampfl (1967) who has the patient vividly imagining the worst possible consequences of a particular fear or obsession (e.g., being arrested and paraded before a jeering panel, being horribly crushed under a subway train's wheels, or covering him with slime and vomit, etc.). The anxiety is gradually extinguished as he repeatedly faces the horrible scenes since, in reality, there is no actual consequence.

To the dynamically oriented and to those therapists of the humanistic emphasis, this smacks of torture and the neglect of human values. Although the behaviorists have now helped to reintroduce the image in therapy, it is not with a keen interest in the patient's inner experiences or fantasies and unconscious processes are generally rejected, uninvestigated.

The Gestalt therapists have made much use of imagination, mainly in conjunction with the patient's dreams, but have limited the possibility of the interpretative value of images and shown disinterest in the imagination as it relates to the patients' past lives. Those doing Psychodrama — especially in the role reversal technique — make use of imagination but the systematic emphasis on imagery, as such, is lacking.

Imagination must not be considered indefinable or cast aside as too vague a subject for examination. Ordinarily, it is thought that imagination is the sole property of writers, musicians, painters, and the like. No prejudice is further from fact. While imagination as a psychological function of the human mind will perhaps never be understood in its entirety, it is not a process reserved for a few creative persons. All of us have imagination, and all of us need imagination for our living, whether we be dull or bright. As the famous American artist Ben Shahn has stated:

"Imagination supplies the banalities of life as well as the inspirations. Imagination is the total conscious life of each one of us. Without it, neither you nor I could make his way to the parked car, or recognize it when he arrives there. Without it, we could not dress ourselves in the morning nor find our way to the breakfast table nor know what we are eating or what was said to us by the morning paper. Without it, we would recognize nothing at all. This seems axiomatic." (Shahn, 1967, p. 14.)

The universality of imagination in each of us as an organizing principle of life is evident. The use of imagination as man's way of adapting in an autonomous manner is even more clearly demonstrated when it is used as a preparation for action. Dr. Salvatore R. Maddi, writing for the Nebraska Symposium on "Motivation," has clearly described imagination used to try out possibilities for future action:

"So the adolescent boy who fantasized making love to a beautiful classmate finds that he begins to think about her, experience her, and interact with her in a more intimate fashion, even though he is frightened to death of sexual confrontation. But the subtle changes that take place in his actual interactions with her, express well the manner in which imagination is a preparation for action. Perhaps she has similar fantasies of him which lead her to avoid him without any apparent reason, while at the same time, she subtly encourages him. Let them be alone together in some unexpectedly secure circumstance, or let another sexual partner loom up to cause jealousy, and the love and attraction they prepared for in their fantasy may find sudden if frightening expression. Similar circumstances befalling two young people who had not fantasized about each other in such fashion might not have had any effect on action at all. What I am saying is that the function of imagination as preparation for action is so potent, and natural, that even fear of consequences cannot demolish it entirely." (Maddi, 1970, p. 151.)

That individual or group psychotherapy sessions should have as part of their process the rehearsal of anticipated and imaged events would appear to be the logical outgrowth of Maddi's thinking. There is the strong possibility of developing general principles about his own dynamics as the patient imagines himself in various situations. Despite the obvious complexities the images permit us to *see,* and perhaps the better we are acquainted with our imagery, the better able we will be to shift toward a new, healthy imagery.

Most American psychologists and psychiatrists are well acquainted with the names of Freud, Adler, Jung, Horney, Rogers, Sullivan and R. D. Laing and could probably relate some incident involving each of these distinguished theoreticians; they could imagine Freud or the others in their minds – how they looked, how they acted. A great many European psychotherapists, contrary to popular belief, are not solely influenced by Freud or Jung but draw heavily from the work of men such as Desoille, Hanscarl Leuner, Carl Happich, Assagioli, Fretigny, Virel, Bachelard, etc., – fellow European investigators who have shared an interest in using "Imagery" and "Imagination" in their psychotherapeutic experience. nd, while the last five years they have sponsored annual meetings, such as the International Societies for the Study of Mental Imagery, I would hazard that few American psychotherapists have been at all influenced by them. It is not possible here to make a thorough examination of their procedures, but it is important to emphasize that it is not the patient's verbal reports but rather his imagination which forms the basis for aiding him to reveal and "work through" his conflicts. Good results have been reported, strongly suggesting that the verbal is not a necessity in psychological change.

The one European name that stands above all in the use of imagination in relation to psychotherapy is that of Desoille. While he was indeed a pioneer in the development of such methods, it is a little-known fact that he himself was first influenced by a physicist named E. Caslant(1927). As early as 1927, Caslant began experimenting with people; he would ask them to imagine themselves rising up into space and observe the ease or difficulty with which they rose; he would ask them to overcome such obstacles as they had imagined by using suggestions of various sorts, such as, " . . . use a sword to cut through that web." These imaginary trips in verticality were an attempt on

Caslant's part to find a method of studying clairvoyance and paranormal abilities.

Desoille is neither a psychologist or a psychiatrist, but an engineer. He personally got in touch with Caslant and was present at some of his sittings. He then tried the method himself, and what started as an entertaining psychological study grew into a considerable psychotherapeutic practice. It must be noted, however, that he initially began working with essentially normal subjects, with the neurotic ones coming later. From Caslant's original notion, Desoille (1965) developed the more involved technique called *rêve éviellé,* or what is known in English as the guided affective imagery technique (GAI). It served as a point of reference for nearly all the psychotherapeutic developments evolving later which employed imagery as a prime mode of approach. It is a method that limits formal analysis of the imagery, suggesting rather that many problems can indeed be worked through by means of that type of symbolic combat, amelioration or transformation which takes place in imagery.

The philosophical roots of psychoanalysis were provided by Freud himself; with the concept of psychic determinism, and the matrix of the triplicity of the Ego, Id and Superego, this philosophical system was uniquely his own. Jung, too, insofar as his concept of the "collective unconscious" is concerned, provided his own philosophical base. A comparable philosophical base but one with emphasis on imagination and imagery was represented by a non-psychotherapist, the highly regarded phenomenologist Gaston Bachelard. A former physicist like Caslant, Bachelard more than forty years ago began an intensive study of man's imagination and his symbolism. When he became the Sorbonne's professor for history and the Philosophy of the Sciences, he pioneered in the exploration of Desoille's two books on the "Rêve Eveillé in Psychotherapy." His appreciation of the importance of Desoille's discoveries as they related to general psychology and psychotherapy was set forth in his book, *The Air and the Dreams,* written in 1943.

Bachelard breaks with the more traditional psychological method of introspection by calling to our attention with a wealth of evidence of fact that the world of things is our home and thus contains the images of human intimacy. A man almost unknown to behavioral scientists in America, Bachelard was something of an armchair philosopher, delving into the symbolism of fire, water, earth and light. The psychology of the crackling fire in the grate, the quiet lake and the restless breakers, the flight of the jubilant lark, the earth calling men to labor, caves temptingly leading to adventure, the black dampness of the tomb — all of these were a part of his philosophical journey, and man's innate capacity for generating imagery and symbolism is a critically important feature of his work.

Singer, referring to Bachelard says, "For the Western European clinician, therefore, the detailed exploration of the intra-psychic or the direct use of imagery have had an acceptance and meaning that is even wider ranging than the classical psychoanalytic influences of Freud in America." (Singer, 1971, p. 14.)

Along with the increased awareness of imagination and imagery, the last decade saw a growing emphasis on phenomenology: the study of how a person sees his world. To my way of thinking, phenomenology requires of a person that he use his imagination as the vehicle by which to ready himself for all that he uniquely perceives, anticipates, defends and acts upon; events to come (as stated on an earlier page) are "rehearsed" in advance of their actual occurrence; a person imagines how it *will be*, thereby preparing for whatever action may result. Thus seen, the increased awareness of phenomenology has been no accident; its integration with the concept and use of imagination was a palpable necessity. Our world of images reflects and represents our being-in-the-world and we can only understand man as an individual, and as a part of mankind, when we grasp the imagery of his existence.

The phenomenologists, and especially R. D. Laing (1962) in *The Self and Others,* have applied imagery to interpersonal relationships. "How does Jim think Mary thinks, that Jim thinks of her?" — This is the kind of interpenetrating imaginativeness that humans are constantly engaged in; and to Laing, the use of imagination in this manner provides the sinews of human interaction. How a person views himself, how he views the other person, how he imagines the other person views him, and, even more essential, how he has learned to be defined by others who have raised him — these are all questions basic to phenomenology. A further concern of major importance is the conflict between how a person imagines himself to be and how he is *told* to be by his parents: to Laing this is the basis of human conflict. It is certainly the origin of bipolarization in neurotic conflict.

I would like to submit the following poem which shows this point beautifully. This was written by one of my own patients:

He loves me for who he thinks I am
but,
who he thinks I am
is not who I am.
Therefore,
it's hard for me to be who I am
when we're together,
because I think I have to be
who he thinks I am.
Of course, I don't know exactly
who it is he thinks I am.
I just know it isn't who I am.
Who am I?
Well . . .
Who I am is something I recognize
when someone tells me
who I am *not.*
At least, I *think* that's *not* who I am.
Maybe who I am *not*
is who I *am.*
If that's who I am . . .
My gawd! He really loves me!

In *Psycho-Imagination Therapy* by Shorr (1972), extensive use is made of the Imaginary Situation ("IS"), in order to elicit the internal bipolarized conflicts of the patient. Imaginary Situations are also used to help the patient focus on changing his self-definition.

With the increased emphasis on phenomenology and the singularity of each person's "world," imagination as a function of the mind has gained new importance for both "viewing" and therapy. At the very least, its use has returned from ostracism and despite the varied shadings of opinion which have greeted it, there is little doubt that it is here to stay, providing, as it does, an invaluable leverage to man's potential.

Idealized Image/Despised Image and False Position

Karen Horney (1950), in developing the concept of the idealized image and the despised image, did not essentially involve the patient actively in imagery; nonetheless, she helped clarify how one can arrive at those forms of self-image which neurotically tend to propel us. If we agree with Laing's concept of an attributed identity − and alien identity in sharp bipolarized contrast to one's real identity − it is to this identity that Horney's concepts are most applicable. The person who is indeed falsely defined by others may make enormous steps toward becoming or appearing quite the opposite of that definition. The image he would want the world to have of him, and to which vigilantly he lends all his efforts to maintain, may be idealized as, for example, the best kind of mother or father, or the most competent performer, etc. In his or her heart of hearts, of course, the person may not *feel* that way at all, and the vigilance against this idealized image from being "seen through" is constant; if it were to be seen through, it would make the person depressed and anxious. At best, that image is a front line, a generally unconscious "good person" defense against the introjected, unacceptable person within; it is an attempt to maintain one's position in the world, but the position is false − one operates in a compensating manner, busily sustaining a neurotic conflict resolution. In general, I would say that the greater the idealized image, the greater the security operations necessary to perpetuate it.

If I were to ask a patient to (IS) imagine your most idealized image of yourself, I believe one would note greater anxiety in the imagery of those people whose idealized image is far greater than their attributed identity. To my way of thinking, when a person is operating essentially from his *true* identity, the need for an idealized image becomes more realistic and the disparity between his idealized image and real self-image is minimal: the possibilities for feeling in false or untenable positions are considerably diminished; depression and anxiety would be lessened as well.

If one falls victim to all the negative attributions ascribed to him by the "significant persons" of his life, if he becomes defined by them, he may come to feel that he is in his "despised image." Add a large dash of guilt, and one soon believes he *is* the rotten self. Disclosure and exposure are feared as never before; security operations may go to the extreme, involving even isolation and detachment. I once asked a patient to (IS) imagine a person other than himself if he were to look into a mirror. He answered that he saw a werewolf. As he continued, he realized the meaning of what he imagined seeing: the werewolf was the despised image that he didn't want the world to know about. He had accepted his false definition as if it were, indeed, him. Subsequently, he was able to change this "alien identity" he had internalized. Another man, who was unemployed, stayed in his apartment during normal working hours so that nobody would see how "rotten" he was. Isolation and detachment were companions to his "despised image."

While Horney did not use concrete imagery to make the patient aware of these self-concept images, her contribution to the understanding of the dynamics of self-imagery is outstanding and brilliant. Especially is this true of her concept of the "search for glory" and the role of imagination in its development. She describes the subtle unconscious use of imagination by people prone to such a search, showing how such people may use their imagination against themselves. "The more injurious work of imagination concerns the subtle and comprehensive distortions of reality which he is not aware of fabricating. The idealized image is not created in a single act of creation; once produced, it needs continued attention. For its actualization, the person must put in incessant labor by way of falsifying reality. He must turn his needs into virtues or into more than justified expectations. He must turn his intentions to be honest or considerate into the fact of being honest or considerate. The bright ideas he has for a paper make him a great scholar. His potentialities turn into factual achievements. Knowing the 'right' moral values makes him a virtuous person — often, indeed a kind of moral genius. And of course, his imagination must work overtime to discard all the disturbing evidence to the contrary." (Horney, 1950, p. 33-34.)

Reaching Out for Meaning

Our minds need to make meaning of some kind out of our life experience, and the capacity to do so has sustained men in the darkest of circumstances. Frankl's "search for meaning" sustained him by the use, among other things, of the imagery of the future of a manuscript he kept hidden in his coat while he was kept in a Nazi concentration camp. Man's concept of imagery of paradise — be it derivative of Persian, Hebrew or Christian thought — has sustained him throughout history; his images of utopia and other concepts of his future have given him similar meaning and hope. Such reaching out for meaning with the aid of imagination is perfectly illustrated by a story told in Romain Gary's novel *The Roots of Heaven.*

"In a German concentration camp during the war, the French prisoners are becoming increasingly demoralized; they are on a down staircase. A man called Robert devises a way to arrest the decline. He suggests that they imagine an invisible girl in the billet. If one of them swears or farts, he must bow and apologize to the 'girl'; when they undress, they must hang up a blanket so she can't see them. Oddly enough, this absurd game works: they enter into the spirit of the thing, and morale suddenly rises. The Germans become suspicious of the men and by eavesdropping, they found out about the invisible girl. The Commandant fancies himself a psychologist. He goes along to the billet with two guards, and tells the men: 'I know you have a girl here. That is forbidden. Tomorrow I shall come here with these guards and you will hand her over to me. She will be taken to the local brothel for German officers'. When he was gone, the men were dismayed; they know that if they 'hand her over', they won't be able to recreate her. The next day, the Commandant appears with his two soldiers. Robert, as the spokesman, says, 'We have decided not to hand her over'. And the Commandant knows he is beaten: nothing he can do can force them to hand her over. Robert is arrested and placed in solitary confinement; they all think they've seen the last of him, but weeks later, he reappears, very thin and worn. He explains that he has found the way to resist solitary confinement – their game with the invisible girl has taught him that the imagination is the power to reach out to other realities, realities not physically present. He had kept himself from breaking down by imagining great herds of elephants trampling over endless plains . . ." (Gary, 1958, p.159.)

With increasing frequency, greater numbers of people refer to their lives as being meaningless. This applies to the general public and especially to patients seeking help. "What's It All About Alfie?," the name of a recent popular song, sums up the problem neatly. But, one may wonder, perhaps it is merely the fashionable attitude in this age of existential thinking, this age of the absurd. Edith Weisskopf-Joelson (1972) undertook a very detailed study of 500 undergraduates, requiring them to write an extensive autobiography; she found that when five clinical psychologists rated the autobiographies for a "life devoid of meaning," 147 of the students were thus classified. The interjudge realiability was 92%. The 147 comprised 96 males and 51 females, she found, and set out to interview each one. After listening to the taped interviews, she concluded that three operational divisions existed:

1. "I have thoughts, wishes and daydreams, but they are in no way related to external reality. I am disinterested in what goes on around me. I cannot produce the mixture between fantasy and reality which makes life meaningful."

2. Some claimed that their lives seemed meaningless in the sense that they lacked explanations and interpretations with regard to themselves in the world in which they lived. Establishing connections and explanations lacked integration.

3. Some felt their lives lacked meaning in the sense that they had no purpose or goal. The goal of going to the bathroom to wash one's hands does not add meaning to one's life.

Endorsing life with meaning requires a relatively comprehensive long-term goal that embraces large parts of life. The goal-directed person integrates various aspects of life with the others, then integrates the whole thus created with goals to be reached. As is evident, approximately 30% of the students were judged to be leading a life devoid of meaning. My own observation is that the percentage would be higher still if one were to include, amongst one's sample group, people in assembly line work, certain kinds of sales work, etc.

Tangentially, Weisskopf-Joelson states, "People tend to focus on meaning more often when they feel it is absent than when they feel it is present." (p. 260.) In a further step, the imagery of the 147 was tested by asking them to react to ambiguous material in the Thematic Apperception Test; the result was a bimodal distribution:

1. They either produced fantasy without paying attention to reality.

OR:

2. They focused on reality without producing fantasy. (They were reality-bound to the point of being talented, but were unable to be creative because they could not "let themselves go.")

By contrast, the control group produces a bell-shaped distribution of their imagery, tending to achieve an integration between fantasy and reality. I refer to this detailed study both to show how important imagery can be in judging meaninglessness in people's lives. In *Psycho-Imagination Therapy* (1972), I have asked patients to finish the sentence: "My whole life is based on proving that _____." Or, "My whole life is based on denying that _____."

One need only to ask oneself these questions in private to see the marked emphasis on goal, meaning and direction which emerges as one attempts to finish each sentence.

The Image in Psychotherapy

An image may appear to a person in the form of hallucination, in a dream, in a daydream, as an unbidden image, in the presence of another person, in a particular situation, in a particular position, etc. These "nonverbal memory representations" are unique to that individual and even should they be fully reported, the listener cannot fully confirm that he has seen the identical image. As with dreams, a therapist may repeatedly inquire into the minutest details and still fall short of congruity. While absolute congruity may be impossible with the use of imagery and imagination — given consistent accuracy on the patient's part in reporting them — still the therapist for all practical purposes may come close enough to seeing what the patient himself is seeing. We do know now that a word may arouse an image and an image may arouse a word; further, the more concrete the word, the more easily is the image aroused. Conversely, the more abstract words do not arouse images easily. The task in psychotherapy is for both patient and therapist to assign meanings to the images and to relate this process to the possibility of new awareness and, hopefully, change.

Allan Paivio (1972) has demonstrated from a strictly experimental point of view that imagery or imagination in the human mind operates synchronically; that is, any part of an image can be elicited instantly without apparent loss of intensity.

For example, if you are asked to imagine entering a room you are familiar with, you may report first what you see to the left of that room; when asked what you see in the middle, or to its right, the one image can be seen as readily as any other. All images synchronize and interchange upon the request of the person who is asking about them, whereas a poem or verbal report can be recited forwards, but backwards only with extreme difficulty. The image of White-House takes one-half less retrievable space than the verbal abstraction of Basic-Truth; White-House is seen as a single image while Basic-Truth requires two separate sequences. Hence, to verbal material which must follow sequential patterns to make sense, Paivio assigns the concept of sequentiality. One need only ask a person to remember the middle line of a long poem, or to repeat the poem backwards to demonstrate this. Imagery, on the other hand, can occur between and among many images synchronously.

Each emotion appears to have its characteristic projection gestalt. We may speak of waves of anger coming over us, the lassitude of grief, gut reactions of hate, the lighteners of joy, and so on. These are more than figures of speech: there appear to be clear, separate virtual images that correspond to the specific emotion. Manfred Clynes (1973) who has studied emotions with an eye toward scientific reductionism concludes this very pertinent example of emotion and the sensory image it encompasses.

"To take a particular example, the emotion of love is often felt together with a sensation of a kind of flow. Flow implies space. But it is not a static but flowing spatial experience. The direction flow is sensed, generally, from central regions of the body outward, towards the limbs, or generally outward. Yet, that sensation does not mean that at such a time, there really is an actual corresponding, substantive flow outwards; rather, this is a sensory projection. Although there is a sensation of outward flow, nothing really leaves the center and moves outward, but the sensation of flow persists without any corresponding redistribution of a substance. It is thus in the nature of a virtual sensory image. This particular virtual spatial sensory image is characteristic of love." (Clynes, 1973, p. 106.)

In psychotherapy, it can be quite advantageous to use imagery and imagination to make a person more aware of his internal state and conflicts. The flow should be quicker and easier than with other methods because of the wide variety of possibilities eligible for recall or imagining. Verbal reports, developing in sequence, must of necessity be slower. As a result, it is certain from clinical experience that asking a patient to (IS) imagine placing a flower between his mother's breasts will elicit much more feeling-material and association-material than merely asking him how attracted he is to his mother. Since one inch of imagery may elicit a yard of associative imagery (or the old Hollingsworth term of redintegration) pure verbal association may be of limited value. We need not relegate the verbal process to the scrap-heap, however; rather, it can be used contemporaneously with imagery to yield a cohesive logic and internal consistency to the psychotherapeutic process. But the patient's unique way of sensing, seeing, or feeling through the use of imagery does not usually produce the same degree of defensiveness that occurs in more traditional verbalized reports. Meaning that can be conveyed or received by imagery and imagination may have more impact than that gained from verbal insights alone.

Szalita cites the experience of one of her patients who sensed a wavering quality to the design on the ceiling of the therapist's office; aware that this was a faulty image, the patient's emotional response was to see it as an "aggressive witch." (1958, p. 60.) Spiegel makes a similar point with one of her patients, writing, "For instance, Raymond, a young man with recurrent schizoaffective relations and paranoid trends, tested himself for improvement early in one episode by noting his percepts on looking at photographs in a pictorial magazine. Sometimes the faces wavered out of the page, coming alive and mocking him with their eyes, and he recognizes that he was still sick; when they subsided into the page and became inert again, he 'knew' he was better. In the height of his elation, he did not challenge his erroneous percepts and delusional interferences."

Spiegel continues her observations: "With the stirrings evoked in psychotherapy, the patient often experiences not only a sense that dreaming is activated but also more favorable imagery."

With the lifting of depression, imagery returns. Indeed, in the writer's experience, one of the heralding symbols is the rebirth of nature, the growth of trees, of new leaves. Mr. Harry W., as his mood of depression gave way to zest in living in going around and meeting people, said, "Trees are soft, green, round. Trees, when you lie under them and look up at the sky, are especially nice. They always move a little and generally there are little clouds — and green of course. The green of trees is always very soft." (Spiegel, 1959, p. 944.)

Reference to the imagination of therapists are not ordinarily referred to in psychotherapeutic literature. Frank Barron in his book "Creativity and Personal Freedom," makes an important connection between forethought and imagination.

"When we say that a therapist's skill has increased, we mean partly that he has learned how he affects the patient, and that he is able to produce desired effects deliberately, with forethought. Forethought requires some degree of imagination, so that is imagination which determines scope in therapy. Because the therapist can imagine, he can understand; and, understanding, he can take action to affect. If the therapist has imagination, no personality is alien to him." (Barron, 1968, p. 81.)

The imagery of the therapist as he imagines the imagery of the patient can help to "see" what the patient imagines. Commonly shared images, as one patient expressed to me; "Do you remember the image of the peach in my head?" "Yes," I said. "I remember what meaning it had for you at the time. Do you have any idea why you have the imagery now again?" Such examples are now commonplace for me and my patients and their imagery is as much a part of them as any aspect of them. The more I share their imagery, the more I understand them and the more they feel understood. Greater empathy is thus assured.

There is no doubt that the patient's imagery may set off imagery in the therapist. This associated imagery or even reminiscent imagery may add clues and further meaning in a more sharpened participant-observer relationship. It is my opinion that imagery lends itself for greater possibility of participation than verbal reports.

Klinger (1971) has found that the content of imagery is positively related to a person's self-concept and holds fairly consistently for many minds of thematic content regardless of whether society supports or punishes a type of behavior. This may make us believe that if imagery can be used adequately in therapy, we indeed may have a "royal road to the person."

Image and Psychosis

The importance of the image in psychosis is probably greater than in any form of human behavior, as a means of communication by the individual as well as a means of understanding psychotic behavior for the therapist. And a vast subject it is. The schizophrenic has sometimes been described as having "cancer of the imagination." The incomprehensibility of psychotic images, of hallucinations, of fragmented and bizarre images haunts the therapist as he hopefully looks to bring meaning and help to his patient. But there are infinite styles and intensities to the patient's use of imagery; meanings are elusive, the therapist's skills are challenged.

It is not uncommon for psychotic patients to hallucinate God's voice. One woman said that it afforded her greater comfort than did her less constant image of her therapist. In another instance, a young man much troubled by object loss and separation was greatly preoccupied with the notion that objects photographed in a certain way might be preserved forever. Burnham, Gladstone and Gibson summarize the role of imagery among psychotics:

> Some patients approach the problem of object inconsistence and separation anxiety by attempting not only to avoid actual contact with the doctor but also to shut out any image or thought of him. One woman who for months had striven to maintain a facade of self-sufficiency, finally acknowledged to her doctor, "You've gotten under my skin; I hate you for it. You don't bother me so much when you are here. It's when you are not here and I can't get you out of my mind that I hate you most. I was sure I could get along without you and take care of myself. I feel that by letting you become important, I have lost my strength and have lost part of myself." Another patient said, " I don't know your name and I certainly don't want to think of you as my doctor. That would mean I might lose you."
>
> On the other hand, patients may prefer their image of the doctor over his actual presence, saying, for instance, "I can be more certain of my picture of you than I can of you. I can talk to you more easily when I'm not with you." This would appear to be variant of eidetic imagery in persons who are fixated midway between the poles of narcissism and object-relatedness, and for whom a vivid image is in some ways more satisfying than the actual object in the real world. They may attain a pseudo-consistence of the object image by systematically excluding badness from the image. Such a purified image can be more readily maintained in the absence of actual object contacts which inevitably arouse some bad feelings which would spoil

the good image. One woman told her doctor, "I know that my image of you will never leave me, but you as a person might leave me. When I think of you as a real person, I get sick."

The mental images of dead persons may be cherished as defenses against separation anxiety. One young woman with severe separation anxiety, clung to an image of her grandfather, who, she was convinced, was the only person who had ever loved her; she vividly recalled that as a child she had pleaded with him at his deathbed, not to leave her. Years later, a boyfriend kissed her goodnight one evening, and as he turned to leave, she suddenly perceived him as changed into an old man. (Burnham, Gladstone and Gibson, 1969, p. 294.)

As one can readily see, the vast and uncharted area of the imagination in relation to psychosis is sometimes comprehensible; more often, however — at least to this point in time — it is beyond our fullest grasp. Especially is this true of fragmented images, hallucinations and delusions. Increased imaginative activity plus living in the fantasy he creates is a common function of the schizophrenic. However, to my knowledge, the active use of imagery and imagination in the treatment of psychotics has so far escaped the literature of our science, even though the importance of its role is undeniable. (That is, besides art.)

Two Schools of Thought on Imagery

Theoretical concepts dealing with imagery fall into two distinct categories, such as the proposal of David L. Shapiro (1970). On the one hand, we have Freud's frame of reference. One proponent of this approach, Kanzer (1958), speaks of visual images coming into consciousness; according to him these visual images have no feelings or movement connected with them, but serve to dissipate the disturbing idea of which engendered them. The image itself remains "an island of resistance." This attitude, while perhaps resembling psychoanalytic procedure, is not accompanied by an insight. In it, the image is taken to be an alternative to the verbalization of ideas, invariably screening the impulses directed towards the analyst as transference resistances. Just as in dreams and in symptom formation, the patient may choose unimportant objects as the subject matter of the image to avoid, the really central and commanding object: the analyst himself or transference reactions. According to this point of view, images are essentially interruptions of the main flow of ideas, motivated by resistance. At best they represent thoughts submerged at the moment. Those who hold to this school of thought are beginning to recognize that the analyst's interpretations may, in turn, give rise to imagery, and they contend that these images are the condensations of inner impulses; if the analyst pays attention to the images, he will merely contact those psychic processes attempting to elude detection.

No mention is made of the possibility that listening to a patient's free association may lead to imagery on the part of the analyst, or the further possibility that such imagery (rather than thought processes) on the part of the analyst might be countertransference resistance. Finally, if a patient free associates and sets off the analyst to indulge in imagery of his own, does the process not imply blockage on the part of the analyst and consequent impairment of the free flow of analytical interpretation?

Fisher (1957), in an experimental period of free imagery, observed a striking similarity to the imagery of dreams. This, of course, suggested that the same resistances found in dreams of submerged thought must be found in the imagery of a patient as well. Warren (1961) speaks of spontaneous imagery arising from free association as representing a regressive state which is more in the nature of narcissistically cathected representations than the — to him — more trustworthy verbalizations. Imagery, he says, satisfies id and superego drives while verbalization is more in line with ego functions and the desire to communicate. Freud (1923) said that thinking in pictures is an "incomplete form of becoming conscious." The visual image represented the return to the "concrete subject matter of things," consequently making the underlying impulses far more difficult to communicate. He suggested that associations to the images be obtained, summarizing that at best the visual image is to be conceived as a screen memory, an innocuous picture represented to screen displaced feelings.

By and large, this point of view conceives of imagery as dynamically similar to dreams in that both are presumably brought about by topographical regression, but dissimilar from them in that the plastic representation is more evident, there is less distortion than in dreams, and the relations to preceding material are often clearer.

The work of Brenman, Gill and Knight (1954) makes comparable observations in discussing the depth of hypnotic trances. "Going deeper" may increase the flow of imagery. These dynamics are very similar to what has been described for the image: a compromise formation like both a defense and a symptom. For instance, going deeper may at one and the same time gratify a passive longing for the therapist and defend against the recognition of that passive longing, since the deeper one goes, the less voluntary control one feels that one has over what one is doing.

By way of review, then, the first point of view, stemming from Freud, concentrates on imagery as screen memories, i.e., what a memory conceals. As in dream work, the emphasis is on the latent content and what it conceals rather than on the manifest content and what it might reveal.

The second point of view stems essentially from the work of Desoille, Leuner and Assagioli; it sees the visual image — in part because of its primitive form — as the direct voice of the unconscious, an expression of the impulse itself rather than a defense against the impulse. This symbolic experience, according to Hammer (1967), is totally transparent requiring no analysis or insight to understand it. It is a level of symbol-making consciousness lying between the conscious and the unconscious; it is the "point of departure for all creative production and healing processes." In this realm of symbols, meetings with unrecognized aspects of the self enable "spontaneous healing through the *transformation* of symbols." The therapist can and does manipulate these symbols, giving some direction and maintaining a degree of control of the patient's fantasy. The therapist may suggest scenes which have symbolic and therapeutic importance related to the basic difficulties in the individual's intrapsychic or interpersonal functioning. According to Hammer, whatever is psychically unresolved will, in the description of the scene, manifest itself though symbolic visual forms and resolve itself at a symbolic level independent of conscious control. The induced visions contain meaningful symbols analogous to dream symbols, but the "psychodynamic organization of affect is projected into such visualizations more clearly than in dreams."

In such procedure, the recall of early memories that hold great affect for the patient is almost totally deemphasized and rarely introduced, since the patient is symbolically dealing with the therapist-directed imaginary situations.

Reyher (1963) used a technique he calls "free imagery" or "emergent uncovering" to make similar points. He asks patients to close their eyes and report such visual images and sensations as occur to them. In 1968, he notes, "As repressed material emerges, it generally becomes represented symbolically, and, as the symbolism breaks down, marked blocking and resistance occurs along with the activation of anxiety and/or symptoms." He goes on to maintain that it is the very appearance of these symptoms which obviates the need for interpretation: the patient directly experiences the affects connected with an image that has been stirred up.

Kubie (1943) advocated hypnotic reverie as an adjunct to a standard psychoanalytical procedure and asserts that it adds more flow of free associations, intense feelings with little distortion.

Reiff and Scheerer (1959), in a study of hypnotic age regression, speak of remembering as the transformation of a previous experience according to ego structures and present schemata. The theoretical difference between the psycho-analytic concept of early memories being a screen for deeply repressed conflicts and the Adlerian idea that the early memory represents a good deal about the person's core-conflicts and the way he structures his life is one which still hangs on unresolved.

Thus, as in memory phenomena as well as in those of visual imagery, there are two very distinct approaches; namely, what memories and images conceal vs. what they reveal. This applies to symbols as well. Analysts such as Jones state with special vigor that one symbolizes only that which could not be expressed, i.e., that which one has deeply repressed, while Silberer (1951) maintained that conflicts were more a conscious level (e.g., the need to work versus the need to sleep) and were almost subject to symbolic representation. Again, interest is divided between what the symbol conceals and what the symbol reveals.

CHAPTER II

Imagery and the Internal Conflicts

A person's inner conflict is brought about by the opposition of two strong and incompatible forces, neither of which can be satisfied without exacting pain, fear, guilt, or some other emotional penalty. From an existential viewpoint, this definition is an abstraction and also, to be sure, something of an oversimplification. No single conflict encompasses the multitudinous fears and wishes that, each with an urgency of its own, swirl about in one's mind. Perhaps the most reliable method to determine the roots of any given conflict is to relate the conflict to the way in which the parental structure has defined the patient, and to the idealized image the patient feels bound to maintain. The difference between how a patient feels he *should* be and how he really *wants* to be can easily produce a gnawing conflict. A natural and spontaneous act may feel degrading and worthless if it violates an "ideal" form of introjected behavior.

It is well known that all of us, in attempting to resolve our conflicts, oscillate between one polarity of experience and the other. Performance, trial and error, interior dialogue which weighs possible alternative acts – we are constantly bringing these elements to bear on our behavior. When the polarization is rigid, immutable, we feel duly stymied, deadlocked.

A crisis situation may rekindle conflicts arrested and/or unresolved during earlier times. At such a point the "usual" ways of responding to the realities of the world may break down, giving rise to a host of symptoms. Too, there occur transition periods in everyone's development which are referred to as "identity crises," during which he is expected to change his identity in the course of solving the unique problems which confront him at the time. These periods add and magnify conflict.

Ordinarily, most of us can say with a good degree of awareness, "I am ambivalent about that man (or woman)." But most people do not nearly so easily accept *the fascination for frightening events:* feelings to temptation preceding disgust, love disguised as hate, tenderness concealing a wish to destroy (or, for that matter, Harold Lloyd movies showing him perched precariously on high ledges). Weisman (1965) believes that the prevalence of such antithetical affects is far more common in ordinary life than is usually recognized; such feelings fan the fires of conflict and confusion. To know these antithetical feelings within oneself, these ambivalences, is to begin to recognize the complementary opposites within experience. To be in conflict is

21

a powerful part of experience and not just an interesting concept for abstract discussion.

Gardner Murphy defines the problem of conflict in human existence when he states: "Most tragedy, whether in the grand style or in the petty style of the daily suffering of common man or woman, is a matter of a personality divided against itself. The awareness of conflict in oneself may be a major basis for self-reproof or self-pity, and the failure to become aware of it when it is strong regularly gives rise to inexplicable behavior." (Murphy, 1938, p. 296.)

In psychotherapy it is inescapable that both patient and therapist should be constantly concerned with the discovery and definition of conflict. To resolve the conflicts, one must first be aware of them. As George S. Klein states, "The central, most pervasive condition for the development of motives and of psychopathology is conflict." (Klein, 1970, p.21.) It is axiomatic, then, that neurotic conflict involves equally compelling forces in opposite directions, *neither side of which wants to move.* The therapist must aid the patient to become aware of this, and guide him in ways to overcome the stalemate.

Psycho-Imagination Therapy, inevitably, places great emphasis on the awareness of conflict. If the therapeutic situation is without movement and the patient seems lost, we must ask the question: Between what divisive aspects of himself is the patient caught, or, between what polarized aspects of himself and others? And it is precisely at such a time that certain useful techniques can be used to advantage: the Imaginary Situation (IS), Finish-the-Sentence (FTS), Most-or-Least question (M/L), and the Self-and-Other question (S&O). The responses to the techniques will assist markedly in illustrating the strategies of the "other" as used against the "self" and the counterreaction strategies of the "self" in dealing with the "other."

As the patient and therapist proceed to clarify existing conflicts, twin approaches are maintained: the phenomenological and the dialogical. They are not mutually exclusive, since most of the time it may be possible for a person to explore his interior life and still maintain a dialogue with the therapist.

Barron makes the point rather sharply: "Conflict in many instances is generative of new solutions rather than a disabling form of stasis. The real question is this: Can an internal dialogue take place between conflicting forces in such a fashion that the speakers do not simply repeat themselves but that occasionally something new gets said?" (Barron, 1968, p. 233.)

Dual Imagery

A rather remarkable phenomenon appears to occur when a person is asked to imagine two *different* forces, dolls, trees, animals, impulses, etc., and then to contrast each of them in line with the projected imagery. In the great majority of the reported imagery (but not all), there appears to be some form of bipolarization between them. This can be better demonstrated when one asks the imager to assign an adjective to each of the two images. The adjectives may reflect opposite forces of some kind. To enhance the opposing or contrasting forces, one can ask the person to imagine one of the images speaking to the other images, then to imagine the answer back to the first image from the second image. Again, this can be reversed with the second image speaking to the first image and the first image's remarks back.

Dual imagery is so fertile that from here it is possible to develop it in many directions. I will demonstrate a few directions:

First image	*Second image*
the person	
Statement to person from image	Statement to person from image

Another direction:

First image	*Second image*
the person	
Statement from person to image	Statement from person to image

Another direction:

Suggest that the first and second image walk down a road together (or appear together in some way) and become aware of what their interaction appears to be.

Another direction:

First image	*Second image*
the person	
(M/L) The most unlikely (or difficult) statement from the image to the person.	(M/L) The most unlikely (or difficult) statement from the image to the person.

Another direction:

First image	*Second image*
the person	
Statement from the image to a significant person in the person's life	Statement from the image to a significant person in the person's life
or	*or*
Statement from the significant person in the person's life to the image	Statement from the significant person in the person's life to the image

or

Statement from the therapist to the image

or

Statement from the image to the therapist

or

Statement from the therapist to the image

or

Statement from the image to the therapist

Experience with Dual imagery as a means of discovering areas of conflict and expanded awareness seems to fall into the following general groupings:

1. Those that compare two images of *things*: two rocking chairs, two tables, two rooms, two bathtubs, two houses, etc.
2. Those that compare two images that *are alive but not human*: two flowers, two trees, two animals, etc.
3. Those that compare two images that *are human*: two women, two men, two children, etc.
4. Those that compare the person in relation to *forces or impulses.* Those include (IS) above you is a force. What you feel and do, etc. (IS) You awake from sleeping in a field at night and there are footsteps over your body. Over what part of your body are the footsteps and whose are they? Or (IS) you walked down a road and somebody taps you on the shoulder, etc.
5. Those that compare *two of you*: (IS) you are in a cave. You are also outside the cave. Call to yourself. Or (IS) you are in a boat in the ocean and you are also in the water. Throw a rope from the you in the boat to the you in the water, etc.
6. Those that compare *two body parts of one person*: (IS) imagine what your heart says to your head. (IS) What does the left side of your brain say to the right side of your brain, etc.
7. Those that compare *body parts of one person to another person*: (IS) what does your heart say to the heart of another person, etc.? (IS) What does the heart of the other person say to your heart, etc.?
8. Those that compare *differences in physical space directions*: (IS) you walk down a shallow river and you see something different on each side. Or, (IS) you look ahead and see something; then turning, what do you see, etc.?
9. *Combined categories* of dual imagery: (IS) imagine two different animals in human situation, or any other possible combination of dual imagery conceptions that may occur creatively in the operational use of imagery that seems to help delineate conflict areas.

In asking a person to image two bipolarized images together and then to imagine them as one image, great difficulty is experienced by the person as he attempts this. Some persons protest and say it is impossible. One person brought the two images together and then exploded them in his imagery so that they would disappear. Apparently, the more bipolarized the dual images the more difficult it is to imagine them in a unitary manner.

In the use of dual imagery with detached or schizoid persons, I have observed changes in their imagery when the detachment lifts. What appeared in detachment as dull and limited seems to enlarge and expand and become more vivid. At other times, with some detached people, one of the dual images has upon examination revealed itself as the "secret self" of that person.

At this point I would like to illustrate some of these directions. A simplified example is to ask a patient (IS) to imagine any two different animals and have them walk down a road together. The patient might continue describing the animals and their "adventures" for quite a time, but at a certain point I would attempt a dialogue so that we can both arrive at awareness of his conflict and its meaning. The dialogue is not initiated for its own sake but to assist the patient in revealing to me and to himself the "what" of his imaginary experience so that he may eventually be able to get at the meaning of his conflicts. This can be true of any imaginary situation posed to a patient. I once asked a woman (IS) to imagine that she was wearing two different earrings and to describe them:

Joan: One is a large looped earring – the other is a pearl earring.
Shorr: (IS) Do you get a further image for each?
Joan: The large looped one gives me an image of me in a slit dress – sexy as hell.
Shorr: What about the pearl earring?
Joan: I get an image of the Virgin Mary.
Shorr: (IS) If you were to imagine the two of them together on a table, what would you see?
Joan: They would hide from each other. I don't think the loop earring wants to be seen by the pearl. . . . It's a battle between the good and evil . . . I've had this relationship with this man, and my husband doesn't know about it.

In learning the language of Psycho-Imagination Therapy, it is best that any given question be integrated into the fabric of the therapeutic procedure. One who picks an individual question at random "to see how it works" may do so, so long as he returns to the particular line of development that tends to elicit the internal conflicts and leads to the focusing techniques and conflict resolution. In this way we can avoid strict computer-like selection of questions, allow for the individual's intuition without straying from that particular individual's unique patterns. My own experience indicates that when a person is involving his imagination in visualizing and feeling, we should allow him to continue the imagery and the reporting of the experience until it seems that he can imagine it no further. In short, it is best not to hurry the patient on to another direction while there is an in-depth exploration of the one at hand. While Psycho-Imagination Therapy is an active therapeutic approach, there is always room for silence, for just plain listening, interpretation, support, human understanding and warmth.

Above all, it must not be assumed that when a person responds strongly to his or her imagery and feelings the answer will conform to the therapist's preconceived interpretation unless further complementary questions and imagery corroborate it. I remember being certain that a response a man had given me in his imagery was definitely related to a sexual problem and continued with this certainty for several minutes before his direction turned away from my expectancy and, to my surprise, revealed that he was referring to feelings of fear of his own death. It was indeed a lesson to me: never *assume*.

The combination of imagery situations together with other techniques and their possible sequence is primarily guided by the direction taken by the patient's early responses. *What is he or she revealing for examination? What is he or she willing to face? Where is he or she going? What is he or she ready for? What does he or she appear to deny?* For the therapist these questions and their tentative conclusions lead to further use of imaginary situations and other approaches that suggest new directions and the working through of unresolved areas of the patient's life. The process of Psycho-Imagination Therapy aims at an integration of imagery sequences with dialogue, in which the dialogue combines reminiscences of feeling and meaning. Findings of a more factual nature are not rejected, but blended, rather, with the other constituents into a picture of the whole existence much the way a good novel or biography brings the central character to life for the reader.

I am reminded of what Freud said in 1895 when he was using the concentration technique to elicit patients' imagery: "The one advantage that we gain is of learning from the results of this procedure the *direction* in which we have to conduct our inquiries and the things we have to insist upon the patient." (Breuer and Freud, 1953, p. 272.) It is my experience that, truly, when imagery is used to reveal the internal conflicts of the patient, the "direction in which we have to conduct our inquiries" becomes clearer. Moreover, as Binswanger has suggested, in our encounters with a patient we must be aware of him as "Thou." His case studies and other writings indicate the actual power of *love*, analysis and imagination combined to break through fragmented and distorted images so as to enable us to see persons *wholly*.

It is an interesting fact of observation that when a patient is asked to imagine two "different" people, animals, things, impulses, etc., and then asked to compare them or have them interact or speak to each other, a delineation of the internal conflict becomes clearer. Clearer, too, becomes the significance of meaning of the conflict. As an example, suppose I ask the patient to (IS) imagine two *different* animals and give an adjective for each. Then I may ask him to imagine one of the animals saying something to the other and the emotional response of each. I might then want to know which would win if they had a fight — or what would happen if the two animals were to walk down a road together. I would then inquire if this imaginary sequence had any relationship to the life of the patient himself. While not all of these dyadic or bipolarized imaginary situations reveal the deepest of a patient's conflicts immediately, one must be alert to those which — especially in the initial stages of therapy — evoke the greatest effect: often it's best to switch to other material until the patient is ready to return to them.

These dual imaginary situations are not standard or constant, though I have found certain specific ones to be very useful. There are countless possibilities, of course, and the variation is infinite. I may ask (IS) for two images and that the images interact, then ask the patient to express his feelings about the interaction. For example, when I asked one man to (IS) imagine an animal from his head, he said, "a fox," and when I asked him to imagine an animal out of his guts he said, "a snake." When I had him imagine the fox and the snake walk down a road together, he said, "The snake would constantly try to choke the fox to death — but would always fail." When I asked what he thought the image meant, he offered, "My feelings are rotten; I am afraid of my feelings — they will hurt people — so I have to be like a fox in my mind, thinking quickly, selecting my thoughts to be what I think I should be — I'll hurt people with my feelings."

Although asking a patient to imagine two different animals may seem a simple avenue into the patient's internal conflicts, complexities are frequent and may not always be obvious. For example, one woman gave the following answer to a dual IS:

Bird . . . . . . *Image* . . . . Fish
Free . . . . . . *Adjective* . . . . . . Free—but confined to water

"We really live in the same
surroundings." (*Spoke first*)

"Yea, I feel you are right." (*Response*)

"I am Zeus, you are Neptune—
we are powerful—king of
different areas. (*Spoke first*)

"Yeah, I agree." (*Response*)

When asked if this answer related to her own conflict, she replied, "The bird says, 'I have it better than you; I can fly through the air.' The fish, however, says 'I can fly through the water and I'm gorgeous.' " She continued, "They both compete well in their own areas." And as she continued to talk she came to realize that direct competition was the most difficult thing for her to contemplate. "If I can be best in jacks (the child's game) because of very special eyesight, I would feel okay, because there would be very few others who would want to compete with me."

She then recalled a reading group in the first grade in which she had intentionally failed in order not to be one of the best readers. Her conflict was to serve her idealized image of being well liked but nonthreatening to her peers. When she was given the same (IS) six weeks later, she offered a different image this time:

Sloth . . . . . . *Image* . . . . Black Leopard
Stationary . . . *Adjective* . . . . Active

"Do you need anything?" (*Spoke first*)

(*Response*) "No, I can handle it."

(*Spoke first*) "You seem ambitious today—
you must have something to do."

"Nothing unusual—just going about
my day." (*Response*)

"I identify with the sloth," she said, "because I go along with things – I really want to be a leopard and move fast and do things."

When one compares this response to the previous imagery, it is clear that some barriers had been removed, making it possible for her to face her conflicts.

It is apparent that the imaginary situation is useful in telling both patient and therapist to what point the patient has progressed, or where he appears to be, or even that it seems he is not ready to proceed ahead. One approach that can be utilized is the "repeated imaginary situation," i.e., repeating an imaginary situation that was used earlier in the therapy – one which elicited strong responses – and comparing the more recent response with the prior one(s).

An extremely useful imaginary situation is one in which patients are asked to imagine themselves on stage as *two of themselves* and then to describe each. When asked, additionally, to say something to each other, many aspects of the self versus the self become more evident; many feelings are exposed as the differences between the "selves" are described. There are instances, however, when the two people on stage are so separate that no communication is possible between them. Too, there are those persons who live so much within their own ego-boundaries that they may have difficulty separating the two. This was true of the patient who said, "Those are two of me on stage and we are making love to each." From this point it was possible to see his internal conflicts when he expressed his feelings in relation to an imagined audience.

As one can see, there are many directions in which this question can be pointed. Often, the answers can indicate the person's false position versus the solid position. Further, it affords the possibility of making comparisons between how a patient views himself (that is, self versus self) during the ongoing course of therapy. An example of this was the patient – an actor by profession – who answered as follows: "I am both of them – one of *me* is sitting in the corner on my haunches, eyes to the ground, looking up furtively to see my other *me* standing guard duty, looking out of a trench window for signs of the enemy." At quite a later point in therapy I asked him the same imaginary situation and this time he responded, "One is directing the other in an acting part. The other has great confidence in his ability to act a truly great part about real people's lives."

The same situation is equally useful as a method of eliciting the internal conflicts and then gradually extending the scope of response to include other people. For example, one man answered the imaginary situation in the following way:

"The Two Me's"

1. Immaculately dressed — brings to this performance years of fine training in the French horn — about to crack from the strain.

2. I'm not dressed up — like I hit the bottom — I lost everything — like I burnt acid in me to get rid of all the shit — I do what I do.

I then had him imagine a statement that he might make to me (Shorr) from each of his "Me's."

"I shake your hand — I say, 'Dr. Shorr, I hope that you enjoy this fine performance.

"Hello, Joe — I am really glad to see you."

He then suggested an imaginary situation in which he was receiving an "Emmy" for his playing and what he would say to his mother from each of his two "Me's."

"Mom, you stuck by me — I really hope I can make a better life for you."

"This is beautiful to win."

Continuing, he said, "The first me talks and is taken in by a martyred mother. The second one is free. I can no longer be defined by my mother as 'her own.' I won't be affected by her subtle martyrdom. She's like an adhesion; wherever I go she sticks to me . . . etc."

Not only was he able to elicit and recognize the conflict within him but by extending the imaginary situation to significant people in his life, he was able to view their influence upon him — to see how they defined him.

One woman responded to the same imaginary situation in these words: "There is myself, as one and another woman on the stage. We are in a play by Strindberg called *The Stronger*, in which two women are in love with the same man. However, one woman says nothing and the other woman does all the talking. It's a half-hour play in which the audience decides the fate of the women. Which part will I play? Which is really the stronger?" She then added, "Why can't people be like the Navajos who play basketball and never keep score? I guess I am caught in a scene of whether to compete or not to compete in this shitty world. Maybe I think my strength would devastate others."

In such dual imaginary situations we often elicit negative self-images in conflict with positive self-images. Sometimes it's possible to draw forth historical self-concepts in conflict with a contemporary self-concept. "Seeing" the conflict may come about through the use of an infinite variety of imaginary situations (or Finish-the-Sentence statements, or Most-or-Least questions, or Self-and-Other questions). All individuals are different, and we as therapists must try to approach each person via that question which seems most useful and appropriate as we continue to develop the ability to "see" what each patient "sees." While some questions might have been posed to nearly everyone, some are applicable to one person only and perhaps to no other person again. Certainly and unequivocally, there are imagery responses that belong *only* to that specific person and no other; I am reminded of an example that demonstrates the point. In response to the imaginary situation (IS) "Imagine two different animals in two different human situations," a twenty-two-year-old woman replied:

1. A groundhog going shopping. It's on all fours and looks at everything around — goes by other people — ladies don't like him and they gossip and talk behind his back — but he goes on shopping.

2. Black rabbit at a circus — big arena. He's sitting in one of the box seats but people don't know he's a rabbit. He gets up for popcorn and still no one knows he's a rabbit — even when he leaves, the parking attendant doesn't know he's a rabbit.

When I asked her an adjective for each human situation, she gave:

Pushy   **Ignored**

I then asked her to conduct a conversation between the two human situations:

"Don't get in my way or I'll run you over with my shopping cart." (*Spoke first*)

"I can get out of your way." (*Response*)

"No, I can claw you with my sharp claws." (*Response*)

"Get out of my way. I can jump on you because I've got big feet." (*Spoke first*)

When I asked her if the two images had any meaning to her, she said, "They are both me — I feel masculine as the groundhog, because my father made me his 'boy' and trained me to ride horses and drive trucks. My older brother was a disappointment to my father so I became my father's 'boy.' I never could be like my mother who was ineffective and weak. As I got older I wanted to be a woman. I don't like to be frilly and weak, and yet I don't want to be another Barbara Stanwyck with a black whip. I like men sexually. But it seems I'm nowhere; I go unnoticed like the black rabbit. I am a female all right, but I can't be weak like my mother or masculine like I was raised to be. Can I be the woman I want to be?"

It's possible to ask a patient for two different birds, animals, or flowers, or even for two different animals of the same species, for example, two different zebras or anteaters. As the differences emerge through the use of the imagination and as the possible conflict between the animals is introduced, an awareness of the patient's own conflict is stimulated.

I try not to interpret; I try to offer more possible ways for the patient to see it for himself. He is, by his answers, becoming aware of his neurotic conflict. The effort is nearly always directed toward the discovery of the *self versus self, self versus the other*, or perhaps the *"new" self versus the "old" self*. If it is possible to use an approach that exploits the 180° polarity in neuroses, the "self" and the "other" can be quickly presented, their opposition immediately available for recognition and study. At other times one may use a "Finish-the-Sentence," or a "Self-and-Other," or a "Most-or-Least" question which permits the person (self) to include the "other" with whom he is in conflict.

In terms of revealing what an individual may feel to be pressuring him and his reactions to that pressure, a particularly useful imaginary situation is: (IS) "Above you and behind you is a force; describe your feelings." Some people sense a force above and an additional one from behind; others report a single force from both directions. My experience indicates that this force is most commonly nonhuman in nature; it might be a "large piece of steel," "a hurricane," "a devil," etc. But, of course, there are those patients who refer at once to a human force: a father, a mother, etc. My own procedure is to eventually ask the patient to humanize the force. One man, in answer to the initial question, said that the force was a large magnet which was holding him in its power; it was fifty feet above the chair in which he was sitting. I then asked him to (IS) humanize the force. The answer, drawn from his imagination, was: "The magnet is my own arms holding me up there. It's my own intellectual control that I won't let go of."

As you can see, equally important as the definition of the "force" itself is the individual's particular reaction to that force. One man felt that there was a huge chunk of steel pushing into his back, and while he felt that he was permitting it to do so, he was not letting the force control him. When asked to humanize the force, it proved to be his subtly coercive father as well as his own subtle countereaction to his father. Another man said of the force, "It's my wife, I feel her controlling me, she pulls me, and I pull against her." A young woman described the force as "power-energy all around me — I have to open my eyes for it to be part of me — it's me against the world." Still another man said the force was "a large block of granite, very heavy. It's just there, in a way it is pushing me, wherever I go, it's there. Same position in relation to me no matter how I move." When I asked him to (IS) humanize the force, he answered, "People that I don't have control over — like a fellow at work who pretends to be boss, who is a co-worker really." In this particular case I was able in time to have him focus his real feelings toward this co-worker. "Get fucked!" he screamed at the imagined image of the co-worker.

There is an additional component to this particular imaginary situation which is worth noting. Often a person will describe the force as supernatural, and it may be that what some people refer to as God is closely related to such a sense of force. When those people who respond that the force is God are asked to humanize the force, it is the person who carries the most authority for them that is invariably mentioned.

When a person has resolved some of his internal conflicts, the dual imagery situation will not appear as radically bipolarized – the essential differences between the two images may be minimal. A fifty-year-old man who had resolved a host of problems, and who seemed very much at ease in comparison to his state of tension earlier in therapy, was asked to (IS) imagine something different in each hand. His right hand held a rose and his left hand held Indian beads. I asked him to have each of these say something to him. The remarks from both objects were gentle, aesthetically warm; his remarks back to the objects were of a similar tone. I then asked him to bring both objects together. He did, placed them over his heart, and seemed to flow in a most relaxed fashion with the peacefulness of the imagery. This was enormously different from his reaction eight months earlier, when I had asked him to (IS) "Imagine someone on either side of you, and have them say something to you." To one side of him he had visualized his grandmother, to the other, his mother; they tugged at him until he was ragged.

The "new" image (and other comparable ones in similar IS exploration) showed little of the original bipolarization, little of the original conflict and greater integration.

One can also pose to a patient what I call Reverse Time Imagery. In such an exercise the person is asked to imagine a situation at the present point in time and then asked to imagine what his imagery to the same situation might have been five years ago, or even last year. I asked one man to (IS) imagine a field, and build something in the middle of it. His response was, "A teahouse where you can see the sun and there is lots of music and food." When asked to retrogress five years in time, he said, "I would have imagined a tall office building, and I would have seen myself walking through it, very sweaty."

If verified by other elements of the patient's development, reverse time imagery provides a viable rule of thumb for measurement of the person's change.

It's beyond our scope to explore all possible bipolarized or dual imagery situations which might elicit conflict areas; I have included only a few in any detailed form merely to demonstrate the technique. But, in brief, one might ask, (IS) imagine your right leg is standing on something and your left leg is standing on something else; (IS) animal out of head and gut; (IS) an image of the day and an image of the night; (IS) ascending upwards into the air and descending down into the sea; (IS) an image within you and an image outside of you; (IS) an image of the past and an image of the present; (IS) an image in front of you and an image in back of you; (IS) imagine looking into a mirror and seeing someone other than yourself and have a conversation; (IS) imagine kissing yourself; (IS) imagine two caves and then imagine a different person in each; (IS) imagine who you would hold with your right hand, then your left hand.

The number and variation of such imaginary situations are infinite. It is for you to experience them and perhaps create new ones for your own use.

Transference Indications

At times, a dual imagery situation may bear directly on transference reactions between the patient and the therapist. A young woman, Joan, who was quite reserved and who appeared outwardly cautious in her first meeting with me, offered the following response to the question (IS), imagine an animal out of your head and an animal out of your guts:

"Imagining an animal from my head, I say a raccoon. The raccoon has a mask on his face and looks as if he is blindfolded, but he can of course see past the mask. He also has long claws which he used to tear apart shellfish. I am like the raccoon in that I felt the need for a mask. Where you could not see in but I could see out. Like the raccoon, I am frightened easily, yet with claws am ready to protect myself. I feel threatened by you as if you were annoyed with me because I wasn't open enough with you or giving the right answers. The rabbit from my guts was trembling as I felt on the inside. It was small and cute. I despise the word cute, because it seems trite and degrading. If something is cute, it is young, weak, and merely appeals to someone's fancy. When someone tells me I'm cute, I get very defensive as if they are trying to manipulate me 'nicely.' My animals walk down the road together amiably because they have to stay together or it seems like they would be destroyed. It is as if my body and mind united to defend me from you."

I then asked her to imagine (IS) any two faces. She imagined seeing Barbra Streisand's face and then mine. She offers the following:

"The two faces of you and Barbra Streisand annoy me because it is me and not Barbra. Yet, I can see, hear and listen to the things she says as if the person Barbra has said them. Yet they are my things I had been thinking about earlier. She feels that she has some need for your help, yet she could do without it and still go on with her career and be successful. Eventually, she would wonder whether she did the right thing and sometimes wish she would have finished with it.

"Some of the reasons I am frightened or wary of you is because you force me to think out situations without doing any of the work for me. Since I don't feel close to you or secure with you, I am left on my own without someone to at least back me up. It is the feeling of being dumped into the middle of a crowd of strangers by you and then merely watch what I do instead of coming over to me or allowing me to come over and talk to you.

"Trusting is hard for me because I'm not sure of what it all means. When one trusts, they leave themselves open to all kinds of pain, ridicule, humiliation and also to a heavy load of responsibility. How far should one trust? Who determines where to stop trusting and why? What happens when I fail in a trust of someone else's? How should I determine when to not trust a person anymore? What are the advantages of trusting? In this situation, trusting would be good because I could accomplish more with you than if I didn't trust, yet if I allow myself to trust you, will I slip and trust others that shouldn't be trusted? Then when they break my trust, will I become more bitter as I have in the past? These are some of the questions that I need to find answers for before I trust. I don't trust because I am afraid, but I don't like my life being ruled by fear. That is why I come here.

"When I trust, I reveal very private feelings that I'm not always sure of. Most people I have trusted take these things and use them against me later when I am not in the same frame of mind. Such an instance would be telling a person that I want to be less hostile with someone. Later when I slip and am hostile toward that person I was working on, the first person throws what I've said into my face. It is as if they are saying, 'See, you are a liar and don't mean the things you say.'"

This response came at the beginning of her therapy and alerted me to her very powerful need to trust me; it revealed all the cautions and emotional brakes she had applied to herself. Further, the need to understand the meaning of imagery was exceedingly important to her; she did not want to feel she was "lost" in a maze of her own imagery. Accordingly, from that point on, I emphasized the meaning of her remarks and their possible interpretations and did not proceed until I felt that meaning was quite clear. In short, I was there for her when she needed me. In time, I felt less and less remote to her; in time I became more real to her and she learned to trust me.

Sexual Conflicts

(IS) Walk into a room and you will notice a *hole* in the floor; now look through it and tell me what you see. In most instances the imagery responses to this imaginary situation are related to how a person feels about sex, how he senses sexuality, and how he deals with sexual relationships. One man said, "It's a dark room with old-fashioned floorboards — like an attic — dust around — there is a nude woman — it excites me — all I want to do is fuck and nothing else — just meat — no feelings — she's a tough looking chick." Well, as one might suspect, this man had great difficulty expressing tender feelings toward women and wanted to control them.

Another man, who was very frightened of sexual involvement, responded to the same IS in the following way: " . . . dark, and (it) gets darker the longer I look — people are swimming or floating in oil — they are vertical — I feel troubled — I might fall in and become one of them — I really envy these people."

Let me repeat that I do not at once push for interpretation or meaning; the responses may serve merely as starting points for mutual exploration, detailed analysis often postponed until a later time and even then with different direction. Still, for the majority of people who do not experience overwhelming difficulty in answering the initial question, it is possible to go further. One person, having imagined the room and the hole in the floor, said that upon looking down through it he saw a bridge swinging back and forth beneath. "How far down is it?" I asked him. "A thousand feet," he answered. "Gee, it's far." And without further prompting he recalled an incident in very early life in which a governess had seduced him in a hammock.

One woman in her thirties gave the following response to the same initial imaginary situation: "(I go) into a room that looks like a modernistic castle. I am looking through a square hole. It's a winding square staircase all rosewood — beautiful gorgeous rosewood — it's a room that opens to the sea — high ceilings with books I haven't yet read. Fireplace — fur comfortably squared over traditional hearth — aesthetically pleasing to get down."

I then asked her to (IS) imagine going down a round staircase, to which she replied, "I go down and down endlessly like an Escher painting to nowhere." Following this I asked her to imagine (IS) a staircase that turned square corners periodically (inspired by her own response). She answered, "It changes so much — it becomes more narrow — at each intersection there is a window or painting — at each window, there is a nothingness wherever there is a painting — they are mixed up and it doesn't make any sense. They are always pretty and impressionistic — then it becomes narrower and the paintings become narrower."

I then asked (M/L): "What is your most frequently repeated relationship with men?" She replied, "Forming the relationship and then dominating it — I had hoped my present relationship would be different. The more I control the relationships, the less happy they become." Then she volunteered, "I guess the squared steps are like my relationships with men as I control the things that will happen."

This imaginary situation is not one to be suggested or taken too lightly, and adequate caution must be employed to ascertain which direction one should take in developing it further. Verification and cross-checking must be used frequently, since we are interested in knowing:

1. How the person defines himself in relation to the opposite sex.
2. How he feels the opposite sex defines him.
3. The specific conflicts involved.
4. His or her readiness to face the conflicts.
5. Finally, the degree to which he or she fears judgment on the part of the therapist or others with regard to his or her sexual attitudes.

I am reminded of a time when I had asked one of my groups (IS): "Imagine looking through a hole in the floor; tell me what you see." And one man answered, "I see a clerk as she is filing all the papers in an orderly neat manner in filing cabinets — keeping it very clean and neat." It was embarrassing to him to hear that this imaginary situation relates to sexual things, and he recoiled from therapy. This reinforces the fact that blanket interpretations are sometimes hazardous, often needless. It is best to use them primarily as a guide for further exploration.

To the same imaginary situation, a woman of twenty-six responded, "It's not very big — the hole isn't — I couldn't get down there because I'm much larger. I see dirt there — ah! — it looks like the Grand Canyon — I can only get one arm in it —

but when I get close to it, it's granite and like the Grand Canyon. There are little people in it, or they are very far away. They have their arms up because they want something — all crowded together — they want out of there. I can't reach them — every time I try, I can't look or I will turn into their size. But, if . . . I kind of concentrate on what I want — I have to look away disinterested and stick out my arm — but I am not sure what they want . . . (Pause)."

Shorr: (S&O) What is your responsibility to them?

Jane: A lot. What do you want? But I can't look. If they saw me as big as me, they would be afraid. If I look I'll shrivel into their size. That's why I have to do it sneakily, like.

Shorr: (IS) Can you go down in there?

Jane: Only if I am little and I don't know if I can get up again. Well, unless I arranged it in advance as the big person. Then I could return — I'd have to have the edge. I must arrange it in advance. They seem kind of hostile. They ain't happy to see me. I'd have to find out what they want. I'd move through them and around them. They don't mind me being there — but I have to justify my presence. I have to help them or make them feel better. I don't want to stay long. My advance plan is for them to want to get out. But, I find they are not too unhappy. I'm stuck. They must be getting something out of it — but I'm getting nothing. There is nothing for me to do. Everybody has got the market cornered.

Shorr: (IS) Imagine your father looking at you.

Jane: He wants my support — he loves me, yet, but, I am paternal to him — not him to me. I have to organize things for him. Just be there.

Shorr: (IS) Imagine your mother looking at you.

Jane: What does she want? A calculated move. I'm apprehensive. Make waves or what? I don't know nothing but arguments — discord.

Shorr: (IS) Imagine Bernie (boyfriend) looking at you.

Jane: . . . More like my mother — yet I'm not sure. He can't take me seriously. He's got to be cold — I want him not to be warm. If he's nice, I don't know what to do — I get sarcastic and push him away. I need the edge. I don't want to fall for anyone or have them fall for me. If I give them a helping hand, they fall for me — then I crush them. It's to get out of it. They bring up sex, marriage or love, not necessarily in that order. (She laughs at that remark.) I run from them.

Another man gave the following account in response to the same imaginary situation: "I walked down the trap door which opened into the room below. The room is bare except for a carpet on the floor. There are four paneled walls. My feeling is that the room is my life and I must furnish it. After looking around for awhile, I first put in a very large round table with a white linen tablecloth. Next came a *very large* three-tiered layer cake all white with much icing, having hundreds of blue, burning candles on it. The cake was thick and took up the full diameter of the table. Next I very strongly threw a naked girl into the birthday cake on her back and she squished into the cake. I jumped onto her (she landed with her legs spread apart) and started fucking her. We fucked until we got tired and lay breathing hard for a few minutes. We both got hungry. I remember first sticking my mouth and face full into the cake and biting the cake and getting my face covered with cake and icing, still clutching the girl, with my cock inside her. It was great. Every time I think of this fantasy, I laugh. It is the neatest, best, cleanest, greatest fantasy I ever had. And you can believe I fully intend to try it in reality!

"It's hard furnishing that room. I feel that I can furnish it any way I like. The carpet is kind of Persian. The walls are wide paneled oak. I would furnish it first with my family (my group) (this included my friend, the doctor). Each one will have a bit of my birthday cake. I want them to. I have feelings about each one and how individually each would react to eating my cake.

"Next, I will have a banquet buffet and I have feelings how each person would react at the buffet.

"Next, I would open the door and let the rest of the world eat at my buffet. They would come in a few at a time.

"I still must furnish the room, Joe, and it's difficult right this moment.

Lest the reader misinterpret the use of the imaginary situation of the hole in the floor and what one sees and feels when one looks through it, I must add that it is one I just find very useful.

There are countless others including dual imagery, such as (IS), Imagine two different vaginas or penises or two different women's faces or two different men on a platform, or imagine taking a shower with one's father, etc. These and many others can help point to the sexual conflicts and serve as valuable reference points for further exploration and eventual focus for change.

Looking at Myself — Looking at Myself

One of the most effective therapeutic imaginary situations is to ask a person to imagine (IS) that you are looking at yourself looking at your "self." Initially I thought that this particular imagery would be too fragmented that it might possibly upset some people. Continual use of this imaginary situation has proved my suspicion groundless even though patients reactions have been profound.

There is no consistent theme that can universalize all people's reactions to this imaginary situation. The variations in reactions are enormous appearing particularly unique to each person. In some instances the first self (or the one that is being observed by the second self) may be the one that is deeply involved with a host of conflicts and negative feelings. At other times the second self may be the target person involved in conflict and negative feelings. The third self or overobserver generally does not have the severity of negative reactions, but his position in the triplicity opens up perspectives sometimes not seen before.

One man, for example, in response to this imaginary situation gave the following response:

1. The first Edward is well dressed, articulate, sincere from a good family — he is hollow — he wears a mask — his body is taut — eyes are not focusing.

2. The second Edward is defiant, insecure, lonely, angry, hostile with sarcastic humor.
3. The third Edward is grounded on earth — follows his own intuition and feelings.

"The first me is all the levels of expectation demanded of me. 'Be this, Edward; be that Edward.' I don't like the first me but I don't say to everyone I don't want to be him, but I slip into my Edward Two and remain defiant and sarcastic. I operate mainly here. When I go to gatherings of my family I feel I am supposed to go as Edward the First (that's funny). And I play the role but I secretly operate from Edward the Second and defiance. It's the Edward the Third I really want to be because that would be rooted in my own standards and I can give up secretly defying the world."

You, as the reader, might get an even better awareness of this imaginary situation if you were to involve yourself in it and observe your own reactions.

My own experience indicates that despite the fact that there are three "selves" involved there rarely occurs a disassociating effect rather an enlargement of perspectives. As a means of viewing the self-image of a person it has proved to be an excellent technique of imagery involvement.

The Three Boxes

An imaginary situation that very often reveals the inner and outer phases of the personality with a view to the person's defenses and conflicts is a seemingly simple question: (IS) Imagine three boxes inside of each other; imagine removing them, and arrange them in front of you; then imagine something in each box. My experience indicates that patients have to "work through" the extrication of the boxes as well as the process of arranging them; invariably, though (but not *quite* always), the greatest effort is involved with opening the boxes and seeing into them. Results from this imaginary situation indicate the following generalizations:

1. The largest box indicates the outer conception of the personality — the veneer or style with which the patient deals with the world.
2. The middle box relates to the person's defenses — the barriers inside him.
3. The smallest box seems to relate to the person's core, or center aspect of himself.

Or so it *seems;* I have no intention of implying that we are dealing with an infallible absolute. One man, when offered this imaginary situation, allowed his imagery to flow and said, "I'm putting the middle box over my head. The large box is full of cobwebs and is stale and dark. The middle box is over my head — it rests on my shoulders. I want to hide — it's a neutralizer — it keeps the old stuff from coming in. It really acts as a buffer from getting into my heart. That's where the heart is, in the small box. At first I thought it was a carefully protected jewel resting in purple velvet, but it's really my heart."

Another patient, a woman, had a remarkable set of responses to the same imaginary situation:

1. "Large box — it's bigger than me. I'm inside of it like a playhouse. I'm the kid — pictures on the side — just a brown box with just a washing machine — it's dark.

2. "Now I've grown bigger, I'm not a kid anymore. I see rows of male organs — like a movie I saw once where there was a thing you held. I guess you call it a stem and you touched people with it and it gave 1-8 on a scale intensity of pain or 1-8 intensity of pleasure. If I touched you with it, you'd be subservient to me because you'd have so much pleasure. (Pause) I dump those male organs out. They are like a box of little steaks you buy in the store. They all roll out downhill.

3. "Then the little box. It's most different from the others. This one has no lid, a jewelry box all tied up in a ribbon. I untie it. In tissue paper inside is my mother's heart and it's still beating and I snip at it and it squirts out some stuff. It's frightening. (Pause) As I stand there, the snipped part grows in the air and wants to grab you like a Venus fly trap. I think it's an embrace, not a strangulation. I stand there to find out. It comes around my neck. I cannot let on that I'm afraid. I offer her a bargain. I say, 'You want my body?' I am caught. I just remain there talking — trying to get out of it. Can I make a good enough bargain to keep it from strangling me? I see money certainly won't help. It must need something. I'll have to figure it out and try and get it."

When I asked her how this related to her life, she replied: "They call me 'the kid' at work. I come off like I'm easy going with no responsibilities. The first box is like my apartment — small and I'm the only one there. The second box stumps me, but when I think of what I see in the small box, it begins to make sense. My mother accused me all my life of trying to be sexual with my father. She was skinny as a rail and had absolutely no breasts. I was afraid to touch my father — because he belonged to her. I am afraid to touch any man because he belongs to some other woman. I can only have the man nobody wants. I guess I really have to show her how contemptuous of men's organs I am — so I roll them down the hill."

To add an additional dimension, I have asked a person to imagine that he *is* what he imagines in each box. One man saw a mouse in the small box. I asked him then to imagine he was the mouse and to Finish-the-Sentence, I am _____. I feel _____. He answered, "I am *weak*. I am *frightened*." This helped crystallize meaning for both of us.

Katherine, a thirty-five-year-old woman, when offered the three boxes, responded, "Three boxes of graduating size stacked like a pyramid. When empty, which they never are, the boxes easily slide one into the other so they could appear to be one box.

"In the largest, which is a magic box, is an endless complete wardrobe from all the best couturiers around the world, from all the greatest, funkiest boutiques everywhere. Everything is characteristically fit for me. When these clothes wear out, the magic box, systematically is a black, flowing, swishy, slinky, silky, clingy, marvelously comfortable thing.

"The second box is very pretty. It is red and white striped — shiny — with a sleek laquered lid — black. When opened, it holds sweet, succulent fruit — much tropical variety — papaya, Kiwi, guava, lychee — as well as all the familiar favorites. The fruit is clean and glowing. It is nicely snuggled in a fine piece of white linen. Nestled amongst the fruit is a silver knife which invites us to sample the contents of the box.

"The third box — the inner one — has a sole telegram in it which reads:

LOVED YOUR TAPES STOP RETURNING THEM SHORTLY
    STOP CONTRACT TO FOLLOW

The telegram is from a large city."

After I suggested the possible meaning of the three boxes, she then continued: "The largest box — the one with the wardrobe — the magic box — is representative of the way I present myself to the world. Or how I would LIKE to do that, perhaps. I seek 'comfortable' relationships. I seek beauty, grace. My being I want to be understood as characteristically, individually me. This individuality I would like to have it magically, systematically, naturally produced without my thinking about it — that's the magic part of the box.

"The middle box — the red and white striped one — is the box which connects the outer box to the inner one. Therefore, the contents of this box tie together my outer self with my inner one. The succulent fruit is indicative of a quest for survival. Further, a kind of survival which is happy, pretty, delicious, good, healthful, and sharing. A sense of aesthetic is always some sort of yearning for knowledge of other places, and cultures and people.

"The smallest box is the one with the telegram in it, and represents the core of my personality, at this point in time anyway. I would like to have valid recognition for whatever it is that I might do or create. I would like it to be meaningful and satisfying.

Occasionally, a person may invest the largest and middle boxes with imagery of a "healthy" nature, then discover a seemingly incongruous image associated with the smaller one. One man reported what seemed like healthy imagery in the large and middle boxes, then saw a tranquilizer in the small one. Similarly, another man saw apparently healthy imagery in the largest box and the medium-sized one — then reported that the small one contained a ferocious possum-cat which ripped at everything in front of it. As our dialogue revolved around this point, powerful areas of conflict and bad feelings were revealed.

One young lady appeared to have seemingly healthy responses to the small box: " . . . a million little things in it — filled with wonderful things in an endless array. I feel gay and joyful. I am chock full of neat things." The middle box, too, was unperturbing: "A beautiful, unique Easter lily. I am full. I feel strong and giving." But, in the large box, she imagined a bedroom, to which she added, "I feel lonely. I am not full enough." This seemed to indicate loneliness and an unshared life, despite her developing strength. It also paralleled a point in time when she knew she had to leave group therapy (in which she practically "grew up all over again") and was faced with a sense of genuine loss as well as other, good feelings. The large box represented her conflict over having to leave group therapy.

The Four Walls

One of the most complex imaginary situations to ask a person is to imagine (IS) "You are in the center of four walls, each wall being ten feet by ten feet and you are to imagine something on each wall." The reference to complexity is based on the experience that no recognizable definite, conceptual framework is evident from the clinical data and that generalizations cannot be made from the material in the other imagery productions. Despite this, on an individual phenomenological basis, the "Four Walls," as an imaginary situation, can be more enlightening for specific individuals as any I have been able to observe.

My original contention was that here was imagery that could comprehend the being-in-this-world of an individual. Indeed, for some persons, this is an adequate explanation and does quite verifiably represent the person's "world view." The usual symbolic predictability of the front view being the future and the back view being the past does not always seem to apply in this imaginary situation. No specific pattern of predictability seems to occur in contrasting right and left sides. Yet, despite the lack of symbolic predictability, the material elicited can be of the most unique and meaningful and sometimes the most powerful of any imagery.

Reminiscent imagery is one direction to which this imaginary situation can lead. Imagery that reveals undetected conflict may be seen on some of the walls. To develop this kind of imagery, I may ask at which wall one would care to spend the most time and which wall one would care to spend the least time.

As the imagery is experienced, one wall may be more emotionally charged than the others. It is possible to ask the person (IS): "Imagine entering the wall and then to continue the imagery." This may serve to clarify conflicts, significant areas of defenses as well as characteristic styles of behavior of himself and those he may include in the imagery. The variations are enormous and the therapist must be prepared to use his own creativity as the patient's imagery leads to points of heretofore undetected conflicts and feelings. It may be necessary to leave the four walls and go onto other areas of exploration if the patient develops his own directions of intensity.

Hazel, a twenty-four-year-old woman, responded to the four walls, in the following sequence:

> *At the Left:* A forest with lots of tall trees and greenery.
> *Statement the Imagery Makes to You:* "Come inside and find me."
> *In the Front:* Big canvas painting with some splattering on it.
> *Statement from the Imagery:* "You are always waving back and forth."

On the Right: Something splattered against the wall almost black.

Statement from the Imagery: "You're dead."

Behind Me: A little box like a peephole.

Statement from the Imagery: "I'm going to frustrate you."

She then said, "I keep looking forward to that canvas — the one with the splattering on it."

When I asked her at which wall she would like to spend the most time, it was at the left with the forest and trees. She said she would spend the least time in the one behind her where there was a little box with the peephole.

I then asked her to (IS) "Enter the right wall." She responded: "I see a long box like a coffin in pastel satin inside (she laughs strongly) with a light shining over it. I'm always a martyr. My mother called me a martyr and said I was too dramatic. Mother could drop dead from one of her epileptic convulsions. I was always afraid of what we children would do if she did, and what my responsibility would be if it did happen. Also I get a view of my grandfather's funeral."

Following this, she entered the Left Wall and said, "It's cool and refreshing. It's full of potential. I'm going to find new things. I'll find a cabin. It gives me feelings of growth and growing."

When I asked her to enter the Front Wall, she imagined, "My life the way it's been. To draw circles extending out. Like I used crayons when I was a kid — I would draw wavy lines over the page. It's like my life crossing lines — wavy — going from the Chicano life into other ways of life."

The strongest imagery occurred when I asked her to (IS) "Enter the Rear Wall." At first she couldn't and said all she could do is look through the peephole. A few moments later, she said, "I can do it now," and she imagined entering the Rear Wall. "I see a kitchen table that's bright, but it's dark all around it. It reminds me of the table we had in our kitchen. Sometimes it looks big. It's the old-fashioned chrome kind with dishes on it. Silverware and food in bowls. Now it changes to one setting. I walk up to it and sit down and look to the left to a door. It's dark behind there and it leads to my old bedroom. My door never opened all the way so you could see and hear things secretly. We could never say what we really thought. It was the house my mother and father got divorced in. I remember now suddenly my high school days. They were dreadfully unhappy. Mother was sick there. She has epilepsy. When she had seizures, I was blamed. I remember painting the four rooms to cover up the misery. It's a house I cried in a lot and got slapped around in. I was told how I must behave. My father lectured me about becoming a lesbian, because my aunt was and I liked her. I never knew what a lesbian was. My aunt, who was one, moved to San Francisco, and when I threatened to leave, they thought I would join her. I'm not a lesbian, but they kept thinking I was going to be one because I liked my aunt's freedom."

I find that usually one wall (which I cannot predict in advance) will be most emotionally charged and lead to powerful uncovering of reminiscent imagery co-mingled with present-day experiences. It can lead to the awareness of historical self-images. Significant people in a person's life may be revealed without interrogation. It can be most comprehensive for some persons and narrow in scope for others, but nearly always a rich source of meaningful material.

Body Routes to Conflicts

Imagining the inside of one's head can be used to elicit awareness of conflict and defenses. One man answered the question (IS): "Imagine entering your own head and tell me what you see and feel." Here is his report.

"As I enter my mind, (head) I see this complex array of machinery working with clocklike efficiency. Parts connected to parts, all interrelated. It seems to be an incredible precision factory except that I notice in one small corner there is a piece of machinery not working, just closed down.

"I try to start the machinery, but it won't work; the parts are all clogged and rusted. I'm going to clean them but seem to have a great deal of difficulty. It's as though it's too big a job and I want to give up. Finally, I ask someone for advice about repairing the machinery and he tells me to drop the parts in muriatic acid, to strip and clean them, which I do. I also polish all the brass parts, install new bands, overhaul the motor, but still I'm not happy, except in a localized way, still not satisfaction. Why not? The machinery is all fixed and in fine order. It's a magnificent sight, the pieces all fit and work together. Why no lasting joy with this? Is it something I did, but not me? I build houses; am I a builder? I'm a musical soul; but not a practicing musician? I collect antiques, but am I just a dilettante?"

In the realm of imaginary situations there is also the possibility for interbody journey, in which body parts travel and communicate between one person and another or between the patient and an other. An example might be, "What does your heart say to the heart of your girlfriend, and what does her heart say to yours?" One can include the head, heart, guts, penis, vagina and relate them to any conflict in the whole spectrum of possibilities. The following is an example of how a young woman responded at length to this form of imaginary situation — an interaction between her body parts and those of her parents:

1. My head would say to my mother's head: "I'm strong and I know how to compete with men on their terms. I won't be weak like you."
2. Heart to heart: "Look at yourself, mom. Become your whole self. Don't allow everyone to destroy your heart."
3. Guts to guts: "Don't play martyr with me. Give up trying to manipulate me. I'm tired of it."
4. Vagina to vagina: "I'm alive and healthy and like to be sexual. It's great!"
1. My mother's head to mine: "Straighten up, think of what people say, think of your reputation. Go to school. . . . "
2. Her heart to mine: "I need you, I love you, I am afraid for you. Let me and your father protect you.
3. Her guts to mine: "You must be cautious, the world is a frightening place, be afraid."

4. Her vagina to mine: "We are prisoner. This is the only part of a woman men like, watch out for them."

1. My head to my father's head: "I can compete with you and do well. I am as good as you."

2. My heart to his heart: "What are you doing? Are you crazy? You are hurting everyone you love. Stop it!"

3. My guts to his guts: "I'm not afraid of you anymore."

4. My vagina to his penis: "Stay away from me! Learn to love your wife."

1. His head to mine: "You are sharp but need a lot of refining. Learn from me how to talk logically and be able to get your point across."

2. His heart to my heart: "Be careful, don't get hurt. I can't stand to see you hurt, because then I hurt too."

3. His guts to mine: "Enjoy life, do all you can, learn all you can. Don't be like your mother."

4. His penis to my vagina: "It would say nothing overtly, but subtly indicate that it was there, just there, not going to do anything but be omnipresent."

Other questions are available too, such as (IS): "Sense your body from your head to your toes; what is the body part core of your identity?" The body part mentioned may be the one which is most protected against — the one which the patient feels to be most "him" or most "her." Indeed, this may very well be the "centeredness" that Rollo May refers to when he says, "I assume that this person, like all beings, is centered on himself, and an attack on this centeredness is an attack on his existence. He is here in my office because this centeredness has broken down or is precariously threatened. Neurosis, then, is seen not as a deviation from my particular theories of what a person ought to be, but precisely as the method the individual uses to preserve his own centeredness, his own existence." (May, 1964, p. 22.)

Situation and Imagery

The concept of being-in-the-world, or man's sense of himself in his surroundings, always involves a *situation*. As long as he occupies space, he is in a situation. Ask yourself where you are right now, and you will be in your home, in school, in bed, etc. The use of the imaginary situation (IS) as part of the psychotherapeutic process is a natural product of this concept. For example, one can ask a person to (IS) imagine his favorite room in the house; then one can ask him to imagine himself in that room with his father. The possibilities of response are countless, the combinations endless; the results depend, of course, upon the reported responses as well as on the therapist's guidance and his own imagination. It is the hope of Psycho-Imagination Therapy to strengthen the role of the situation, to encourage patients in their *choice of actions* within the situation, and ultimately lead them to greater choice and freedom in their being-in-the-world.

Too, if one asks a person to imagine himself in a situation, it is also possible to be aware of his hesitancies, doubts, freedom, fears, anxieties, etc., as he imagines his feelings and actions in that situational context, be he alone in it or accompanied by an imagined "other."

By way of demonstrating the permutations of situations, we arrive at the following list:

1. In some instances, the self is alone in a situation.
2. Then there are those instances in which the self is imagined in combination with an "other" in a situation.
3. There are those instances in which the self imagines only the other in a situation.
4. Then there is the self who imagines the other imagining the self in a situation.
5. And the self may imagine an other imagining yet a different other in a situation.
6. Finally, the self imagining the other imagining a different other who is imagining about the self in a situation.

On the Use of Imagination and Imagery

It is better to have the patient close his eyes or focus on a spot on the wall. All of us have been with people who, while sitting with us, have become engaged in mind-wandering; you have probably mind-wandered yourself. It is generally noticeable in that the mind-wanderer will be focusing his eyes on one spot. If he were not fighting social decorum, he would prefer mind-wandering with his eyes closed; therefore, I suggest that the patient close his eyes when he is asked to imagine something. I personally prefer the patient to sit in a reclining chair; a person in a horizontal position has greater avenue to imagery than when he is vertical; when not using imagery, the chair can be returned to its erect position.

While the relationship of the patient and the therapist is basic, since we are both interacting upon each other, the use of imagination in the therapy should not detract from the establishment and enhancement of this relationship. As therapists, we must assist the patient's exploration but the actual direction of any imagery situation rests with the patient's responses and feelings. The more the imaginary situation illustrates the conflicts and strong reactions with the patient, the less necessary are interpretations that might ring of psychoanalytical pontification.

The patient has greater responsibility for his daydreams and for his responses to imaginary situations than for his dreams over which he has no control. So when he imagines a response to an imaginary situation and is "surprised" by his imagery, he is quite aware that it came from himself and, thus, unquestionably relates to him. Certainly whether he is the participant or the observer in the imagery is important. When a combination of different imaginary situations is offered the person, the responses are more and more illustrative of his inner world of experience.

Through *imagination* we can help reveal the person's *conflicts* as a way of seeing together. The therapist and patient can share the experience. The *pain* and *anguish* are expressed for both to feel as the patient involves himself in imaginary situations. Certain *resistances* are seen by the *difficulties, hesitancies* and *blocks* expressed in imagination. Certain *vital memories* are *recalled* as a result of *association* to specific *imagery*. *Parental strategies* are revealed in imaginary situations, as well as the patient's *counterreaction strategies* to the parent. Transference reactions with the therapist are revealed by reactions to specific *imaginary* situations. Thus, imagination is in *the awareness of conflict*.

On the Manner and Style of Imagery

Not only do people differ in their responses to various imaginary situations, but there are countless variations of observable body reactions as well. Some patients have particularly strong reactions; they may laugh or cry as they imagine, yet show very little body movement. Others may move their arms or legs as they experience certain strong imagined feelings, but invariably − if my observation is correct − not until after the *felt* experience of the imagination. To one man, asked (IS) to imagine himself struggling out of a giant web, it seemed that he was involved in violent, muscle-exhausting movement; but despite all his loud grunts and groans, there was little large-scale activity of his body at all.

Each person seems to develop a style of his own as he involves himself in imagery and imagination. Some continue their imagery without requiring further stimulus from me, while others will rarely enlarge upon their imagery unless urged. It is precisely when a person seems to change an established "style" of response that I want to check further for possible significance. One man who seldom opened his eyes during imaginary situations finds it difficult to close his eyes when imagining his mother.

Then there are times when a person may report vivid and terrifying imagery without indicating any feelings which match the intensity of that which he is imagining. This may sometimes be due to the patient's having so internalized his imagery that he does not show the overt signs of his terror; at such points my experience indicates that it is best to ask the person for his feelings, to asses his intensity without stopping the flow of imagery. I once asked a man to (IS) imagine two chipmunks, one on each hand. He said that they both came up to his eyes and scratched them out. It was to me an obviously terrifying sequence of imagery, yet his reporting of it was neutral as reciting the time of day. Asking him to finish the sentence (FTS) "I am afraid to see _____" at once brought his body into rapid movement as he squirmed and finally answered, "My penis."

Thus, a feeling may yield an image and an image may yield a feeling. The more congruent the feeling and the image, the more impact, meaning and awareness.

Occurring less often is the phenomenon of the patient's thoughts being different from what his or her imagery reveals. I remember asking Clara, a young woman, to imagine (IS) walking up to herself and seeing herself asleep. She expressed an immediate thought, "I would wake her up." Then she added, "But I see her sleeping and I let her continue to sleep. I guess my head says one thing and my real me says another thing."

This phenomenon can sometimes be evoked when one asks the person to imagine a situation that involves sexuality. If the person shows embarrassment, he may instantly make a remark (many times quite funny) that precedes the actual imagery production. In such cases, the person is quite aware that the thought is a mild defense against what he fears his imagery may reveal.

Phenomenology

Merely stating that each person is unique is useless, unless one respects the specific uniqueness. Phenomenology is a way of revealing and respecting this uniqueness. When a person is confronted by images, statements and imaginary situations, he is the only one in the world to "see and feel" them *that particular way*. For example, asking a person to (IS) imagine being nude in bed with his nude mother and father will elicit solely that individual's unique and special reaction. One need only ask this of a patient to verify the point.

While parental admonition invariably contains a frequent or occasional "Don't say that," or even a "Don't think that," it rarely prohibits a child to "Imagine that . . . " It is common in the experience of children and adolescents as well as adults to have "unbidden images" and imaginary situations come to mind. Essentially, the phenomenologist asks the questions "What?," "Whence?" and "Wherefore?" and all later questions are guided by the answers to the first.

From the Universal to the Specific

There are those imaginary situations which are seemingly general, neutral or noncontroversial, such as (IS) imagine some clouds, what color they are, etc. There is no specificity — the person must organize the imaginative sequence with very little to go on. From this point, one can increase the details of the given imaginary situation and still arrive at a more or less generalized image. A further example might be to imagine (IS) that above you and behind you there is a force; what do you imagine it is and what does it do? Or, (IS) imagine looking through a telescope and tell me what you visualize; then turn around 180° and tell me what you imagine you see through another telescope stationed there. Or, (IS) imagine you have telepathic powers and you can imagine someone in a foreign country; tell me what they are thinking and in what country you imagine them to be. There are a hundred other examples, but suffice it to say that the initial emphasis is on the universal or the general, with a gradual shift toward specificity. There is, of course, no perfect scale by which to calibrate increments of specificity, but if I should ask a patient to close his eyes and (IS) imagine my face in front of him and imagine my saying something to him, then I am indeed getting quite specific. After a good trusting relationship is developed between the therapist and the patient, the therapist can offer specific imaginations very directly without encountering a great deal of defensiveness.

One woman who had made considerable progress in her therapy and had expressed a strong desire to work on her sexual problem found it relatively easy to accept an imaginary situation which would have been an impossible assignment months before, i.e., imagine (IS) entering your father's penis. A tough imaginary situation, undoubtedly, but she accepted it well and despite a certain obvious anxiety, she attempted to allow her imagination to operate.

One may frequently be surprised by some individuals who respond to the most specific imaginary situations in the earliest moments of therapy. Their readiness is apparent in their attitude and in the degree of involvement; they seem open, too.

Spontaneous Imagery

The most common form of imagery in man is spontaneous and arises before our "inner eyes" without any apparent stimulus from any specific source. Augusta Jellinek, originator of the term "spontaneous imagery," put it most aptly when she stated, "These images are experiences as they would originate independently as though we were only spectators and not the source of these productions." (Jellinek, 1949, p. 372.) Anyone who has asked a person to "just imagine anything that comes to you," with no regard for direction or specific content, will know that surprises never cease for the person imagining, who may express discovery, amusement or shock and for the therapist himself, who may be quite astonished by the unexpected nature of the imagery. Most frequently the imagery seems to flow into a continuous stream of scenes and actions. It is quite likely, from observations, that verbal reporting of spontaneous imagery, when uninterrupted and prolonged, provides the same function of release as painting or similar diversions. Nearly everyone is able to describe adequately his imagery, and these word pictures are usually much more complete, much more open to meaning and awareness of unconscious processes than other, more "artistic" means of expression and exploration.

As a person grows to trust his spontaneous imagery during the therapeutic dialogue and beings to see meaning and direction from it, he can begin to trust his spontaneous imagery when he is outside the therapy situation and can begin to derive his own meanings and directions. These "waking dreams" allow the person to consciously observe and interpret his own productions. We are likely to remember our imagery with greater clarity than our dreams; indeed, there are some people who claim to never remember dreaming who may suddenly report having dreamed after having been involved in spontaneous imagery for a time, such is its impact.

Directed Imagery

Directed imagery intends for the patient to react to images presented to him. This does not mean that the patient's spontaneity is sacrificed, however; the directed image may very well serve as a springboard for continuous spontaneous imagery. In essence, no matter how direct the therapist's suggested image may be, 1e does not suggest the entire imaginary sequence. He may offer direction whenever ne feels it is needed, and if the patient offers a spontaneous scene, he would certainly regard it as an appropriate point for further study by imagery. Directed imagery by no means takes the patient's responsibility for his own image productions away from him.

Horowitz and Becker found in studies of intrusive thinking "that the specificity of instructions for reporting visual images increases the tendency to form as well as to report images." (Horowitz and Becker, 1971, p. 39.) As such, directed imagery has certain obvious advantages for the therapeutic production of images.

Nonsymbolic Imagery

"Imagine you are casting a fishing line into a river and tell me what you will come up with," I asked Tommy, a thirty-five-year-old man. He answered, "My grandfather's law books," and began to talk about his conflict with authority and his fear of being "caught," even though he had done nothing to be caught for. It is with such an example that I introduce those images that elicit conflict from a nonsymbolic imaginary situation. These imaginary situations are countless; they are often enormously indicative of a patient's internal conflicts as the image is unveiled and the concomitant feelings explored. This is not to say that such imaginary situations cannot yield some form of symbol, or that they are devoid of all symbolism. If I were to ask (IS): "Imagine that you are drunk; say something to your wife," a patient might imagine, in response, that terrible monsters are descending upon him. There might be no direct reference to his wife at all, but the symbolism is palpable. Clearly it is impossible to draw any absolute line of demarcation between the symbolic and the nonsymbolic, but my experience indicates that there is a category of nonsymbolic questions which tend to evoke imagery of a generally nonsymbolic nature; in asking a person to (IS) imagine a hoax he might play on someone, it is rare indeed to get a symbolic answer: a specific, concrete image is virtually always elicited.

The important aspects of imagery are the mode of its use in the therapeutic process, the degree to which it affords awareness of the patient's internal conflicts, its value as a tool by means of which to focus the need for change. Past experience, the continual use of imagery vis-a-vis patients and their responses — these will fashion my selection of image-questions whether they be symbolic or nonsymbolic. Within each patient lies the kernel of image possibilities. Within the therapist lies the kernel of intuitive application, plus the knowledge of human dynamics and psychopathology. Moreover, while I stress here the use of imagery, the reader should not be ignorant of the Finish-the-Sentence technique, the Most-or-Least question, or the Self-and-Other question, all of which can be introduced as needed.

One of the nonsymbolic imaginary situations that I find useful is (IS): "Imagine you are a baby in a baby's room and that in the space of three to five minutes you grow to your present age." This exercise affords the person a chance to view his development, the strategies of significant people in his life, and his own counterreaction strategies. Critical points of identity development and conflict resolution may be illustrated. It · rare that the person will not want to break out at some point and leave the room. Those patients who cannot, or don't want to, are troubled by other areas of conflict resolution which need to be examined further.

(IS) Imagine carrying yourself up a mountain, or imagine various people carrying you up a mountain; relate all the connected feelings. This imaginary situation is helpful in revealing a patient's awareness; should the roles in the IS be reversed, further feelings are elicited; invariably the responses are nonsymbolic.

Included in the domain of nonsymbolic imagery are those imaginary situations in which one is asked to imagine holding or touching another person, or being touched *by* another. When I once asked a woman to (IS) imagine her father's hand on her back, she shrieked, "Oh, I can't stand that!" leading to an exploration of her relationship to men. Further, the imagery may be related to body focusing, i.e., (IS) imagine whispering something in your father's ear; then imagine him whispering something into your ear. Once again, the number of similar imaginary situations is vast, the answers almost always nonsymbolic. Jerome L. Singer (1965), in his book *Daydreaming,* reports on a daydreaming exercise of his own device, a fairly extensive personal experiment. In observing and collating his results, he concluded that " ... the more general trend, however, was for the occurrence of memories or fantasies that were not specifically symbolic in content." My own experience tends to confirm his view: most imagery reported by patients is nonsymbolic. But be that as it may, clearly it is what one *does* with the imagery – how one uses it to help the patient – that really matters.

Symbolic Imagery

The history of symbolic imagery can be traced back to the work of Caslant, Desoille, Leuner, Assagioli, and – to be sure – Freud and Jung. It might be expedient (but perhaps overly simplistic) to say that symbolic images are those which are representational of certain people in the patient's life or certain elements of his life without his awareness that that is what they signify.

As Gendlin (1962) and others have shown, the act of symbolizing is a creation of meaning out of experiencing. It is a formation of an organized pattern which comprehends and clarifies what might be diffuse, plural, or a combination of different elements. The Guided Affective Imagery of Leuner uses ten standard imaginary situations; they are presented to the patient in order to elicit symbolic aspects of conflict. He offers, for example, (IS) imagine a swamp in the corner of a field and imagine something coming out of it. Should the patient imagine some sort of monster or dragon, the therapist will aid him fight the creature by direct confrontation, offering all sorts of aid to the patient to help him win; possible methods involve exhausting the monster, feeding it, or engaging in other neutralizing procedures. It is from the symbolic process of confronting the monster and successfully destroying or neutralizing it that an improvement in life situations springs. The monster may very well represent a father figure in the patient's life, but his possibility is ordinarily left unmentioned as the patient proceeds through the symbolic imagery of the situation.

My own experience leads me to conclude that symbolic figures are frequently translated into nonsymbolic ones. Assagioli (1965) quotes a case history of Robert Gerard in which the patient was instructed to imagine that he was descending to the bottom of the ocean. As he descended he was attacked by the image of a powerful octopus. The therapist asked him to visualize rising to the surface and taking the octopus with him. Upon reaching the surface, the octopus seemed to change into the face of the patient's mother; this revealed the extent to which she was at the root of the neurosis.

I include symbolic imagery in this discussion both for the evaluation and definition of internal conflicts as well as for focusing change. My experience indicates that the use of symbolic imagery alone is insufficient to deal with all the needs and problems of a patient new to therapy. The complexities of human dynamics are so vast, so fantastically different, that effective treatment demands the integration of symbolic *and* nonsymbolic imagery within the fabric of the therapeutic dialogue. Symbolic imagery alone falls short, does not allow the patient to leave his session with the awareness and insight necessary to permit him to cope in his day-to-day functioning. My own experience with imagery impels me to utilize as many forms of imagery as may be necessary to reeducate the patient, to help him deal with and resolve his conflicts. One of the advantages that symbolic imagery provides is a decreased ego-involvement on the part of the patient as he engages himself with the imagery. *Increased* ego-involvement within the context of the imaginary situation, however, does not necessarily handicap the patient, especially as it often leads to conflict resolution – as the focusing techniques. For example, in the following chapter which deals with focusing, a man in the course of therapy is asked to imagine himself in his mother's vagina and fight his way out, this as a means of breaking his feelings of castration. He succeeds, with a very positive result. Ego-involvement was certainly at a maximum and the symbolism at a minimum, but the technique was a powerful and effective avenue for change, nonetheless.

A given imaginary situation may produce either symbolic or nonsymbolic imagery. Take the following example: (IS) Imagine something behind you and something in front of you. One woman saw her mother behind her in a rage, and her husband in front of her, smiling. There was nothing symbolic about her imagery and we were able to proceed from that point to certain specific awareness. Yet a man, when asked the same question, imagined a very comprehensive symbolic imagery which he fought through in a symbolic manner. No psychologist has yet been able to predict which type of imagery will occur to any given person engaged in any given imaginary situation.

Here is a written report of the man describing his symbolic imagery session:

"I went into Joe Shorr's feeling better than I had ever felt — than I have felt in a long, long time, feeling very positive from the previous group session, for many reasons. I came in basically feeling terrific. We discussed all the good things and some of the progress, and so on, and what the previous group perhaps represented. Then he gave me the imagery of 'there is someone in front of me and someone in back of me.' I immediately saw someone with an erected penis in back of me — nude — a woman — a nude woman in front of me and I was nude. And I got very nervous and fought the image and tried to change it. It was very hard at first to change it. And it took me a few beats. Then finally I did change it — it reeked with the phallic situation, homosexuality and so on, and that scared me, so I got away from that and saw myself on a large, open plain, like a desert, and in front of me was an old kind of covered wagon — a western wagon — crickety thing, and I was walking towards it as it was going in front of me. And then a jet airplane — the nose of a jet airplane came and prodded me towards it. It kept pushing me, pushing me, making me go faster and faster, as though it wanted me to make more progress. So I stopped and I told Joe that, and he said, 'Let's get back to the other one.' So I went back into it, and he asked me to turn around and to see who the man in back of me was, and when I turned around, I couldn't tell. It was all very dark and it was like there were black strips — he was covered like a mummy, but very sloppily covered And I looked and I tried and tried to figure it out — who that person might be. And I couldn't do it. I told him it was just total darkness. It was like I didn't see anything at all, but I knew something and someone was there. So he asked me to tear away the strips of whatever that was there and — oh, no — before he said that, he said, 'Put a flashlight on the thing,' to find out what it was. I couldn't figure out whose face was there and so then I put the flashlight on it and I saw strips of 35 mm film, so it was like the guy — the person — was incased, like the mummy, with film, so then he told me to clear away the strips of film to see who was underneath it. When I did, I saw a large sword, a very pointed, very dramatic and beautiful sword, and sort of surprised me. It was sitting on a pedestal and on the pedestal was a dried prune and a walnut, and I told him and we were both a little confused about that. So then I stayed with the imagery and all of a sudden, the point of the sword started tilting towards me and it caught me underneath the chin, and I said, 'What the fuck is this?' and then all of a sudden a hand came into frame and he lifted me high in the air and I was hanging by the point of the sword tucked underneath my chin. And when I took a better look at who it was, it was like a mythological God. It had a helmet on, like Mercury without the wings. It was a huge person, like in metal or whatever. It was a cross between Father Neptune — or Neptune — and Mercury. The face had a beard and so on — there was nothing — I couldn't really define the face. I tried to figure out who it was and I couldn't. And all of a sudden, Joe asked me to deal with it — or Joe asked me to give it a name and I felt like I was in a cartoon strip and then all of a sudden — oh! and then the thing had a two-foot erection — his penis was two feet long. And the name I saw — I called him God. I called it God, and then Joe later asked me to find — to put another name across its chest, although I didn't see it clearly, but what came out was 'King' — K.I.N.G. King. And the chest was throbbing, very big and powerful and proud. Then I had to deal with the thing a little more, and blood was coming out of my chin from the point of the sword and I looked very small up on top of the sword — the person was a giant. And so I started to deal with it, trying to get down, and he took the sword and flicked his wrist and sent me flying, and I got clobbered against the wall, as though I was very impotent and had no chance against this monster. And then I said, 'Well, I don't like that, so let me do it again.' So he flipped me again on the — from the point of the sword and I went sailing, and before I hit the wall, I — I made a hole in the wall for myself, or I allowed a hole to be there and I went soaring into the universe, and Joe later said, '. . . went soaring into oblivion.' I think that's what he said. So what I had — it was — uh — dark, I was flying through space, it was dark with the sky and the stars and so on. And so I stopped and was very confused and — I was confused about how I could've walked in there so happy, so positive and so much enjoying the seeming progress, and so Joe, realizing it was important for me to get back at this big fucker, made me deal with coming back to deal with it and so I flew back — flew myself back — and I saw myself coming towards him from far — from high above — and my feet — I came down feet first and then I belted him in the head, then knocked him over. And as he fell, it built and built and built, like I was an animal — a vicious animal — and I started punching the shit out of him. I — uh — I went and broke his cock over my knee and I took my knee and I started belting him in the side of the face — in front of the face — his nose — with my knee and my fist — I kept pounding and punching — I kicked his body several times — I took my knee and I — I squashed it into and rammed it into his groin — I — I beat him mercilessly — I just didn't stop — I kept on going — and — and then in reality as I was sitting in the chair relating this or seeing this, the impulse was such that even my foot kicked out once, — my whole body was tense and I was uptight and I wanted to, like, scream and I felt a need — I even expressed it — I told Joe I wish there was something, like a huge, stand-up bag that I could keep belting now — I felt the need to want to punch and punch and punch and punch. And as I said, a couple of times my body jerked — and I felt like kicking out or punching or whatever it was I did. And, God, I wanted to kill this thing — I — how I wanted to kill it — I kept at it and I kept at it and I just — this son-of-a-bitch wouldn't die. Then I went and I stomped on his eyes and two geysers came up and again it was like — it was like rendering me impotent, it just threw me up in the air with these two gushes and whatever fluid was coming out of his eyes and I couldn't get down off of it and I knew I had to, so I finally broke loose and I jumped — I was about twenty, thirty feet high, and I jumped off that geyser that was holding me up there, and I jumped on his stomach, and that hurt him — and I kept up and I — I just kept it up and I went and grabbed his sword and — oh — and then his tongue — I — he started flicking his tongue out or something and I started clawing at it and then — and my hands wouldn't do anything — so I started biting and I was biting his tongue and spitting out the pieces. I kept telling Joe how much I wanted this thing to die — I wanted to kill it — I wanted to kill it desperately and he told me to get at the heart — go get his heart — rip his heart out and I tried and I started clawing away at his chest and I couldn't get to it to — uh — I couldn't break open his chest and uh — and uh — oh, his chest turned — as I was beginning to make progress, his chest turned into metal — into iron — it was like he had one of those iron chest protectors on. So again I was rendered helpless. I couldn't make headway with this prick, so I kept going and kept going and I finally went and I grabbed — I knew I had to kill it and I went and grabbed his sword and I — the thing — you know — it was — boy — it was trying to get away from me and it was almost getting away from me after all the pummelling I did, the son-of-a-bitch — and I was squeezing his throat — I was squeezing his throat. He uh — no, no — uh, yeah — right, and he started crawling away from me, so I went and grabbed his sword and I — uh — went for his heart and finally it pierced his heart and — uh, he let up a roar that was just incredible. The sword pierced the iron and went into his heart and out of it came a black — a gush of black fluid like that which comes from a squid — the ink from a squid — uh — but it was huge, like an atomic mushroom blast, that's what — it was all black and gray. And his face came closer and closer to me — it was roaring, it was like he was still coming fucking after me, he didn't stop, then I jumped down and I made sure I missed his mouth, of course, and I jumped on his neck and — uh — evidently the weight of that finally got him, and I went down with him and it was like we were falling twenty stories, and he came down with a crash, and again I started kicking and punching and fucking, kneeing the son-of-a-bitch — I — I hated him, I wanted to kill him so and I — he still would not die, after all of this. And — um — I had his throat — that's what it was — I had his throat and while I was squeezing his throat, he could barely breathe — his tongue came out and that's when I started biting his tongue and spitting out the pieces, while I was squeezing his throat, and he still wouldn't die, so I took his sword, and I — uh — sliced his neck and I — uh — severed his head and his head came off. And the bod — while the body was still just moving around a little, the fuckin' head was still coming at me — uh — uh — I mean it wouldn't stop, so I didn't know what to do — oh, and then I punched its eyes — oh, I looked at its eyes and there were — they were black with fire in it — and — uh — then I remember telling Joe it was like watching a Saturday cartoon — uh — on TV — and then I took some implement, I don't know what exactly, and I started scraping out of his skull — the base of his skull — uh — the head — all the stuffing — all the stuff that was inside his skull, I started pulling out like you pull stuffing from a turkey and I did that and the fucking head still looked at me and still started coming at me so then I took his flesh and skin and I started ripping it off his skull — and — uh — there was — uh — that, and — that still didn't stop him. It was as though he were still alive and I was still ineffectual in terms of destroying and killing this thing, and then finally all I had left was the skull, and bare — bare-boned skull, and I said 'Okay, that should do it, hopefully,' and then I put it on a shelf, and then all of a sudden it started moving and there was — there was Joel Grey — uh — with the same makeup he had on in "CABARET" and he slid the skull across — uh — that was hiding his face; and there he was, smiling at me and then he brought the skull back in front of his face to cover it and I felt again that I had lost, that I had no chance to win against this fucker — uh — I am now consciously aware — I am not going to be put — the — the thing is, I'm ready to do battle and I wanna — I want to kill — I want to get all that hostility — that hatred that I have in me — uh — for these — all these years, well — I will kill him. I will win. I do win. I am me."

The point I am making is this: the same imagery situation might have produced nonsymbolic imagery — the image of the patient's boss, the patient's sister, etc. Both possibilities can exist. If symbolic imagery is produced, I will attempt methods of resolution using symbolic imagery. With specific nonsymbolic imagery I may use some of the focusing techniques, or an interior dialogue psychodrama resolution.

Dreams

Looking back historically we find that soon after Freud abandoned his "concentration technique" of eliciting patients' imagery, he published his monumental work, *The Interpretation of Dreams.* Rather than negating the imagery, the book elevated its value to a new plateau. Still, wider possibilities remained unexplored, and Jung's preoccupation with active imagery essentially involved dream work.

While the major emphasis of this discussion has to this point been on waking imagery, I welcome and encourage patients to remember and report their dreams. Images from our dreams are pictures of our conflicts and intimacies and basically reflect what we think of ourselves and what we really think of others. Beyond doubt, they are a useful guide to the internal conflicts of the person. Dreams as such are a complex and varied phenomena, and I can only limit my discussion to a few points.

Psycho-Imagination Therapy approaches dreams from several viewpoints. The first is simple, relating as it does to those dreams that have clear and obvious meaning which can be shared by patient and therapist. The second approach encompasses any or several of the four basic techniques generally used in Psycho-Imagination Therapy, with prime focus on meaning, direction, and conflict, i.e., what the dream signifies, what mode of experience or behavior conflicts with other possible options.

The Most-or-Least technique may be brought into play with regard to a given element of the dream or even in regard to the "title" of the dream. One person gave the title of her dream as "The Train." I then asked her to tell me (M/L) the most unlikely person to be on the train. She answered, "My father" (who played no part at all in the dream). She then reflected that she " . . . never did anything with him as a youngster." The dream, in this light, began to make sense to her, and she connected it to her present behavior with her boyfriend. Also, the phrase "to please" appeared in her dream several times. On the basis, I inquired (M/L) who was the most difficult person for her to please, and (M/L) who was the easiest person to please. At this point, she experienced a flash of anger at her boyfriend for the difficulties he had set up to be pleased by anything she did. In a way this cleared the path for her; she became aware of how she was being defined by him and resolved to take action.

Her dream involved a train ride in the course of which she was trying to please her boyfriend Frank. He did not seem to respond to her, did not seem to know how to handle himself in the social situation of the dining car, etc. She was frustrated as she tried to buttress his self-confidence and overlook his lack of sophistication. I asked her to imagine (IS) two different trains, using dual imagery. She gave this response:

1. Very streamlined — sleek, sophisticated.

2. Big chuggy — old fashioned like my mother.

She then volunteered that she was the sleek train and her boyfriend was the unsophisticated, big, chuggy train, just as she had always felt about her mother. The meaning of this did not escape her, nor did her boyfriend escape her feelings of anger.

Sometimes one may ask for a title to a dream; after getting it, one can then ask (M/L) for the most *opposite* title. This may or may not provide clarification as to meaning, and can sometimes serve to refine the feelings connected with the dream.

Many dreams naturally indicate some internal conflict. We must try to recognize the elements in opposition and ask the person to contrast these elements. It is helpful to ask where the dream took place (the "setting" of the dream itself); often one location has greater emotional significance than another. It also seems to me a good idea to ask the patient to imagine the people in the dream, and to imagine what they might say to him or her. Then I ask the patient to "guess" the names of the unidentifiable persons in the dream. The "guessed" names may relate strongly not only to the dream, but to the patient's life.

I agree with Jung's suggestion that in the therapy session the dream be "continued" beyond its actual termination, that the patient be encouraged to imagine the consequences that might occur from this further development of the "story." At times I will ask the patient to imagine any one of the dream's personae speaking directly to me, the therapist, and then to imagine what I might say in reply.

The reminiscences of imagery evolving from a dream indicates residual feelings and conflict; thus, a springboard is provided for further imaginary situations. Furthermore, asking the patient to imagine that he himself is each of the various parts of the dream (as the Gestalt therapists are fond of emphasizing) is beyond question a valuable approach. I suggest additional scrutiny of meaning and interpretation.

What follows is a dialogue in which patient, Kenneth, reported one of his dreams to me. My own comments are inserted parenthetically throughout his report.

"I dreamt I was in the living room of a house with another man. He had a large bag of marijuana and I had a small one. I knew that someone was coming to get the stuff. The other man and I hid our bags and he left. Then I dreamt that a 'gangster-type' came into the living room and asked me for the stuff. I quickly gave him mine, but panicked for a second because I couldn't remember where the other bag was. Then I remembered it was hidden under the cushions of the couch. Very relieved, I found it and gave it to him. He told me that they would still have to kill me because I knew too much. I told him it was OK and that I wouldn't tell anyone, but he said I would still have to be killed. He disappeared and in came the 'killer.' He was thin, with shoulder-length black hair, and good looking He came at me making hand movements that appeared to be ballet-like. He was also wearing some type of costume which I vividly remember was white with colored polka dots. He came at me and I grabbed his arms. I remember trying to twist them with no apparent effect on him and getting frustrated at the thought that he must be double-jointed. I then started scratching him which seemed to have an effect on him. However, he backed away and revealed that he possessed fingernails several inches long and gave me a look as if to say that if scratching was what I wanted, he could do it in spades. I then remember deciding to charge at him, no matter what happened, so I put my head down and charged at him. I got in close to him, picked him up, turned him upside down and bashed his head into the ground.

"In discussing this dream with Joe, the following came out: 1) When asked to name the dream, I immediately thought of the title "Rebirth." 2) The most obvious meaning of the dream (certainly as to its conclusion) was that in my pretherapy days, I probably would have given up any hope of fighting the killer and chosen the easier way out of just letting him kill me. Now, as a result of therapy and, as evidenced by various little incidents in recent months, I decided not to be afraid of what might happen (putting my head down and taking my chances) and to fight back even though this required more effort than allowing him to kill me."

(I asked him the Self-and-Other question: What choice did you have in the dream? I also asked him for imagery of the small bag, and what it would say to the large bag.)

Small Bag	Large Bag
"I want to be as big and cool as you."	"You're OK. You're fairly cool — but not one of the 'in' group or one of us."

He volunteered, "I have always been on the periphery — never an outcast — not completely accepted as a true inner group."

3) "When asked to think of the person *most opposite* to me in the dream, I couldn't think of anyone right off, and then I flashed on 'old Jews' which I'm sure included but was not limited to my father. To me, historically, 'old Jews' are weak, can't fight back and are therefore killed at the killer's whim. I'm sure that despite my rebirth in the dream, I still see myself as an 'old Jew' to a certain degree."

(I asked him the Finish-the-Sentence: Old Jews _____ ; to which he said, "never fight and play dead.")

4) "One of the most interesting insights was the interpretation of the movements of the killer. In describing the dream, I referred to them as ballet movements, but in the subsequent discussion, I realized that they were the type of hand movements made in karate routine. This fit perfectly into the 'masculinity measured by strength and toughness' trip that I guess I'm still into, wherein I've many times fantasized being proficient at karate and how impressive (especially to women) that would be; I actually once started karate lessons but quit shortly thereafter."

(I asked him to (IS) imagine the name of the killer. To which he answered, "Steve." "Steve" led him to associate the name "Doug" a few seconds later. I then asked him to (IS) imagine Doug and himself on a balance scale when he became aware that Doug was the trim man who was divorcing the woman whom Kenneth, a lawyer, was representing.)

5) "The last, most nebulous and therefore, most frustrating, recollection was the attempt to determine who the man was that had the large bag in the beginning of the dream. I finally decided it was the husband of a client of mine in a divorce case. What was frustrating is that this man does not, at least consciously, impress me; I have never thought of, or have any present desire to be like him. The only thing Joe and I could think of was that, by virtue of being a relatively good-looking, trim man for his age (early forties), he represented the attractive, self-confident man I would like to appear as."

Depth Imagery

A depth reaction can be viewed from many directions. A person may have a deep set of reactions to just the mere presence of the therapist. I have also observed intensive emotional reactions to a mildly reflected statement in the Rogerian fashion. Furthermore, one cannot help but observe enormous individual differences of intense emotional reactions to the same imaginary situation. But, there are certain imaginary situations that nearly always elicit a profoundly deep set of reactions, no matter who the patient may be.

These highly emotionally charged imaginary situations should be employed with caution and with some awareness of where the patient is and what he appears ready to face. Needless to say, at these times the mutual trust between patient and therapist should be at its optimum. Support and therapist encouragement may be of vital importance during such imagery sequences.

One can ask, for example, the imaginary situation (IS): Imagine that you are a child and you are crying; now imagine your mother and father 'licking' away the tears.

In all but a very few instances very powerful reactions will emerge. Some people do not wish to cope with their strong reaction and say such things as "I'll punch her out" or "I'll hit him in the teeth." For the majority of the persons the imagery continues with surprise, horror, anger, shame or love and tender feelings. What becomes clearer is the way in which the mother or father defined the patient and how he began to define himself. Sharp differences between the actions of the mother and the father are frequently noted.

I ask you to imagine the following response is being related by a twenty-seven-year-old woman and then ask what your reactions might be.

"My mother is licking my tears and as they drop from her tongue, they fall on my breasts and vagina and burn holes into them until there is nothing left of me."

Or the response of a forty-five-year-old man:

"My father licks all my tears just as they emerge. He is determined not to have mercy. He then proceeds to lick me all over my body including my asshole. The obliging bastard."

I am certain that you cannot fail to note the intensity and the depth of the feeling presented.

One young woman, Wilma, reported the imagery in a halting manner. She was breathing very heavily and sighing frequently. Here is her report of her depth reaction:

"Imagining one of my parents licking my tears is impossible with my father. It is only possible with my mother if I am a baby who isn't aware of what is going on. Then she would really have to be in a really different mood than I've ever seen her. My mother is very clean. From her I have learned to cringe when sleeping in anyone else's bed unless they have freshly laundered sheets. She can't even handle it when I lick a spoon, after trying whatever is in a cooking pot, and putting it back in the pot. Even though the heat would kill any germs. My mother would be able to hold me closely but I couldn't handle it also if she licked my tears unless I was an incoherent baby. In some ways I have forcibly gone against her. I allow my cat to eat off of my plate. My friends and my younger brother are welcomed to share my glass or silverware, plate or food. Besides my mother just doesn't get that close physically. We can go up and hug her easily. When she plays with my brother or me (a year ago or before) she would tickle us or hold us so we couldn't get away. But as a rule she isn't overly affectionate. To touch us, she does things like holding one of our faces to the light to look for blemishes. When she does this it doesn't feel like she is being critical. It is more of a way for her to be physical with us, I think.

With my father it was impossible to imagine even if I were a tiny incoherent baby. I guess I couldn't imagine it because I always have such a strong feeling that he would be sexual and not just tender and loving. The feeling is that he gains out of any touch instead of giving. He is taking and getting a thrill off me that he has no right to. I always feel powerless with feeling of being taken − that is another reason I used to not want to be a woman. As a woman I feel very powerless or am reduced to the level of a child, who, of course, has no power. When a man looks at me or says things I always feel anger because I have no means to stop him from visually raping me. That is usually what it feels like when men "look me over." Usually, if I am feeling especially hateful, I try to outstare them. Of course, from my mother I learned that when men look you over that they are mentally raping you. Maybe not. She probably never said it that directly but the feeling came from her. The words probably just came from someone else. She doesn't trust any men. I, of course, went against her about the age of 16 or so. I started going over to a guy's apartment, calling them and just wholeheartedly trusting them. In fact, I went overboard. I would trust anyone that gave me half a chance. Immediately I would do anything for them and give of myself till I was eventually knocked down, everytime. It interesting the spectrum I've gone through. From complete trust to no trust and a lot of hate and suspicion. I am aware that my worst area for mistrust and terrible feeling are towards Mexicans and old men. They only take for themselves. They can't give as far as I am concerned, of course, it's far too generalized. There are probably some who are quite giving but it just is too hard to get past my feelings to find out. It also seems like these two groups are the most attracted to me of all men. So I also hate it because I want to be wanted by young liberal longhairs who don't want me."

As each of these persons continued in their imagery it led to reminiscent imagery of crucial incidents in their lives. Awareness of the self image versus the prescribed image was sharply focused. The intensity serves as a natural bridge to the focusing procedures to change the person's self-concept to a more authentic position from the previous false position.

Other imaginary situations that nearly always elicit a depth reaction are as follows:

1. Wake up as a baby. What do you feel and do?
2. You are in a cave and you are to call for help from your mother or father.
3. Take a shower with your mother or father.
4. You are in a playpen with your mother and father and you are all one year old.

5. Father or mother beating you up.

6. Look into a mirror, but instead of seeing yourself imagine someone else. Speak to each other.

7. Your mother or father walks into a room and finds you dead on the bed.

Again, it would be wrong to assume that certain imagery produces profound feeling reactions and the others have little or no effect. Experience with imagery indicates that strong emotional reactions can come with any image if the patient is ready to face something difficult within himself even if certain seemingly nonemotional imagery, such as a train or sled, is presented. Such a train or sled may be associated with guilt and shame feelings and would then need to be dealt with.

My own references to depth imagery here emphasizes those imaginary situations that seem to almost always elicit powerful reactions. Clinical judgment must be exercised in their use. They are most effective in impasse situations and other points in therapy where the clinical judgment of the therapist comes into play.

CHAPTER III

Imagery and the Focusing Approaches

In the long run it is not enough for a person to be aware of his inner conflicts: a change must be made in the way he defines himself. The resolution of an internal conflict is more important than a mere solution; sleeping pills offer a solution to insomnia, taking a vacation offers a solution to an unpleasant situation, but in neither case is the actual problem resolved. Superficial solutions are easily conceived and more easily prescribed, but it is the duty of the therapist to ignore such temptations and deal constructively with the problem itself, however difficult it may be to liberate a person from a neurotic conflict resolution.

The focusing approaches are designed to free the patient from a deadlocked position in his psychological life. Suppression, avoidance, distortion and withdrawal provide avenues to sustain conflict and escape from resolution; approaches must be implemented to provide healthier, more positive avenues. As their cornerstone, these approaches depend upon the concept of self-definition. It is essential that the patient be assisted in changing his self-image and in combating the inclination to let others define him falsely. It requires little effort for the neurotic person to be placed in false positions, and the focusing techniques provide a starting point for the patient's inner resources to work for him in fighting these uncomfortable and painful situations.

Interior Dialogue/Cathartic Imagery

In order to demonstrate the focusing approaches, I am presenting a portion of a taped discussion with a twenty-five-year-old man, Arly, who had been in therapy for about six months. The discussion involves interior dialogues between Arly and his mother, as he imagined they might take place, during which he confronts her with the purpose of changing his self-image. Essentially, the method makes use of cathartic imagery though it also includes use of the "impossible scream" and powerful expressions of anger feelings — a valid force in liberating the individual from a negative self-image. Let me emphasize that these techniques — imagery in interior dialogue, body touching and holding, body focusing and task imagery — are not employed capriciously. Clinical judgment is required to assess the ego strength of the patient, to determine whether the patient is *ready* to mobilize his forces against an archaic bastion of defenses. The therapist must also align himself on the side of the positive forces, consistent with the patient's true identity; obviously, it is only when the trust of the therapist is secured that the individual can allow himself to be free to face elements of his life which have heretofore seemed overwhelming.

Arly: Um, I feel sort of like a something is expected of me — something I should be *giving* more than I should be doing, and all the ploys she used on me, it reminds me — remember that time in group when I said I went real stiff? — somehow that all related in there, like I could associate it with dear old mom and me and stiffness.

Shorr: (S&O) What were some of the ploys she used on you?

Arly: Mom? Well, mainly just faking the sadness and hurt and not being able to make it, I mean — it's like I know all that in terms of her.

Shorr: Faking sadness — clueing you in, sucking you in.

Arly: Yeh, I never, you know what — I never even thought about it. I mean, I always associated sadness with her as being genuine, this is the first time I've ever said faking.

Shorr: Yeh, it slipped out?

Arly: Yeh, how about that, not a bad slip, huh?

Shorr: (Focus) (IS) No. Okay now, your mother faked sadness; I want you to imagine pointing your finger at her face.

Arly: Okay, I'm imagining, do you want me to say something?

Shorr: (Focus) Yeh, what are you going to say?

Arly: (Focus) (Angrily) QUIT FAKING YOUR SADNESS OR I'LL PUNCH YOU IN THE MOUTH — (Laugh) I'd like to belt her one.

Shorr: You're pretty angry, huh?

Arly: Yeh.

Shorr: 'Cause you were taken.

Arly: Yeh.

Shorr: She seduced you with fake sadness, therefore it behooved you to _____ . And it's your responsibility to _____ .

Arly: To be there all the time to make sure she didn't wither up and die of fake sadness, hum, (Sigh) so that, hum. . . . .

Shorr: (FTS) So I have to convince every woman that _____ .

Arly: (Sigh) That I'll always be there.

Shorr: (FTS) Every woman has to convince you that _____

Arly: (Sigh) Um, that she is incapable of making it without me.

Shorr: How do those two jive?

Arly: Oh, they jive real well unfortunately, yeh. . . . .

Shorr: (IS) Do you want to go through that scene again where your mother comes on with a fake sadness, try to imagine it, she coming on toward you now with a fake sadness of some kind, now you react to that.

Arly: (Sigh, sigh) It's hard to react, it's hard to picture, the only reaction I have, I mean I'm not even sure that I can picture it — or it's just to hit her in the stomach.

Shorr: Well, how do you feel after you do that?

Arly: Yeh — Wow! I just had like a strange flash, as I was hitting my mother I could almost see my father like a shadow in the background, you know, like he's coming into focus too, so I had to let him have it on the jaw.

Shorr: (Focus Scream) Yeh, and what do you want to scream at him?

Arly: I'm not sure, just "get away," you know, it's like I could punch the – if I – like I can picture punching them both toward the door and just closing the door and locking it.

Shorr: (IS) Okay, just imagine closing the door.

Arly: Well I, well I can still hear them banging on the door.

Shorr: You have to get rid of them you mean?

Arly: Yeh – it's guilt you know.

Shorr: What are they screaming at you?

Arly: Don't shut us out or something like that.

Shorr: (IS) (Focus) And how about you screaming at them with "How dare you" – What would you say to them?

Arly: (Sigh, sigh) Um, (Loud) HOW DARE YOU PLACE SUCH A TERRIBLE DEMAND ON ME.

Shorr: (Focus) (FTS) I don't need _____ .

Arly: God, I don't need YOUR PROTECTION, I don't even know what that means but, but it's, it's sure in there someplace.

Shorr: Is it hard to scream at them?

Arly: (Sigh) Hum, no, I think I could do it.

Shorr: All right.

Arly: (Yelling Loud) I DON'T NEED YOUR PROTECTION – I think that was my dad, my mom's still there –

Shorr: (Focus) (FTS) I am not_____ .

Arly: (Loud) I AM NOT YOUR LITTLE BOY ANYMORE AND YOU DON'T NEED MY PROTECTION (Quieter) YOU DON'T NEED MY PROTECTION (Sigh)

Shorr: Do you feel better?

Arly: No, still feel a. . . .

Shorr: Still hooked into it?

Arly: Yeh, like I want her to go away and I, I guess I'm surprised cause I don't – I wasn't feeling very hooked into her either, you know. I'm pissed off that I still, have some hangups that I thought I got rid of. It really bugs the shit out of me. (Sigh)

Shorr: And she still persists.

Arly: Um, seems like it, everything started feeling better the last few weeks, much more aggressive and full and everything and (Laugh) I still feel these kinds of shadows of mom or whatever you call them.

Shorr: Well, what is it you want to do to get rid of her then?

Arly: I don't know, kill her I guess, would be the best way, but if I could do that without (Laugh) feeling guilty, which is the problem.

Shorr: Yeh, would you like to just put her away separately and go your own direction?

Arly: Yeh, that would be fine.

Shorr: Where would you like to put her?

Arly: Well, it's hard to do, that's what it is, it's like going my own direction is, almost comes out in terms of something like distance instead of, (Sigh) you know, not like I don't want to see her anymore, I just want to be free of her, it's the only way I can —

Shorr: How can you become free of her?

Arly: That's the thing, I mean . . .

Shorr: (S&O) What is your obligation to your mother?

Arly: It's still to be there, (hum), nuts!

Shorr: What do you owe her?

Arly: I don't owe her anything.

Shorr: Except your life.

Arly: (Laugh) Oh yeh, you know about that.

Shorr: That's no little item.

Arly: Yeh — shit.

Shorr: (Focus) (FTS) How about I don't owe you _____.

Arly: I DON'T OWE YOU ANYTHING, NOTHING. (Laugh) I'm having this fantasy of me with a double-barreled shotgun and her right there and it's like, if I pull the trigger, it's like I'll blow her away but I'm not sure what the after-effects will be. Well, I'll see what happens. (Sigh) (Long Pause)

Shorr: Did you do it?

Arly: Yeh, I did it but I don't trust it, it's like I don't see her anymore but I've got the feeling she's still lurking around back here someplace, like I —

Shorr: (IS) Could you put her in a net?

Arly: Put her in a net?

Shorr: Yeh.

Arly: Okay.

Shorr: (IS) Then hang her from sort of a crane.

Arly: (Laugh — Sigh) All right, this is hard to do, okay, all right I'm on the edge of this chasm and I take the crane and I put the net on the other side, it's like there's no way she can get back and I leave it there — a — okay, that wasn't too hard, now comes the hard part, and that's like walk away. I'm walking and I can hear her yelling like "Don't leave me" (Sigh) and suddenly I see my father standing alongside of her and he's waving to me and I feel very sad about the whole thing but —

Shorr: How will you break your responsibility to them, how will you break their guilt induction to you?

Arly: How? I don't know, it's like I just feel like if I can just keep walking —

Shorr: How about — what do you want to scream at them — can they take care of themselves?

Arly: Um.

Shorr: Can they get along without you very well?

Arly: Well, that's, that's where it's at, isn't it?

Shorr: Can they take care of themselves?

Arly: (Sigh) Yeh, they can take care of themselves.

Shorr: Tell them that. (Focus)

Arly: Okay. (Firmly) YOU CAN TAKE CARE OF YOURSELVES, YOU CAN

CONTROL YOUR OWN DESTINIES AND YOU — YOU'VE GOT TO DO FOR YOURSELVES, I CAN'T DO IT FOR YOU.

Shorr: (Focus) (FTS) I am not responsible _____.

Arly: (Focus) I'M NOT RESPONSIBLE FOR YOU, FOR TAKING CARE OF YOU, FOR SEEING THAT YOU SURVIVE, FOR BEING THERE AT YOUR HOURS OF NEED ALL THE TIME, FOR (Sigh) FOR SEEING THAT YOU MAKE IT FROM DAY TO DAY, FOR SEEING THAT IT ISN'T TOO HARD FOR YOU TO WORK, YOU KNOW THAT WORK ISN'T SUCH A DRAG. IF YOU DON'T DIG IT THEN GET OUT YOURSELVES. Um. (Sigh)

Shorr: (Focus) How about (FTS) I am not your caretaker _____.

Arly: Ouch, I AM NOT YOUR CARETAKER.

Shorr: Are you really saying that from your gut?

Arly: I'm trying. (Slightly Firmer) I AM NOT YOUR CARETAKER.

Shorr: Doesn't sound from the gut.

Arly: (Laugh) It doesn't, but it sounds pretty close. (Exhale, exhale, exhale) (Firmly) MOTHER YOU CAN SURVIVE ON YOUR OWN, I AM NOT GOING TO TAKE CARE OF YOU ANYMORE, YOU'RE GOING TO, YOU MAKE IT BY YOURSELF, I'VE GOT MY OWN LIFE TO LIVE. Whew.

Shorr: Don't explain it, just state the position and act on it, don't prove it, just state it and that's it.

Arly: (Focus) I'M NOT GOING TO BE RESPONSIBLE FOR YOU ANYMORE.

Shorr: Well that really sounded like that came from the depths of your core.

Arly: Yeh, I'm still mad — (Laugh) — I feel better though, I'm still pissed off. Oh, this is like a shaker. Whew, I mean I see where freedom lies, I really see it so — I'm just (Loud) *pissed*, I'm tired of being where I'm at, I just want to be completely and unequivocally free. I mean I knew something was bugging me and I didn't know what it was, now I know but I don't feel completely free but at least I know where it's at, like, all the strings are not clipped — most of them are though. (Sigh)

R. D. Laing said: " ... as one grows older, one either endorses or tries to discard the ways in which the others have defined one." And, " ... or one may try to tear out from oneself this 'alien' identity that one has been endowed with or condemned to and create by one's own actions an identity for oneself ... " (Laing, 1962, p. 84.) These quotes serve as a basis of the theory to help the patient change his 'alien' identity to his "true" identity. One patient referred to a day of shame in his life, giving the following account:

"I was in terrible shape in the bathroom. I was barely twelve years old and all my brothers who were older were laughing at me as I retched and twisted, holding my stomach in pain. They didn't believe me. They thought it was an act. I felt so powerless to have anyone believe me. For this had happened countless times before. I once came home with a bloody nose from a fight at school and they wanted to know, "Where did you get the ketchup, baby?" On this particular day that I remember lying and squirming on the bathroom floor, my mother joined in and said sarcastically, "Leave the little baby alone!" In time I was able to crawl onto my bed and cried all night in pain, feeling so alone and unbelieved. I felt powerless like this again and again. How long would a kid go on with everyone laughing at him like he was just a sick baby?"

The patient was twenty-six years old when he related this emotion-charged account of his day of shame. Although he felt a certain humiliation in revealing such a terrible event in his life, he had been in therapy long enough to trust me; looking at my accepting and compassionate face as he concluded his talk, he felt relieved and seemed ready to deal with the agonizing "sick baby" concept.

When a patient has recalled a traumatic incident, together with its attendant feelings, I may urge him or her to utilize some interior dialogue which I will then suggest. Sometimes it may involve *The Impossible Scream* in which I ask the patient to (IS) imagine his mother or father in front of him and then ask (M/L) what would be the most difficult thing to scream at them. The patient usually responds with hesitation to this emotional task, but I persist in encouraging; I would not have initiated the procedure if I had not been certain of the patient's "readiness" to redefine himself. Further, I am willing to accept his feelings of rejection and humiliation, and this acceptance helps bridge whatever difficulties he may have in expressing anger. During that period in which a patient is growing up, the expression of anger toward significant people causes him to feel guilt, subject to retaliation; thus, the therapist's support and encouragement is of special help.

The twenty-six-year-old man described above was asked to (IS) imagine his brothers in front of him and to express (M/L) the most difficult thing to say to them. Slowly, but with great strength, he clenched his fists, focused a scream of considerable magnitude which came unmistakably from his core. "*I am not a sissy!*" he screamed, "*I am not a sissy! I am a man! Man! Man! You bastards!* I put my hand on his shoulder for reassurance. He seemed shaken but relieved, having indeed faced that which he had thought to be totally impossible.

It is worth reiterating that specific techniques should be used within the precise context of each individual's neurotic conflict resolution, with the aim of achieving a *healthy* conflict resolution. It would be useless and perhaps perilous to have a patient engage randomly in any of the focusing techniques if one did not have a clear awareness of the neurotic strategies which enchain him to his neurotic treadmill.

A focusing approach involving the interior dialogue was of particular help in dealing with a puritanically raised young man who had become obsessed by his "proper" behavior. I had him (IS) imagine himself walking down Wilshire Boulevard wheeling his wife in a baby carriage and answering to a number of men who were asking him why he was doing such a thing. Initially, his responses to them were expository, to the point of begging their permission to be allowed to continue pushing his wife along in the carriage. While quite patently not a reality situation, it evoked great fears and accountability. I had him repeat the sequence three of four times before he could tell the men to "fuck off." When he did this, he blushed markedly and hid his head in his hands, and when I asked him why he was reacting so strongly, he remarked, "I never said 'fuck' before in front of my wife."

The use of an obscenity was not important in and of itself; what was essential was to liberate him from his puritanical mold. At first he felt there was no possible alternative, then through imagery he allowed himself to feel a new way of behavior. Gradually, as a consequence of his therapeutic experience, a definitive and healthy change occurred in his life at home.

(IS) Imagine yourself in the gondola of a ferris wheel with members of your family; the gondola is stuck at the top for a long time. This imaginary situation often reveals a fear of heights, a loss of control; but more importantly, within the imagined interplay between the family members, it discloses heretofore unrecognized intimacies and hostilities. It is helpful both as a delineator of internal conflicts and as a focusing technique, especially powerful when the patient is ready to confront the situation. At times patients have imagined the experience of throwing various members of their families out of the gondola entirely. Combined with the liberating screams of (FTS) I am not_____; (FTS) I am_____; or (FTS) How dare you_____, it has often helped free patients from false definitions imposed on them by significant others. A patient's development can often be gauged by the therapist and revealed to the patient himself, if this technique is used in the early phases of therapy and then again later on — first to highlight internal conflicts and later as a focusing approach. Sometimes, however, a patient will at once involve himself with it as if it were a focusing approach, though I do not recommend its use as such in the early stages.

Clearly, there are other comparable imaginary situations which offer the possibilities of cathartic focusing for change.

Resistance and Imagery

It is commonly agreed that the censorship over imagery is less than in verbal reporting. It should not be automatically assumed, however, that imagery productions are relatively free of resistance. Diversionary imagery may occur. An example of this was a man who was engaged in imagery, exposing strong feelings of shame about his "cowardly" approach to people. As the imagery expanded, he noted images of food and guessed he must be hungry. In subsequent imagery sequences, he himself began to become aware of food images as being diversionary images. In time, as this would occur, he would smile and say, "I know I must be resisting. I'm getting those food images again."

Another man was asked to imagine his father hitting him. While he was a vivid imager, this seemed like an impossibility for him, despite continued attempts at imagining this situation. In time and with repeated focusing, as his self-confidence grew, he was able to visualize his father as a cartoon figure. This, too, was an atypical imagery for him and it persisted in subsequent sessions.

In time, when he seemed more ready to face his real feelings towards his father, his imagery lost the cartoon character and he visualized his father as a flesh and blood person. The expression of his strongly repressed hostility and the ability to truly visualize his father appeared to coincide in time. As his self-image became more positive and he was able to overcome his guilt feelings at having marked hostility towards his father, the resistance to related imagery about himself and his father disappeared.

Another form of resistance occurs in certain people when they are seemingly ashamed that they are revealing immature imagery and that would result in my possibly mocking them.

Here is the report of a young woman and her resistance to imagery that she thought would cause me to laugh at her. I had asked her to (IS) "Imagine someone standing behind you."

"Standing behind me, I saw George Segal. He placed both of his hands on my shoulders. It was a very warm comfortable feeling. Then as I turned in the chair to face him, he became angry. The next thing I knew, we were standing on a street corner and he was yelling at me. I couldn't figure out why I had made him so angry. He shouted, 'I've had it up to here!' For the life of me I don't know what he was referring to. At this point I also realized that I had the old feeling again of you and your desk being a long ways away from me. Suddenly, George took my hand and stormed across the street and into his car. I asked him again why he was mad at me but I only got a 'I've had it!' back. We drove down to the beach and went into the house. He seemed to be mellowing a bit. He came over to me, took both my hands and sat down on the couch with me. 'I'm sorry but I want our things for just us. If you want to share things with Dr. Shorr, fine, but not our private things.' This was probably the hardest fantasy for me to relate to you. It is one of 'my' fantasies I have when I'm by myself. I feel like a little girl who is dreaming yet none of them can come true. I am afraid of you laughing at me and thinking I am just a child. I had the feeling that George Segal is also another side of me that got mad because I was revealing things that are too personal."

This led to a discussion of "shame" in her life. Both her parents and her religious training made her feel shameful about her sexual daydreams. In time, she realized I felt no shame towards her for such fantasies and, on the contrary, I felt they were quite understandable in her present condition of loneliness. This served to make it a "natural" imagery for her and later on, she did not view me at a telescopic distance.

Transformation of Imagery

The directed daydream technique, used almost exclusively in Europe by Leuner in Germany, Desoille in France, Assagioli in Italy, has been reintroduced by Max Hammer (1967) in the United States as an effective means of psychotherapy in dealing with the unresolved conflicts of childhood treated in symbolic terms. The patient brings his symbolic conflicts into the open to deal with them. As Hammer says, "In a sense, the patient is asked to enter 'hell' in order to conquer the 'fiendish demons.' This meeting with unrecognized aspects of himself brings about spontaneous healing through various symbols. . . . Symbolic experience requires no analysis or intellectual insight for therapist effect, although such insight may be used adjunctively." (Hammer, 1967, p. 173.)

Hammer suggests that this type of visualization is autochthonous, i.e., largely independent of conscious control. Typical scenes are introduced, all having symbolic value in which the patient is asked to visualize himself in a meadow, in a house, in a cave, forest and climbing a mountain.

The emphasis is away from dialogue and conversation that might occur in a normal waking state, since it is felt this detracts from the free expression of feelings. The technique operates best when the patient is in a deeply relaxed or hypnoidal state.

Theoretically, the assumption is made that the use of this procedure facilitates the process of extinction of those harmful reflex responses which, "though relevant to the conflict, are active only in the patient's imagination and are not being reinforced by the patient's current reality situation. Through this process, we help the patient to develop new dynamic patterns which he will subsequently transfer from the realm of imagination to reailty." (Hammer, 1967, p. 174.)

One of the techniques is the active approach of Symbol Confrontation, in which the p tient is asked to face, for example, a big snake that he imagines coming out of a sw imp. The therapist suggests to the patient to stare into the eyes of the snake until the snake is transformed into a bird, later into a mammal and finally the threatening mother figure stands in front of him, showing that the original symbol was a mother derivative. The end result of successful confrontation is strengthening of the ego.

Other suggested techniques are the Principle of Feeding, The Principle of Exhausting and Killing, the Principle of Magic Fluids and the Principle of Reconciliation. All of these principles stress the transformation of symbols through visualization into better symbols with which the patient is much more comfortable. The work of transforming the symbols, with the support of the therapist, is therapeutic.

Keith Johnsgard (1969) has utilized symbol confrontation in a recurrent nightmare with dramatic success by reexperiencing the nightmare.

My own experience utilizing these methods has found them to be quite helpful. However, there are times when certain patients do not seem to have the readiness to respond to symbolic confrontation, and rapport in this direction seems difficult. The hypnoidal state, while readily accepted by some patients, is resisted by others who wish more of a dialogue and conversation. With these patients, I will attempt task imagery which may not be as highly symbolic. I will discuss task imagery in the next section.

While Symbolic Confrontation techniques are designed to deemphasize analytic understanding, again my experience indicates that many patients in "working through" imagery get more benefit if insight and understanding are combined with the imagery sequence. In general, task imagery offers more of this possibility. In any case, however, one must conclude that transformation of imagery can have a highly therapeutic effect. Transformation of nonsymbolic or concrete imagery can have a powerful therapeutic effect just as the transformation of symbolic imagery can. What appears to be basic is that a person can find better ways of dealing with conflicted areas by transforming, reexperiencing or redoing imagery whether it be symbolic or concrete imagery.

Task Imagery

Certain imagery situations useful for focusing involve the patient mastering a piece of work or action, and I refer to this approach as task imagery. Invariably they involve the redoing or reexperiencing of the imagery. An example would be to ask a patient to (IS) imagine climbing 1,000 steps to the top. As the patient undertakes the imaginary task, he often reveals a particular style or attitude of approach, doubts or feelings or mastery, his need for power — or the absence of such a need. He might meet other people in his ascent; they might exhibit certain feelings about each other; he might meet someone at the top. To be sure, there are those persons who cannot go more than ninety percent up; others take the steps two at a time to the very top in no time at all. One woman got to the top readily enough, then held her hands high above her head and spoke of meeting the archangel Gabriel and a host of other angels, all of whom clamored for her to perform. It is often surprising for patients as they describe what happens to them and the dynamic stresses they feel. Repressed feelings may emerge; the degree of hopelessness or optimism in a patient's life is seen, together with distortions of reality should they exist.

Another imaginary situation would be (IS) imagine building a bridge across a gorge to the other side. The ways of imagining such a task are infinite, often revelatory of the patient's attitudes toward himself and the world. One man said he would build a bridge, and a very good bridge — but when he finished he imagined that a flood would wash it away. The meaning was that he could operate very well under great challenge, but once the challenge has passed, his interest diminished.

Another man, Hank, responded to the same imaginary situation by saying, "I'm getting the shit beat out of me while I'm building it but I continue on with it. I start out from one side and it's all right for a while and then I fall into the gorge. I come up anyway, like a cartoon character. I throw a rope to the other side and swing over but I slam up against the other side. I'm battered but I make it up the side, but I don't complete the bridge. I do something I set my mind on, no matter what the cost. I guess I'm masochistic."

The reader will see how readily task imagery reveals the patient's internal conflicts, his style and manner of approach, his defenses and fears; also that it serves as a vehicle for focusing a changed self-concept in the "working through" of the imaginary task. The important ingredient following the initial flow of imagery is to reexperience or redo the imagery in a manner that leads to a possible healthy conflict resolution.

One man, after prolonged imagery, could not get himself to the top of the 1,000 steps; remained at the 995th, clutching desperately to hold on. I urged him upward, supported him until he could get the courage to climb to the top. Working at the problems with palpable intensity, he was able to strengthen himself in his struggle against always being "second best." His greatest conflict was to succeed — without alienating others in the process. To complete successfully and still be well liked kept him always in the second position. His resistance to get to the top was enormous. "I can be best man on the second team," was his constant statement. In working through task imagery he seemed to be able to change sufficiently to assume a "first" position in his professional work. If his involvement with the task imagery had been anything less than assiduous, the change would probably not have taken place. That I supported him during his arduous struggle helped him accept the fact that he could succeed without incurring dislike.

A very intensive exercise in task imagery (for most people, but not all) involves (IS) walking out of a plane wreck. Some people respond with very little emotion; even if they imagine all of the other passengers to have been killed, they may appear remarkably uninvolved. Others are guilt-ridden and may cry. One woman was so overwrought with guilt that she sobbed uncontrollably for a time. Her imagery was that all the other people in the plane had been killed, and to her this made her responsible for their deaths. This was traced back to an interior dialogue between her and her mother, her mother having constantly made her feel strongly responsible for any aches and pains, no matter how minor, which she (the mother) experienced. Even with this recognition, it was some time before the young woman was able to utilize an impossible scream (FTS), "I am not rotten!" (FTS) "I am good!" The Task imagery brought to a sharp focus the "certainty" of her rottenness, and the impossible scream liberated her from the false designation.

The variations to this particular imagery situation are remarkable. Some patients would have flown the imaginary plane themselves; others would have their loved ones with them; others might be in a foreign country; others yet will imagine walking away from the plane wreck to start a new life after experiencing such a close call with death. At the very least, one can gain insight to a patient's attitude toward death.

Task imagery affords the possibility of a patient's facing himself and then attempting to change his self-concept. When I ask (IS) imagine yourself in a tank of the foulest liquid you can think of; describe the liquid; what are you going to do? — we are probably dealing with a well-ingrained feeling of rottenness if the patient finds it difficult to get out of the tank after describing the foul liquid in all its terrible aspects. The therapist must be alert to helping and urging the individual not to be submerged by his rottenness. It is sometimes nothing short of amazing to observe people's obstinacy in refusing to leave the tank, refusing to take a hot shower (or a cold one, for that matter) and remove from themselves all of that foul liquid. One woman wanted to drink the liquid and just stay there in the tank until the hangover was gone.

This imaginary situation is not offered indiscriminately to everyone, but to persons who stubbornly cling to a rotten self-image despite the efforts of the therapist and/or other members of a therapy group. Such a woman was Beulah. She was made to feel "rotten and worse" by a mother who related to her in a snobbish and superior way. She actually felt she was rotten to allow for change. When I asked her the abovementioned situation, she reported this reaction: "It's all menstrual stuff − like before Kotex was invented − it's blood and mucous − it's sickening. I do not know what to do." At this point I urged her to fight being drowned by the stuff. She paused, muttered something and then appeared to want to stay in the stuff. I continued to urge her to fight. Several minutes went by, during which she persisted in her silence. Finally she spoke very quietly:

"There is a plug in the tank and I'm going to let it all go out. (Long Pause) Now I'm going to take a hose until it's chlorine fresh. I'm going to get perfume and pour it over me and the whole tank − I'm going to fill it with clear blue spring water and let the kids swim in it. I suddenly see a meadow beyond the tank. I can feel a relief of pressure in my head."

At the next meeting of her therapy group, she surprisingly initiated talk without being asked and seemed to exhibit behavior of a positive form she had never shown before. When she was bypassed by the group discussion (as she often had been) she fought it by asserting herself. She challenged anyone who referred to her as a "sourpuss." Her readiness (albeit initially reluctant) to do the task imagery and then actually fight her way out of her rottenness seemed to have a direct bearing on her changed behavior.

Asking a person to (IS) imagine himself in jail; imagine breaking out serves as another useful focusing approach as well as a method of assessing the individual's style, his behavior characteristics. Some people refuse to leave the prison, representing as it does their neurotic conflict resolution. Such people must constantly be urged to make the effort to leave. Among other information available from responses to this imaginary situation is each person's characteristic way of coping with conflict.

A large number of patients − unfamiliar with the realities of prison − refer to movies they've seen which deal with the subject. Nonetheless, the imagery is a product of their own choice and no less significant. One man said he would hide under his cell mattress until six p.m. The guard, arriving with food, would not see him, would leave the cell door open and run for help, at which point the patient (the "prisoner") would escape down a long hall and out the back exit to the prison. When asked what was characteristic about his imagery, the patient replied, "It's me, all right. I hide in life. I'm the old observer himself. I won't confront − and I guess I do run out on people."

I made him revisualize the incident in such a way that it would involve direct confrontation. He imposed strictures upon himself in visualizing any form of confrontation, however, and balked, saying, "I just can't." But I urged him on, and slowly, with great trepidation, he imagined " . . . rushing the guard when he came in with the food. I knocked him out. I then went through the long hall and out the back. Somehow I don't care as much as I did the first time because in the long run they will find me innocent."

How a person feels as he leaves the prison, where he goes from there, what he feels as to his innocence or guilt — these become especially important. Theresa, a twenty-seven-year-old woman, pole vaulted herself over the wall to freedom while in the recreation yard of her imagined prison. But once she had gotten her freedom, her anxiety was noticeable. "I have to run," she said, "but I can't go through life running. The thing is, I always get caught. Somebody is going to catch me. I can't say I'm innocent because even if I were, they would still condemn me. Some people would sympathize but there is nothing they can do about it. Someone would find out."

I then said, (IS) "You are in court now. Look for the person who would find you out and condemn you." The sequence of imagery which ensued led eventually to Theresa's violent condemnation of her father. From there we made use of cathartic imagery directed towards the father.

As you can see, many dimensions can be unfolded from such an imaginary situation, leading to the possibility of focusing for change.

A particularly powerful example of task imagery involves (IS), imagine yourself as a fetus about to birth. Well? — Some people seem not to want to give birth to themselves; others relate directly to their own birth from their mothers' uterus and express some of their strongest feelings, imagining their parents' respective attitudes to the event. The awareness that they were unwanted may emerge. Still other patients react with hostility as they imagine the task; it was one man's desire to " . . . crawl on all fours away from my parents so that they never can find me."

A common reaction is the sense of being born anew, with new possibilities in life. But beyond these typical examples, the spectrum of response is limitless; rarely does the task fail to evoke strong feelings; and as with other forms of imagery, this one can lead to a sequence of other imagery or reminiscence, allowing finally a focusing for change.

Here are other examples of task imagery:

(IS) Imagine going down the road and doing something worthwhile.

(IS) Imagine cleaning an oily, scaly piece of metal.

(IS) Imagine starting at ten inches of height and growing to your present size.

(IS) Imagine walking into a middle of a field and then build something.

(IS) Imagine walking down a road and confront a stranger.

(IS) Imagine hacking a road through a dense forest.

(IS) Imagine working your way through a web with a sword.

(IS) Imagine a huge wave is coming over you. You are to get free and safe.

(IS) Back up and go through a paper wall.

All of these and many more are helpful and offer the patient the possibility of working for change. But it must be remembered that the patient must be *ready* to focus for change. The elements determining this readiness are the patient's awareness of his internal conflicts; the release of feeling connected with contributory traumatic incidents; cognizance of the undermining strategies of behavior of the significant others; and recognition of his own counterreaction strategies.

The Repetition of Imagery

In repeating the same imaginary situation with a person, one can attempt to increase the intensity of the desired response, focusing for greater feeling response each time. This is especially true when the feeling response seems devoid of effect. In repeating the same imaginary situation, one may offer the instruction to "say something with more feeling." An example of this was asking a man "to imagine two different rocking chairs and then to imagine somebody different in each." He imagined an old man in one rocking chair and a young man in the other. I then instructed him to make a statement to each of the men. He started with an abstract statement in his initial response. His second response was a factual statement about the furniture. I repeated the imaginary situation urging him to make an emotional statement to each man. This time, he was more feeling in his statement and expressed some concern about "the older man's son who was lost in Vietnam." From this initial feeling spark more profound expression of feelings emerged.

Body Touching and Holding

Sheila, a twenty-nine-year-old woman, often spoke of the anger she felt at herself for being just like her fragile martyred mother. "Oh! I hate myself for being like that." she would repeatedly lament. I asked her to (IS) imagine holding her mother's face in her hands. She did this, holding her hands as if she felt her mother's face between them. After a long silence she started to cry. "It's very hard to do," she said, "I'll get her sickness. I feel really threatened by touching her — I feel unclean."

She was then asked to reverse the imaginary situation and picture her mother holding *her* face. Responding slowly, Sheila said, "I don't get feelings that way. I can feel her playing the game, that gentle fragile way of hers. I feel like stone between her fingers. I feel dead until she stops. I have to turn off so that I'm not susceptible."

From this point on, I tried to focus for her to separate from her mother by using the (M/L) question: "What is the most difficult thing to say to your mother?" Her immediate answer was, "See me." She was then guided to the impossible scream, "I am not _____ ; I am _____ ." After a long hesitation she was able to respond, "I am not *you*. I am *me*." It was necessary to repeat this at subsequent sessions until she was able to reach the feelings that would establish her autonomy.

This focusing procedure is very valuable both in individual and group therapy; it is a powerful instrument in breaking intimate deadlocks or gaining access to areas where guilt is especially strong. It may also elicit the most tender and gentle feelings or provide a focus for the softening of feelings which some patients may badly need.

Here is a report submitted by a thirty-six-year-old woman who describes her experience in body touching and holding:

"I was talking about being ashamed of my vagina. Ashamed of its being wet. Wishing to hide it. Pretend like it wasn't there. Disown it. Avoid it. Joe asked me who did my vagina belong to. I said, 'My mother.' Then Joe said something about my telling my mother that my vagina didn't belong to her; it belonged to me. Or in other words, told me to find a way to make it mine — take it back from my mother.

"I had my hand on my vagina (over my clothes) and I started trying to get it back. Each time I spoke, it came out in a begging, pleading tone even though the words were, 'It's mine, it belongs to me.' I struggled over and over and each time Joe kept saying you're begging, saying it again and over again. You're begging — louder.

"It became a frantic exchange between me, Joe and my mother. Just as it seemed I wasn't going to make it, I think Joe reversed things and I felt closer to the ownership than I knew, and the suggestion of relinquishing it triggered the floodgates — from the depths of my being, perhaps my vagina, or up through my stomach, chest, throat, and mouth. I started to scream at my mother. I could *feel* for the first time the full change of resentment, anguish, rage, hatred, abuse and pain as I called her vicious, evil, hideous bitch and on and on and I kicked and bashed the walls with all the strength I had and rolled in anger and agony on the couch. Then I remember yelling and pronouncing, "It's mine, you hear, it's mine, it belongs to me." the shrillness gone from my voice and deeper resonating tones coming out. It was the first time I can remember feeling whole and unfragmented since early childhood. I could sense my own presence and being. That afternoon after my session was the first time in many years that I'd driven the car unafraid. I drove happily about the town feeling that I belonged and *was*. That I was master of myself and not needing to grasp and gasp for confirmation from every person and object in the world that I passed."

Body Focusing

History records countless cases of people who were accused of being "obsessed" or who claimed to be "possessed." Invariably accompanying such claims and accusations were statements relating to the person's body; it was assumed that being "possessed" by the devil, God, evil spirits, involved some foreign presence within the body. It was (and is, if you're a believer in that sort of thing) as if the person no longer owned his own body (or parts of it) — as if some outside force or presence had not only occupied it but taken control of it.

As often as not (but primarily in more recent times) these cases were attributed to psychosis. Ignorance regarding such a condition resulted not infrequently in the isolation or ostracism of the person afflicted lest by touching him other people become similarly "possessed."

Normal people, of course, and even neurotic individuals do not become victims of these forms of illness in the course of everyday events. But in my experience over the years with hundreds of neurotic people it has not been uncommon for me to hear that a patient "senses" or "feels" a part of his body (or all of it) to belong to parental figures, if not demonic forces. When a person feels little or no identity of his own or if he operates constantly from a false position, he may make bodily identifications with a strong parental figure and incorporate that figure internally. Seidenberg (1969) reports a case of an individual who was completely dominated by his mother and by the feeling that "he was owned by his mother." The patient talked of a "protoplasmic bridge between them." Shutz (1967) used guided daydreams to help explore "one's own body" in the case of a woman who had excruciating pains in her stomach. He asked her to imagine herself as being very small, then to enter her own stomach. In the course of her journey through her body she encountered many imagined obstacles, and with the aid of the therapist was encouraged to overcome the obstacles. A considerable improvement in her physical health and social relations was reported.

The phenomenological aspects of people who report similar "possession" are various and unique. A question I ask is, (IS) Imagine your body as a whole; now see if you can sense the part of your body in which your mother or father resides. Most patients are not overly surprised by the suggestion and respond quite naturally. Imagination is the vehicle by means of which such associations can be made, leading ultimately to therapeutic experience and change.

Below is the verbatim account of the use of imagination in this context. The patient's symptoms in this case included inarticulation and speech hesitancy. He was thirty-one years old.

Shorr: (IS) In what part of your body does your mother reside?
Bob: In my vocal cords.
Shorr: (IS) I want you to imagine that you are entering her body.
Bob: I enter through her vagina — I go up under rising water — through the intestinal area and glands. (Long Pause)
Shorr: Why are you frowning?
Bob: Well the truth is, my first image was to enter her mouth — but I was afraid I'd be stretching her jaws apart — that's repulsive and ugly, like tearing it apart.
Shorr: (IS) Try to enter the mouth anyway.
Bob: O.K. I'll try — I'm standing on the back of her tongue, looking around — I slide off the tongue into the vocal cords. It looks like a prison. I am a prisoner of

the vocal cords. In fact, I am an enemy of the vocal cords. They should recognize I'm not an enemy. Now they appear more like they are alive and they are not steel bars. They can move.

Shorr: (IS) Pluck the cords as if they were harp strings.

Bob: O.K. — good music — but I'm still a prisoner.

Shorr: (S&O) How can you define your vocal cords so that they don't define you?

Bob: I can fight back.

Shorr: O.K., fight back.

Bob: (Long Pause) How do you fight back? I am tickling the base of each vocal cord and uncontrollably each one is opening up — so I can get out — I run up the tongue and I jump out of the mouth to freedom.

Shorr: Now how do you feel about your own vocal cords?

Bob: I can define them and then show me how it works. I can say anything I want to, whenever I want to.

Shorr: (S&O) Keep defining them.

Bob: They are nothing but my servants, they are only mechanisms of sound.

Shorr: (Focus Scream) Try screaming "I have the final authority over you."

Bob: (Focus) I HAVE THE FINAL AUTHORITY OVER YOU — (Continues Normal Tone) — They are nothing but a bunch of vibrations. They can't think, they will not define me. They are my prisoner.

Shorr: I get the feeling you gave the vocal cords a separate identity.

Bob: It became alive and told me what I can say or what I can't say. Like my mother, "Never say anything wrong to anyone or they would leave you" — that's my conflict.

Shorr: (IS) Enter your mother's body again.

Bob: Through the mouth. All I feel is revenge; this is what you did to me — now I'm going to show you what it feels like. (Pause) It deprived me of my hostility towards her. I couldn't liberate from her person. I had to be perfect or I could expect the worst.

Imagine in What Part of Your Body Your Mother Resides

The following is a report of a patient, Jim, in group therapy. He includes a running account of the events leading into the group experience, his experiencing of his mother in his stomach, and his efforts to liberate himself from her influence.

"I don't really remember too well what actually happened. I know that I had been suffering from extreme stomach pains for two days. Everything had been going extremely well in school for three weeks. Karen and I had just had the best two weeks of our relationship. For the first time in my life, I felt protective, social, myself, and in love with Karen at the same time. My fantasy of a "sunshiny winter afternoon" was coming true every day. I felt like everything was going well, except for some unknown reason, my neck and shoulders were tightening up harder than steel — more than I had ever known.

"Back to the stomach pain. At first I thought I had the flu. But I had extreme pains that were very high in my stomach. At the same time, I felt like vomiting, but I couldn't. I even stuck my finger down my throat and I couldn't, I wouldn't vomit.

"Tuesday morning, I went to work. I talked to Helen before I left and she said it sounded like I had an ulcer. Right then I got extremely depressed, angry, tearful and alone. I went home and I was really angry. I felt shitty (guilty) for having an ulcer. I felt shitty that I was still so uptight and fighting and unproductive as to have an ulcer. I was also really mad and untrustful of group and my last two years in it. I went back and forth, from guilt and anger.

"Then I called Bill (group member). The *one* thing I remember from the conversation was him saying, 'I care that you are in such pain' — and 'I really like being around you and Karen when you're happy.' When I got off the phone, I was wide open. I cried by myself and for myself without hesitation. For the first time, I let my guts hurt and I cried without any thoughts or judgments. I then felt like I wanted to cry "mommy." I wanted someone to love me and take care of me. I wanted a mother. But I knew I didn't want *my* mother. And it made me angry to realize I never had a mother.

"When Karen came home, I was very aware of not wanting to show her my feelings. But I had called and asked her to come home. That was pretty hard to ask for. If I ever let it out to my mother, she used it for her false motherings and to shrink my cock and consume my balls.

"By the time I got to group, my stomach was really hurting and I explained that everything was good but I was dying of pain."

Shorr: What part of you hurts?

Jim: My stomach. Right in the middle of my guts.

Shorr: Can you hand that part to someone? ("When Dr. Shorr asked that, all I could do was cry. He asked me several times and it seemed impossible. It seemed it would be giving the most vulnerable and dearest part of me away.")

Gwen: (Group Member) No wonder it hurts so much. It always hurt you and you were always alone with it.

Jim: What bothers me is that I never got anything with my pain, and I'm not now.

John: (Group Member) You must have gotten something.

Jim: Yes, I got to stay home. I didn't have to go to school and compulsively achieve. I got protection against my father. I didn't have to feel alone at school with the kids. I felt like I got some love. Even though it was being used to manipulate me into taking care of her. She had a way in, through my pain, and I had a way in with my pain.

Shorr: (S&O) Who does your stomach belong to?

Jim: To me. It's a good stomach. Good color on the outside. But the inside is all jumbled.

Shorr: (IS) Give that part a name.

Jim: Me.

John: How does the rest of your body feel?

Jim: Fine. It's all mine.

John: Then your stomach must not be yours.

Jim: No, it's not. It's the shit part of me.

Shorr: (IS) In what body part does your mother reside?

Jim: In my stomach.

John: Isn't it true that you still want your mother and you want to call to her?

Jim: Yes, no — I want a mother, but I don't want mine.

Shorr: (Focus) (IS) Reach in and grab her out.

Jim: She's in there with tentacles — it is all around me of — (Pause) all through my meat.

Shorr: (Focus) (IS) Rip her out. She's scared of you.

Jim: That's really true. That makes a difference. She's god damned scared of me. I scream at her and she shrinks like a sea urchin. I'm not really the scared one, she is. (I remember the dream where I jacked off on my mother and then I screamed I was going to kill her.) I pulled her out with my right hand, and held her there and talked about her. She was like a huge, sickly cancer cell. I talked a lot about her, and the more I talked, the more she was back in my stomach and the more my stomach hurt.

Shorr: (Focus) (IS) Rip her out and throw her in the fire (a dream I had about the ending of the world). Scream at her and tell her to get out.

Jim: For a long time I didn't feel like I could. I just couldn't reach in and get her out. I decided to stand up and try it. I had to. My stomach hurt so bad. I couldn't let her stay in. Thinking of her as scared of me helped. But I still couldn't do it.

Group Member: You won't be alone — we're all here.

Shorr: I'll be right here.

Jim: I know you all love me and you'll be here. But I'm afraid once I scream, I won't be able to call for you anymore when I really need you. (This feeling is the same feeling when I get sick and am scared that I'm all alone and I wouldn't get any help if I really needed it.)

Shorr: You won't have to call for me. I'll be right here with you, anyway. (That did it.)

Jim: AND THEN I SCREAMED. I SCREAMED WITH ALL MY MIGHT. WITH ALL MY PAIN FOR MY WHOLE LIFE. WITH ALL MY ANGER FOR MY WHOLE LIFE. WITH ALL MY GUTS. I SCREAMED FOR HER TO GET OUT. I SCREAMED FROM MY GUTS. WITHOUT ANY HESITATION. I SCREAMED FOR MYSELF. 'CAUSE I WANT TO LIVE FOR ME. 'CAUSE I DESERVE FOR ME. AND SHE GOT OUT. YOU'RE DAMN STRAIGHT SHE GOT OUT. AND SHE CAN NEVER GET BACK IN. SHE'S SCARED. I KNOW NOW. I KNOW IN MY GUTS. I KNOW WHO I AM. I KNOW MY STRENGTH. AND I KNOW HER WEAK, SADISTIC, INHUMAN GAME. I DON'T NEED IT. I DON'T NEED YOU. I'LL NEVER NEED YOU. SHE'S GONE.

"As soon as I screamed, I bent over and clenched my fists. I felt like I was screaming to hell and back. Dr. Shorr straightened me up and told me I didn't have to bend over. She couldn't get back in now. He hugged me and protected my stomach with his belly. It felt good, I really needed the warmth. I don't really remember what happened after that. I was shaking a lot and Dr. Shorr stayed next to me and hugged me and sat down next to me. He really cared. And he was really there. And I didn't have to call for him. And I looked up and people really looked human and warm. And especially the women looked different. I guess not so much like my mother. They looked human and fleshy. My stomach actually felt like it had a wound in it. But it was a clean fleshy wound. And now it can grow back together with me. It's mine."

Several months have passed since that group session, and the patient has shown considerable change; he is much calmer and there has been a marked decrease in his strong suspiciousness. His own analysis, verified in time, suggested that he felt accountable for his behavior to his mother, behaved according to her standards and felt great guilt if he did not. Since she was "inside" him, the accounting system was acute and ever present. Just as the paranoid person is defined by nearly everyone he meets, this man on a lesser scale was defined by his mother and substitute mother figures.

Lest the reader misinterpret that the mother is the only target person, the same question can be asked emphasizing "in which part of your body does your father reside." Whether the question involves the mother or father would depend upon the prior communication and feelings of the patient as well as other prior imagery. Of course, in some instances, both parents can be imagined.

One man, Lester, when asked, "In which part of your body does your father reside?" responded as follows:

Lester: In my brain, sitting on it like it's got handlebars. He's up there trying to pull my head. He's the size of a mouse and exerts lots of pressure. I want to move my head in the other direction. I'll show the son-of-a-bitch. But he has the power to stop me.

Shorr: Try to imagine putting your hand into your head and try to get him out.

Lester: OK. (Pause) I can do it. It's like a snail and I step on it. But it jumps up like a rubber ball. I get a knife and cut it in many pieces. Then I throw it on the street and cars run over it. That feels better. (Pause) I can now walk down a street tossing my head high. My own hands go onto the handlebars and I hold on to it like it's a motorcycle. I feel in control. I feel I am my own master.

It is possible to reveal feelings of self in relation to the other by imagining entering the body of the other and then imagining the other entering one's own body. Many deep feelings may be revealed, numerous aspects of the interrelationship brought to light. Here is a verbatim example of such an imagined journey on the part of a twenty-four-year-old woman; she was ordinarily detached, not too verbal:

"I enter my father's body through his stomach. His stomach is thickly congested with fog. Blindly feeling my way through the fog, I find a safe deposit box. Inside it is filled with cobwebs. At the bottom of this box lies my father's heart. What a terrifying sight! His heart is dark brown and it's dead. I can't stand to look at it. It's revolting! It's morbid! It's rotten! I say to his heart that all of my life I have been most curious to know what you are all about. I've *always* felt that there was something much deeper about yourself that you have never exposed. Now I am looking at it before my eyes. Only a man with a dead heart would have to live off of the lives of others. And only a man with a dead heart would use his daughter for his own means and at the same time try to suffocate me from my own sense of self. Inducing in me what you couldn't accept in yourself — that *you* are the rotten person, not me. Of course, my father's heart could not reply — it's dead.

"And — my father enters *my* body through my guts. He feels threatened and frightened by the echoes of truth that the depths of my guts reveal. My guts are echoing to him that I am *not* what he has tried to make me. I will not accept responsibility for his own rottenness. My father cannot bear the pain that it brings him, so he violently fights back with sudden anger as he intellectually and physically makes every effort to degenerate me with his degeneracy. When he finds my heart, he is overwhelmed by its intensity. It is bright red, healthy and well endowed with warmth, human depth, and a great eagerness to *live*. My father's reaction to my heart is disapproval. He cannot afford to accept it. If he accepts my heart, then he has to accept his own rottenness. I don't feel that my father could say anything to my heart — he would merely deny it."

I asked a woman of thirty-five to (IS) imagine entering your mother's body. Her immediate answer was, "Her womb — I just go in — it's dark in there and round and I fall asleep." I then asked her to (IS) have a dream while she was sleeping there. She reported her imagined dream as follows:

"I see colors, dark, red and purple. There are cubes glistening and bouncing all over. I am slipping over them all and I build a little house with them — I build a little igloo — it's all snow everywhere I look — it's crisp and cold and I have a fur coat on. I walk around in the snow and lie in the snow and Mona (her dog) is with me. I ski down a hill into a green valley — old Western town appears — it's one of those old Western bawdy towns — I take off my coat and have on a dance-hall dress — I get on stage and dance — the applause is terrific — I have a boyfriend who owns the club. It's a great dream!"

Shorr: You feel good?
Vicky: Who wouldn't feel good in their mother's womb? Even now when I'm in trouble I cry for her. Mama, Mama. I have lots in that womb. I can have lots of freedom. I can be a hooker, singer, dancer and a child. *The womb is the door to the world.*
Shorr: Can you visualize a sign in the womb?
Vicky: HERE YOU ARE.

"Responsibility is taken over by the womb. You see, my mother was authority. I felt safe with her. I let her be responsible in allowing her that power. I was not preparing myself for life. I started to look for things to be dependent on like drugs and men — a cozy place because it meant dependence. I walked away from my mother at seventeen — and then to drugs — then to people who took care of me. (Pause) Like I get into bed — then the tube will take care of my mind — I know there are trees out there but I won't go — I want to go but I won't — it is as if my mother said, 'Thou shalt not be without me!'"

One man of twenty-eight had talked about having a "filter" inside of him that constantly prevented his feelings from coming through; the filter made him "switch up" to his head from his reactions. If his wife reprimanded him for playing chess for hours with his friend, his immediate reaction was anger, but he transferred it "to my brain, by a filter inside of me" and answered her with an innocuous remark.

I then asked him, (IS) "In what part of your body does the filter reside?"

Gene: In my chest — as a round filter, right around my heart, like a.big basket. I see it as somewhat overloaded. It needs cleaning. It doesn't seem to be working in conflict with anything around it.

Shorr: What does the heart feel?

Gene: Some kind of pressure. The heart is able to do very little except to maintain itself.

Shorr: What material is the basket made of?

Gene: Made of wood, very finely constructed high-quality wood — it's actually immobile right now.

Shorr: Is there anything you can do to change that structure?

Gene: Not really unless I concentrate.

Shorr: Imagine entering your body and go to the heart area.

Gene: It's very large. It's got to be ten times larger than me. The heart is five times bigger than me. I can walk right through this basket thing. It's quite easy to do. But when I get inside the basket the heart stops. (Long Pause) It gets very dark. I am staying there pretty scared because I am pretty small compared to all this.

Shorr: Can you get the strength to break the basket (Focus) and eliminate it out of your system?

Gene: I might falter.

Shorr: Try to.

Gene: Oh! I'm not big enough. In order to do it I'd have to be big enough — I'm only one-half as tall as the basket. (Pause) O.K. — I can imagine myself as tall as the basket. It's extremely heavy. It's not made of wood, it's made of iron — (Pause) I manage to tip it over. My heart wasn't beating until now — now it's started again.

Shorr: Can you go inside your heart?

Gene: I can't go in my heart. I'm sorry for my heart. That's strange. I would hurt it if I went inside. (Pause) I'm standing there.

Shorr: Say something to your heart.

Gene: Why haven't you grown bigger?

Shorr: Your heart answers.

Gene: Because you haven't taken this basket away from me. Now that you have entered me *I will open up and show you what's inside of me.* It's immaculately clean. That's saying a lot (Laughs) — immaculately clean for my whole heart. It's a very good feeling. It's a very good heart. We have a very good thing going there. The basket wasn't doing much good at all.

Shorr: (S&O) Who does your heart belong to?

Gene: It belongs to me. It's having a lot of trouble with the basket. But's a good heart. It looks at me and says, "Quit screwing around."

One young woman, Clara, was asked, (IS) "In what part of your body does your anger reside?" Her reply was as follows:

"My anger is the central part of my being — a central core of hot carbon. It's solid and static inside me. In fact, all my feelings are contained in that carbon rod — it's hard to imagine the good feelings apart from the anger.

"It takes a special effort to separate the anger from the other feelings, but I can imagine them sort of falling off the rod as little black specks, and I'm left with a strong carbon rod with little piles of soft black specks around it.

"I want to take the carbon rod out of me — but it's too hot to touch — I've got to use tongs to extract it.

"I can take it out but there's no place to put it. It's glowing red hot — then white. Joe says to put it in a furnace, but that won't help. It only acts as fuel for the furnace — it won't be destroyed.

"I can destroy it with water — simple, but effective.

"But there's still this hollow inside me where the anger was. It's hard to fill it with good feelings — but I can. I feel guarded, as if it weren't possible to be rid of my anger. The good feelings fill me very slowly. There's an insecure feeling of lightness (vs. the dense, heavy rod) — a floaty feeling that I don't really exist. If I can drink the cool water of a fresh stream — that makes me feel more real — but then there's the feeling that the stream isn't real. I'm not really convinced."

In time as therapy continued, she was able to develop a better self-concept; and one might say she "filled up her body with good feelings" instead of her "hot carbon."

I Enter My Own Body

Another man describing his journey on entering his own body:

"I enter my head through my nose. I go up just under the surface of my skull. I don't like my head. It keeps playing tricks on me. It won't cooperate with my body. Hey head, you're ridiculous. Why don't you just pack it up? One minute you're a peach, and the next minute you're concrete. I'm tired of your game. It looks like you're going to keep it up for awhile though. You've really helped me survive, but god damn it, the war is over. You are another General Patton. In the face of danger you can turn my eyes to cold steel and take anything on. I thank you. But now it's time for something more. You don't seem to help me much when it comes to warmth and love and soft things. I guess I can't blame you too much, after what we've gone through in the last twenty-six years. It was a long battle, wasn't it? Hey, I think we made it! You protected my heart pretty well. But now it's time to live and I need you to relax a bit and slowly come along with me. I'll be easy with you though. I know how you get going in vicious circles and then you panic. Just take it slowly. In fact, why don't you just take a vacation and let the feelings take over for awhile. I want you to keep one eye open though, 'cause I'm still a little tender. And my heart hasn't seen a hell of a lot of sunlight yet. Slowly, slowly, slowly, with lots of love and care. Friends? Friends. I travel down the back of my neck. God, it's uptight. You need to relax neck. I give you the same advice I gave my head. It's all okay. It's time to feel good. I travel down my throat and into my chest. My chest is kind of a traffic jam right now. I would imagine just like after the war in New York City. There still seems to be a lot of tears and anger running right down the middle. Those motherfuckers never loved me for one minute. And now I know it. I have called the game. It's still kind of hard to accept those feelings all the way. I've always felt so god damn isolated. No wonder. The more alone, the harder I tried, the more I sold myself, the more alone I was. Those fucking assholes. And that fucking cunt of a mother of mine. She never squeezed me once or told me she loved me. She didn't love me. She didn't, she didn't, she didn't. I can feel the tears and anger in my chest right now. I think it's going to have to come out in group. I'm just so tired, I need a rest. But it has to come out pretty soon, and be done with it. I go over to my heart and that feels much better. My heart is round and red and plump and just really full. What a beautiful heart. It's thumping away, and alive, and so full of love that it looks like a little kid's cheeks full of air. It is soft and strong at the same time, and it's full of hugs and kisses and dreams of sunshine and really loving myself. I think that dream is pretty close now, at least I know that now I have a chance for it. It's hard for me to picture, but I feel like there is a possibility of a slow sunshiny life that is really enjoyable. As soon as I think about that I get scared and the old head starts in with 'How am I going to do it, and what do I have to do now, and what to achieve. That's what I have to stop. I guess it's going to take some time and practice. Maybe some just sitting around.' The next dream in my heart includes a woman. I'm in my house. It's been a slow day and sunny. My back hurts a little and I'm enjoyably tired from maybe building something or from gardening. I get into bed and there are small paned windows completely covering three sides of the room. There's a hill behind the house and there's no curtains on the window. A couple of the windows are open inward and it's kind of warm out. My wife comes in and she looks out the window and just stands quietly for a minute, and I know she's happy and smiling. She's pleasantly tired, too. She has been excited all day. She's been excited about some project she has going, and she's most warmly excited about being pregnant. And I've been so excited my heart is twice its normal size and still growing. And my head feels like a peach. Anyway, she slowly gets undressed and I can faintly make out the silhouette of her beautiful body. She lets down her hair and she's soft and simple and earthy and beautiful. She comes over and just sits down on the edge of the bed next to me and she says, 'Golly, I love you so very much.' And I say, 'God I love you.' And we just stay right where we are for a second and just really love each other and just let the warmth flow all over us and fill up the room. Then she just hugs me and climbs in bed and we hug each other so tight and so warm and so naked.

"That's what's in my heart, and it's so beautiful. When I think about it I start to figure out 'what to do' and it screws me up. I just want to let it be. That's the kind of life I want to have.

"There's a direct line running from my heart to my penis and balls. When I just go ahead and let my heart feel good, my cock and balls feel so full and just kind of natural, like they're really my cock and balls and really belong to me. When I woke up this morning, I looked at my cock, and it really looked nice to me. Really mine and natural and just the right size. I looked at my cock for a long time and if I may say, it even looked sexy and sexual to me. For the first time I realized that a woman could really want to make love to me in a really feeling and hungry way. Imagine that — a woman with her feelings wanting my body just as much as I wanted her. That sounds far out. When my heart and my cock can feel that way, baby, I'm making hay — you might say.

"There also seems to be a direct connection from my heart to my head. When my heart swells up, my head feels so much lighter and it can dream and create and laugh too.

"Right now it feels like all these things can happen, but they don't seem really together. They are all there, but they don't seem to be able to flow. I think the flow might have a lot to do with just sitting back for a change and climbing into my stomach and not worry about things. And when my stomach says, 'Hey, I REALLY want to taste some of that,' go ahead and taste some. It's okay, and if I don't like it I don't have to be discouraged. I can crawl right back into my stomach and just be. I'm afraid it won't just happen though. And that's what I've always done; I've been responsible to do something more if I wanted something to happen or if I wanted to be loved. My stomach is real hungry, but I can't force-feed it. I would rather sit back and be hungry and just get one little thing at a time than eat what everybody else is eating.

"Who knows, maybe I could really let someone love me and love them back and do what I want, and feel good and feel slowly, all at the same time. If that's not the way the world really is, then I think I'll stay in fantasy for as long as I can."

I Enter Your Journey

Sharon reports feelings of desperation for her boyfriend, filled with fear that he will abandon her. When she is with him, she can only think of what to do that will please him so that he will stay.

In previous discussions she had become aware of how little she mattered to her father — she made no difference to him. I asked her what was the (M/L) most difficult thing to say to her father. She answered, with great difficulty, "You are weak; you can't see me." At that point she became faint and asked to lie down on the couch. I told her to do so.

(S&O) "How did you punish your father," I asked. Her reply was that she would be angry at him for his peculiar breathing, and then leave the room to punish him for it. Nobody else apparently thought her father's breathing was peculiar.

Shorr: (IS) Where does your anger reside in you?

Sharon: In my chest.

Shorr: (IS) Can you enter your chest and go to it?

Sharon: (Sobbing) Yes, I go in and there is a large steel plate and it's very wide.

Shorr: I want you to use the largest blowtorch you can think of and melt it down.

Sharon: (She continues sobbing and moves her hands as if she is using the blowtorch) Yeah, I can do it – but it takes a long time.

Shorr: Take all the time you need.

Sharon: (Long Pause) I've melted it down.

Shorr: What do you see?

Sharon: I see a bright blue sky and fields.

Shorr: Can you walk into it?

Sharon: No, I can't. (Sobs some more)

Shorr: Let me come with you.

Sharon: (After another pause) O.K., but it's sloping out there. There's a large mound and then a steep slope. I'll fall.

Shorr: I'm holding your hand. Let's build a bridge from that mound. I'll help you build it.

Sharon: It goes to another place, but there is a lot less slope. Then another bridge, then flat fields.

Shorr: You come across a pool of spring water and drink some of it.

Sharon: I want to bathe in it.

Shorr: Go ahead and enjoy yourself.

Sharon: All right. But will you go away?

Shorr: No, I'll just sit here and watch you. I won't go away.

Sharon: (Pause) I'm bathing and I look over at you and you are writing.

Shorr: Enjoy the water. I'll be here.

Sharon: I can't believe you're not going. (Pause) I'm letting myself enjoy the water and it feels good.

Shorr: How do you feel?

Sharon: Very good. Maybe I can believe men won't abandon me.

Good Guts Vs. Bad Guts

Some patients are so thoroughly convinced that they are their alien identity – that they are rotten in (or *to*) their core – that only after a loving relationship with the therapist can they finally allow themselves to examine this so-called rotten core.

Shorr: (IS) Can you sense or imagine a body part of you that is rotten?

Murray: My penis. (Pause) No – guts – yes, a sinking body feeling comes over me. My guts – for a moment I thought my penis, then I decided my guts are the worst part of me. My penis is O.K.

Shorr: Why guts? (Long Pause)

Murray: They're rotten – (Pause) – It's very hard to say. It's that they're – (Pause) – putrid. That word is very difficult to say.

Shorr: Can you hand them to me using your imagination?

Murray: (Pause) — I don't know. It seems easy and yet — I know I have to make sure I do it with my feelings. (Long Pause — Murray, after several half-attempts, reaches across belly and scoops out 'guts.' Holds them down, not wanting to expose them to full light by holding them up.)

Shorr: What did you see?

Murray: They're — (Pause) — slimy — (Pause) — putrid. They're not good.

Shorr: Can you hand them to me?

Murray: Well — (Pause) — I'm feeling anxious. (Then very reluctantly hands them over to Shorr after making several false starts. Shorr holds them with care.)

Shorr: Do you know what I see?

Murray: No.

Shorr: I see good guts. They are brave, strong, courageous, healthy, loveable, loving. They're not putrid at all. This is a case of the good guts vs. the bad guts. (We both laughed.) You have very good guts. Can you seem them this way?

Murray: Well — (Pause) — (Starts smiling — anxious look starts to fade) — I don't know.

Shorr: Here, hold them. (Passes guts back to Murray.)

Murray: (Holds guts a little nervously while examining them.) I guess they're OK.

Shorr: Can you put them back?

Murray: (Slowly lowers them into his belly and carefully seals them in. Suddenly he starts patting his tummy. At first gently, then more vigorously.) I like this. These feel good. I like them.

Shorr: You have good guts — everyone does naturally. You were taught that they were bad guts. What do you think that the bad guts did for you?

Murray: They — (Long Pause) — they prevented intimacy. I couldn't have any close contact or people would discover how rotten I was. I had to compete and keep control of every situation to retain my secret. I feared discovery of my rottenness — my inadequacy.

As will be seen later, many of the focusing techniques may occur in group therapy. The interaction of the group members seems to be a valuable point of integration for the person attempting healthier methods of coping with his conflicts; it allows the possibility of strength, of individual growth, and the demonstration of new life values. Of course, all of life outside the therapy room (whether the therapy is individual or group) serves as a point of integration for the new behavior.

Liberation From the Body of the Other

This young man felt castrated, duty-bound and obligated to his mother. He feared women could enslave him if he didn't perform. Coupled with this was a constant suspicion that women were about to entrap him. He would become circular in his self-accusations; first, that they were regarding him only as a problem and not as himself, and second, that they wanted him but didn't care about his problems. There was no way he imagined a woman could please him, no way he could please himself.

In the course of a session, the strong enveloping hold which his mother exerted on him became clearer and clearer. The imaginary situation (IS) "Imagine entering your mother's vagina and fight your way out" was presented to him. So embarrassed and ashamed was he that he could not do the imagery in front of me. Here is the verbatim audiotape of the imaginary situation which he finally managed to complete in his own apartment.

(There is one minute or so of silence — clattering noises — heavy breathing.) "I feel embarrassed doing this — don't know if I can do it — (Sigh) — it's really scary — I guess I'm afraid of the riducule for even doing this right now — Joe asked me Friday to — crawl into my mother's vagina — and come back out again — and I feel like I'm in there (Sigh) — and it's — it's like all of therapy — coming back into a circle again — it's like it it's really the life, it's life or death struggle to be here or not to be here (Slight Chuckle) — and we talked about it Friday — the overwhelming feeling was — that I was embarrassed to do it even with Joe — it's like really a baby. (Sigh) We talked this morning and it's really being the castrated man — it's living in my mother's vagina — the incredible power she had over me — and it's embarrassing, every fucking thing I've been through — it's like (Slight Chuckle) it's all been kind of a survival thing, like getting rid of the paranoia — at least getting my mother out of my body — keeping her out there — but it has to go beyond that, it has to be me living my life with my balls — (Sigh) — there's a, this imaginary situation brings together like the whole shot, it's — well — that's life — finish the sentence, 'Never refer to me as,' it would still be — 'Never refer to me as the baby,' and (Sigh) the way my mother related to me was keeping me as a baby, keeping me as hers — and (Sigh) what I did back was, the way I punished her was — 'Okay, I'll be a baby — but you won't get any more of me — so I'll go ahead and relate to you as a baby,' (Sigh) which is how she got her hate out of me — she would keep me that way — all I would show her was my 'baby' — and all I will show a woman to this day is my 'baby' so that I don't get taken over — it's like she could take me over as a baby and I would relate to her and I went along with that, that was fine but I'll be damned if I'll let you take the real Steve over, I'll be damned if I'll let you have my balls — but, that neurotic conflict resolution screws me in the end — because I still relate as the baby — the other part of it was the humiliation from my brothers and from my father — it's like as I imagine myself, not actually doing it but as I imagine what would happen, me fighting out of the womb — it's like it's the most difficult thing that I've ever done — at the same time as I imagine myself doing it — the thing that — one of the things that is just so fucking impossible about it — is that as I'm fighting out — as I'm fighting not to be the baby — as I'm fighting to be the fucking man I am — it's like my brothers and my father are laughing and ridiculing and still calling me baby — no matter that I'm beating my way out with machetes or — or flame throwers or whatever the hell I'm using; it's like they're still laughing at me as the baby — and that's the way they related to me as a kid — (Sigh) my imagination says that even, it's like I fight my way out of my mother's vagina — and it's like then they're still there and it's like having fought my way out and being a man — which none of them are, I feel — it's like then I threaten the hell out of them — and I imagine violence coming from them because they're so damn threatened at that point — at the same time I guess actually doing it I might find that the strength I have and the power I have, I might threaten the hell out of them so much that I might not even have to worry about them — in the end — Sooo (Sigh) that's where it's at, being a baby with my mother — my father and my brothers always referred to me as a baby. I always felt like a fucking baby, no matter what I do — it's like in the end I will always be the baby — and that feels really fucking alone — it's like it doesn't work for me anymore — to be the baby — just talking right now, I was feeling really self-conscious about sitting here in my own room talking to a tape recorder, but it feels better, like being here alone, because of the fucking humiliation — it's like that would get me into a bind of not even being able to move, not knowing which way to go no matter what. I would be a baby — I go to my mother and that's a baby, I try and fight out of it and that's a baby, and like the constant ridicule, the constant laughing, the constant humiliation, the thing of laying on the bathroom floor, the time I fainted — it's like that was the total humiliation, and at that point it's like it didn't make any difference anymore — (Sigh) — (Sounds of Crying) — Ooh — (Sigh) (Sniff) — the dreams that I had last night — had some incredible dreams — one of them was of Lucille Heatherton — and like I hadn't even been able to remember her face but in the dream last night her face was right there, exactly as her face is — about the whole thing with her and Logan — the other dream was that my brother was giving me a blow job and that's the point that I feel I've gotten to, it's like — hopeless with a woman — and yet realizing what's going on now, the hopelessness is kind of — I feel like there's something I can do about it — I forget the other dream, (Deep Breath) — (Sighing) — well anyway I guess that's enough for the dreams, those dreams themselves, it's like, (Sigh) it's the part of me I guess I've always been afraid of — it's like, finally the impotence I feel like — Jesus Christ — you know, I would rather be a homosexual than — than a — no, I wouldn't be (Slight Snicker) — that's the way it feels — feels castrated, feels helpless — (Sighing) — I don't know, but a — (Loud Sigh) — this is really hard — my a — sitting here with my eyes closed I can imagine being in the womb — (Chuckle) — I'm really scared to do this — (Sighing) — it's like my feeling is — it's like I'm laying down in the womb — and if I'm just laying there not making a move, or not standing up for myself or not being the man that I am — not being sexual or not being — competitive or anything else, like as long as I don't make any problem — I'm okay — I — I mean not okay but — I won't get the retaliation — it's like as soon as I start to make a move — it's like the retaliation is going to be there — the — the picture I have is an — it's like as soon as (Voice Cracks) I — or I start to get up and press into the meat of her womb or whatever it is — inside of her vagina, it's like it's going to smother me to death, it's going to clamp down on me and it's like once I make my move it's going to be all or nothing — and it's like, it's going to be the battle of my life — (Sigh) — it's humiliating (Teary Voice) — it's humiliating — (Sigh) — I don't know if I can do it right now without support of some kind, I feel like I have the support, it's like (Sniff — Sigh) talking to Joe this morning, Joe will be there — aah — I can call all sorts of people if I want to — maybe I really do have to do it on my own — (Sighing) — I don't know maybe I'll just — (Clatter Noise) no, no, like this has to be for me — (Sighing) — it's like I'll be god damned if I'm going to go through this again — it's like it's got to be for me my way — there's no way to perform this anymore — only perform is to get the recognition and make sure that I don't get the humiliation instead — those sons-of-bitches — (Sigh) — (Sniff) (Voice — sound of crying) This is a — I was thinking the other night — it's like with the humiliated — with warmth — when I used to have it, it's like any kind of feeling, it's true it was any kind of feeling but the more specifically — the feeling that they humiliated the most in me was the warmth — it's like they — they couldn't stand the warmth and joy is included in there — the time I was skipping down the driveway and I got the ridicule for the joy that I was feeling — it's like that's when I shut it off, there was no way that I was going to feel warmth in that family — um — it's so incredible, it's like it takes some of their power away, I guess even — even thinking about that (Sighing — aaah) just like they weren't men at all (Slight Chuckle) — I remember my father used to watch television and if any kind of — if any kind of sad scene, a movie, or a love scene, or any kind of feeling that would bring feeling out in, in the rest of people in the family, my father would sit there and he would have to laugh and make jokes and ridicule until the scene was over. I mean it was so fucking threatening to him to have any kind of feeling go — it's like — feelings were to be ridiculed and humiliated — the only other, the only time, I mean (Deep Breath, Sigh) it's like I say warmth, it was (Voice — Snicker) still humiliation, I mean it wasn't warmth at all, but the only time my father even really touched me, in a semblance of anything, but it was just a bunch of bullshit and that was that I was crying on the floor as a little kid — he picked me up in the rocking chair and I was like about probably four years old or something like that, and he said, 'Poor, poor baby' and made me stay there — he grabbed onto me and wouldn't let me go and just humiliated me for crying — (Chuckle) and that was the only touch I ever got from my father except for, for getting hit or, or swung on — (Sniff) — just kind of like to break that humiliation, to break the babyness — always a fucking battle, am I a baby, am I a man, am I a fag, do I have balls, can I make it with a woman — (Sighing) — it's like no matter what — it's fighting my way out of the vagina — (Sigh) — Joe asked me — it's like I've been saying, you know, like the girls at school, it's like they're babies, they're, they're — they're not for me, they're not enough or something, they're not mature enough — and he asked me if my mother was a baby, well I didn't answer it right then, but yeah my mother, my mother was really a baby and that was the one way she really got to me, it's like the only thing I identified as warmth as a kid was my, was my mother's babyness, her, her, her martyrdom, her inability to fight back, her helpelessness, her, her just laying down and taking it all, and it's like, it's like I would — fight her battle for her — I would scream at her, 'Why in the fuck don't you, you know, get what you want or something like that'; (Sighing) — it's like my, you know, it's like my own battles (Sighing) — why in the hell couldn't I get what I wanted — (Sigh) — she was a baby and that's, and, and I guess her tears, her babyness is, is what I identified with — as being some sort of feeling, I mean that's the way I felt — to my mother — I was her sick comrade, in her sickness — but I don't think I need to go on anymore with that (Big Breath) (With a teary voice) — I will go ahead and try it — I don't know how many of my feelings I got in here right now (Big Sigh) — I'm pretty much there I guess ⇢ pretty much laying down in her fucking womb — (Sniff) — I think I'll lay on — I think I'll lay down on the bed — (Sigh) — god damn son-of-a-bitch — (Long Sigh) — begins to feel so, so fucking difficult, feels so fucking difficult — (Sigh) — I don't know what's going to happen — it's like once I start I don't know what's going to happen — I don't know what tools I need but I guess I can have any tools I want — just feel like the fucking meat is just going to surround me, it's like, no matter what, it's like it can crush anything, it's, that it's just, the retaliation is just incredible — (Aaagh — Sighing) — (Big Sigh) — (Sniff) — (Clatter on the mike) — (Big Sigh) — (Big Sigh) — (Sniff) — that's funny, I got a big machete — it's like there's meat on the other end (Chuckle) — I'm afraid, and just keeps coming down, I wish I could just be tight around me — (Heavy Breathing — Sigh) — (Angrily) fucking cunt — she sucked me in, she sucked me all the way in and that's where the fuck I've been — (Sigh) — GOD DAMN YOU — (Heavy breathing — few seconds) — keep it screaming, it's what they want in there, it's like the helplessness and the powerlessness to, to scream and be crazy, it's like that didn't work all I got was humiliation — (Sigh) — FUCK YOU, YOU FUCKING CUNT — (Sigh) — you horrible evil bitch — you slimy shit — (Sigh) — I'm just so scared — (Sigh) — just have to take my time with it — (Big Sigh) — (Sigh) — so afraid of the humiliation — shameful to be a man that's what I'm saying, it's shameful to be a man — (Sigh) — (Sniff) — I'll sit up in the chair — (Noise of walking and noise of the mike) — (Sigh) — SWISH — (Sigh) — track of blood comes trickling down — it's like it's starting to envelop me — SWOOSH — (Sigh) — it pulls back a little bit — then it starts coming down — I stand up — (Sigh) — I have a little bit of room — it, like it's closing in right around me — (Sigh) — SWISH — SWISH — (Sigh) — as long as I slash at it — I can keep my room anyway — keep the room right around me — (Sigh) — I'll use the flame thrower just to, just to singe it back, just to burn it, just to make it pull back — SWOOOOOO — SWOOOOOO — SWOOOOOO — SWOOOOOO — SWOOOOOO — SWOOOOOO — (Sigh) — Oh balls (Agonized Voice) — Ooooooh — (Sigh) — (Breathing heavily while talking) — it's pulled back, I don't know what direction to go in now, I don't know which way is out, it's like everything is sealed up — I feel it's in front of me, I feel like the pathway is — feel like it's in front of me — (Sigh) — take one step forward — it's like there I am, it's like there's just a fucking wall of meat in front of me — (Sigh) — I feel real weak in my knees — (Sigh) — take a long, like a long spear — (Sniff) — god it's hot, it's a hot spear, it's like the ends — a red hot — right on into the fucking wall — it pulls back a little bit, it's like I can see there's the slit, there's the opening (Sigh) — (Sniff) — and I just keep poking and poking and it opens up a little bit — it's like I can see the opening, can't see any light, can't see the light but I can see an opening — (Sigh) — (Sniff) — like I see a tunnel, I see a tunnel there — (Sigh) — I don't know if I want to climb into that or not but I got this — it's like the womb is like seared, it's like seared open — (Sigh) — (Stronger Voice) — I'm coming out — fuck all of you, fuck you man, I'm coming out — god damn I'm coming out, you're not stopping me now — you're not stopping me — (Sigh) — (Sigh) — Joe's out there — Joe's out there — (Sniff) — (Sigh) — Joe's out there — (Sigh) — all I got to do is make my way out — (Sigh) — (Sniff) — I can do it, I know I can do it, I can't do it right now but I know I can do it, I know I can do it — (Sigh) — (Sniff) — (Sigh) — just as I take one step, this just starts the stuff just fucking closing in on me again — like all over around my neck and my back — (Sniff) — (Sigh) — SWISH — take a slice out — SWISH — (Sigh) — cuts the meat all up and down the sides — SWISH — just *whack* the meat away, just *whack* the meat away, just WHACK it away — it's not closing in so much — I'm scared of having my feelings, I don't know, I don't know right now — I'm just feeling — (Sigh) — I don't know if I can do it ------- see, (Sniff) ------- said it before, don't want to perform it — I don't want to perform it — (Sigh) — I don't want to perform (Sigh) — I got to do it — (Sounds of throwing up) (Tape went dead) — I feel my cock — like I can have my cock for me, I'm having my cock for me — fucking bitch — (Sigh) — (Louder Voice) — my cock for me — my cock for me — MY COCK FOR ME — MINE — IT'S MY COCK — (Sigh) just get it out — SWISH — SWISHHH — SWISHHH — SWISH — SWISH — SWISH — SWISHHHH — SWISH — SWISHHH — SWISHHHHHHH — (Lots of foot noise during this) — SWISHHH — SWISHHHHHHHH — SWISHHHHHHHHH — SWISHHHHHHHHH — SWISHHHHHHHHH — SWISHHHHHHHHH — SWISHHHHHHH — SWISHHHHHHHHHHH — SWISHHHHHHHHHH — (Sigh) — SWISHHHHHHHHH — (Heavy breathing for one minute) — I don't know where I am — I feel like I'm on the outside — it's like I can see her cunt from the outside — I don't know where I am with it — feel like I can use the fucking flame thrower and like just burn it up — swooooo — ugly fucking cunt — looks like her vagina just ripped open — try and stand up now — (Sigh) — (Sigh) — (Sigh) — she's lying down, she's little — all the fucking shit all my whole fucking life — I'll get the machete — SWISH — SWISH — SWISH — SWISH — (Sigh) — SWISH — I just want to cut it to pieces — SWISH — (SIGH) — fucking ugly cunt — (Sigh) — (Sigh) — (Sigh) — I want Joe's arm around me — put your arm around me Joe — (Prior line said with sad voice) -- I can see your face — I don't even know if I need your help or not — (Sigh) — but it's okay I guess if I have to do more, I have to do more I don't know — I've held myself inside — I don't know if I got out the old things or not, feel like I'm on the outside but don't know if I went through it or not, I don't know if I can trust myself or not — (Sigh) — (Sigh) — try and see her face at least, she's dead — she's just dead, she's . . . dead, it prided me, didn't surround me but it, but any way I cut, it's okay — (Sigh) — put your hand on my shoulder (Sad Voice) — (Sigh) — you (Chuckle) have a nice face — (Loud Exhale) — I'm scared I'm still back in there — (Sigh) — I don't know — I must be — (Sigh — Sigh — Sigh — Sigh) I don't know — (Sounds of walking) — don't think I've quite made it out — feel like I got into the, like I got into the canal, like, the vagina itself is closed up tight on the end — it's like I can go in the canal and not be smothered like I thought I would be — I'm stronger, I'm a fuck of a lot stronger than I thought I was — (Sigh) — it's like, it's like I'm still in the canal — at least I got — anyway I begin feeling sexual just like, just like getting to the, to the, to the, vagina itself, it's like the outer genitals makes me feel sexual, even to cut it up makes me feel sexual, like to cut her vagina up and have my cock — yeah — I'll make a slash crossways — SWISH — yeah, just kind of makes it open up a little bit, see light out there and there's Joe grinning out there — I can't, it's not wide enough yet — (Sigh) — I just start slashing the sides of it and just cutting meat off, just, just, cutting meat out — SWISH — SWISH — cutting across the top and on the sides and just whacking it, cutting hunks of meat out — just cutting it out, it's like behind me is just pus, shit, just — evil as — cutting and cutting — SWISH — (Sigh) — it's like it's open, like the vagina's open — I put a bar across the opening, one at the top and one at the bottom to make sure it stays open, just stand there (Sigh) — I turn around and look back — it's just ugly and black, dark in there, what a horrible place to have lived — it's horrible — and it's not even powerful — just like a vacant hole — turn back around — and here's the opening and all I have to do is step out — Joe's sitting there laughing, 'Come on Steve' — says all you do is step out — Oh yeah, I won't worry about my brothers and my father being out there someplace right now, 'cause they could destroy me — (Stronger Voice) — I ain't no fucking baby no more, I'm not a baby — I can have my feelings, and I can hack my own way out, I can be a man, I don't need to live around in a fucking vagina, I don't need you, I don't need your vagina anymore, I don't need your fucking vagina — I don't need your god damn womb, I don't need what you told me was love — I don't need my own fucking tears — I don't need my own impotence — I don't need to feel sorry for you, feel sorry for your own fucking self — you felt sorry for yourself your whole life and died that way, you died of cancer — a death well deserved — I'm a man with my own fucking cock and I'm going to use it and it's going to be happy and strong and my balls are going to hang between my legs, and you guys, you can, you can laugh and you can ridicule and you can sit there and slop in that fucking vagina and hate each other and kill one another — and suck off of her dead pussy — evil sons-of-bitches — you're no men — you're weak, you're weak, you're really weak — you're the babies and I thought you were men — fuck you — it's like I push that opening of the vagina with my hands, I push it open — it went away — step out — (Sigh) — feel like I got balls right now (Sigh) to here, like I'm stepping out, turn around — let it close — it's an ugly vagina — it's like the vagina's still not as tight at least, feels like my shoulders are getting bigger — my chest is expanding a little bit — (Sigh) — pull myself out — (Sigh) — I'm growing up bigger — (Sigh) — I'm a man, I'm a man with balls, I'm a god damn man — fucking a — I don't need to be in your vagina, I don't need to be there no more, I don't need to be in your vagina — I don't need your vagina — I don't need to be a baby — I need to be a man — need to feel good about my balls and my cock — don't need to feel ashamed, don't need to feel like I have a little cock — I got a nice cock, I got a nice big cock — and balls that are mine — and I can fuck with them, feel good about them natural, not uptight, not embarrassed, not feel like a little kid, not humiliated — you fucking old man, you don't even know what a cock is — you got a fucking angry cock — you got a weak cock, it's limp — you gonna all live together, you fucking cunt and you fucking sons-of-bitches — live together, I don't need you, I don't need you at all anymore and I don't need to be crazy, I don't need to be in an impotent rage all the time either — I can have Steve — I want to love a woman of my own choice — and I don't have her right now but that's all right — I don't want what you guys have — I want my balls and my cock first of all and I got 'em — anybody want to argue about it, any fucking brothers want to argue about it — want to try laughing — aah you're scared shitless aren't you — you want to try something, come on — beat the fucking shit out of you — I don't need no machete for you guys either — come on you chickenshits, you laughed while I was in there, now laugh that I'm out, come on — what's wrong, can't you do it — yeh, turn your tail, run back in there and hide, hide in the vagina, go ahead, go back in there then you can laugh in there, you can laugh your hearts out — cry for yourself — sick people, you're sick, you're really sick — and I thought I was the only one who was sick — I got feelings my whole life and a hell of a lot of strength and I played baby instead, it was the only way I knew how — you can take it from me, fuckers, you can all go wallow in your own puke and your own shit, I'm sick of it — (Sounds of walking about) — (Clattering noise) — (Sighing — aaah) — I feel sick to my stomach, I feel like I want to throw up — I'm so sick of 'em all — I can see them all around the vagina — they're all little and they're all crazy, like little midgets — I feel just really sick — I want it all out of me, all of it — yaaaaaaagh — yaaaaaagh — (Coughs) — (Sounds of throwing up for approximately one minute) — (Sniff) — (Sigh) — feels like one of them is caught in my throat — which one — Ron, good old Ron, you weak son-of-a-bitch, you shit (Sounds of throwing up four times) — it won't come out and I reach in and (Sounds of throwing up) (Sighing — Saying, aaah — oohh — aaggg) — Yaaaaag, it's out — ooooooh — ooooooh — (Sighing — oooooooooooh) — ooooooooooh — (Sigh) — Sigh) — ooooh — (Sounds of throwing up) — (Sigh) — (Sigh) — oh that feels better — (Sighing — aaah) — wallow in the puke you shits, wallow in your puke — (Sniff) — (Sigh) — OOOOHH —

(Sniff) — (Sigh) — (Sigh) — (Sniff) — now I need to wipe them up and put them in the toilet (Sounds of walking away) — (and return) — (Cough) — (Sounds of wiping up) — (Sniff) — (Sigh) — (Sigh) — (Sigh) — (Sigh) — (Sigh) — (Sounds of walking) — (Toilet flushing) — (Loud cough) — (Walking back) — (Sniff) — (Sigh) — (Sigh) . . . . (Clatter noise — walking to door) — (Sigh) — in fact there's light outside, looks nice outside — it's beautiful (Noise) — (Sigh) — fresh air, a glass of cold water — (Sighing deep — oooooh) — another one — (Exhale) — and another one from a brook, aaah with the cold breeze and trees and people — my friends — hot sun, cold water — (Sigh) — (Sigh) — (Sigh) — (Sigh) — (Sigh) — that tree outside my window is beautiful — it's what I love, mountains and a blue sky and the trees and the grass, it's so beautiful out — it's mine and I don't have to be alone — I've got me — I don't think I'll ever go back into the vagina I'm scared I will — I'm scared I'll go back in — I don't think I want to, I don't want to, I don't want to go, I don't ever want to go back in — not unless I want to wallow in shit and pus and puke with them — I got no reason to go back in — (Sigh) ---- it's like it's so new for me to be myself — and I'm not even sure where I'm at right now — I'm not sure what it's like to be me and not be so afraid of humiliation — I feel like I can calm down now — and still be me, it's like I can laugh but I can be calm or I can be angry and I can be calm, like I can have all my feelings and be calm — like some inner strength, a core of strength. I can feel my cock like a core right now — like my cock and my balls and my whole crotch are like coming right up the middle of me into my chest — especially my balls -------- (Sniff) ---------- (Noise) ---------- that's enough for now ----------."

In the months which followed this rather powerful imagery experience, a marked change in Steve's feelings took place. He reported feeling more masculine, less inclined to anticipate his former "obligatory" mode of behavior towards women. Occasionally, he still experienced "entrapment" feelings in his relationships with women, but the likelihood of any real entrapment was appreciably diminished. Being defined by women and being without a choice were conditions of decreasing probability. Steve had become freer and enjoyed a more positive self-image.

CHAPTER IV

Imagery and Dialogue

I have audiotaped several hundred hours of sessions between myself and patients, utilizing the methods set forth in the previous chapters. About a year ago I attempted a videotape of myself and a woman named Lynne who had been in group therapy with another therapist but had now been out of direct contact with therapy for several years. Lynne had heard of some of my methods from her previous therapist (who is my colleague) and expressed interest in doing a videotape. Of course, I was interested too. She had appeared on TV years ago and expressed no self-consciousness about the possibility of videotaping a therapy session. What follows is a verbatim record of the audio portion of the videotape. Other than what I have mentioned, I knew nothing more of her than her name.

In choosing this session, I am aware that it is limited insofar as it could not possibly cover each and every point encompassed in the preceding chapters. The reader is asked to be aware that this is only *one* session and essentially the beginning session between me and Lynne. The range of possibilities is vast and I could only attend to the subject which arose in this session. There are no *typical* sessions, as each session takes on the feelings and attitudes of the people involved. The reader should be also aware that a printed text of necessity leaves out many nuances, voice changes, physical movements and other nonverbal manifestations of the session.

A year or so after the videotape was made I asked Lynne to return, listen, and comment about the tape at any point she wished. (She volunteered to inform me that she had been too busy to get any therapy in the last year.)

Spaced below the text are her comments, taped one year after the original recording.

(A note to the reader. From previous experience with patient-therapist printed texts accompanied by patient comments, it seems clearer if the reader would read the entire patient-therapist text first and then read the patient comments second, in that order.)

Shorr: How do you feel, Lynne, coming here?
Lynne: Oh, I guess I feel all right about it, just a little bit shook up at first.
Shorr: Shook up? You mean . . .
Lynne: Well, you know, I think my getting lost really was a sort of a — I mean I tried not to get lost.
Shorr: Before you came here, you mean?
Lynne: I really tried because I was afraid of getting lost for the simple reason that this is sort of a strange thing for me to go back to. I have avoided, tried to avoid being in front of a camera altogether.

Shorr: Well, we're on the camera right now. How does it feel?

Lynne: Well, that's fine. Hi there. (Laughs looking into camera)

Shorr: Good. Where can we start? How should I not refer to you? In other words I can refer to you in any way but what's one way you would not want me to refer to you as?

Lynne: I don't think that at this moment that there is anyway. There was awhile that I would have resented being referred to as Lynne in any way because I consider that a part of a dead past and I think at this moment I . . .

Shorr: (S&O) Well, what about what quality would you now not want to be ·referred to as, any quality you can think of?

Lynne: You mean in order that you are going to avoid it or in order that . . .

Shorr: No, if I said to you (FTS) never refer to you as whatever quality that would be.

Lynne: Well, I think an actress.

Shorr: That's the worst?

Lynne: Uh huh. That's sort of − oh, I guess that's sort of like saying you're bad. I'm free associating right now. But it's like saying you're bad and you're insecure and you're not loved. Now that makes me feel like crying. (Pause)

Shorr: (M/L) Who is the most unloved person that you know of?

Lynne: My mother and me. And I don't particularly like my mother at all.

Shorr: I want you to try something. I want you to − it might be that you close your eyes or focus at a point with your eyes opened and I want you to imagine something − O.K.?

Lynne: Will this be pleasant or unpleasant?

It's very significant, I think, that I forgot all about having said anything like that even though I felt that − it's interesting because I actually never did want to be an actress; however, lately as I progress in therapy, I feel that there wouldn't be much . . . oh, phoniness in acting. I think it's more or less a betrayal of the truth as you see it. That's strange because at one point I had to use the cobalt treatment for cancer on my face and I was just petrified − absolutely petrified of the machine even though there was no pain whatsoever associated with it and I think the crushing very possibly could have been pressured into anything.

On the part where I say I feel the pressure is my mother. Oh, I think it's amusing that I say that I'm blending with it because I really actually don't feel that at this moment. That I would want to be a part of my mother − she is more like a child that has to be taken care of and I am more of a grown-up, but, oh, I don't know − I guess I could humor the child but I don't feel it's all that threatening anymore.

On the mention of the people that I have used through the telescope, they were sort of tied into one another. Only recently, I have begun to feel that there might be a possibility of my being open to other people and accepting them, therefore accepting myself. At the brink of the recording I feel I was less able to accept myself or feel that I would be receptive or open to other people.

Shorr: Well, I'll tell you and you will imagine whatever you wish — let your own imagination go as it will.
Lynne: O.K.
Shorr: I don't have a preconceived idea — you just let your imagination roam — O.K.?
Lynne: O.K.
Shorr: (IS) I want you to imagine that above you and behind you is a force — now you try to imagine that force.
Lynne: What kind of force is it?
Shorr: That's what I want you to do. Using your imagination.
Lynne: Well, I see it as a crushing force.
Shorr: A crushing force.
Lynne: Sort of, if there were heavy, you know, one of those radioactive machines that they use for cancer — one over here and one behind me and they are both trying to crush me and I'm resisting them.
Shorr: You are resisting them. Now what I want you to do — still imagining (IS) — see if you can imagine that particular thing you mentioned as the force — humanize it in some way. In other words, give it human form if you possibly can. Use your imagination and let it be your guide.
Lynne: Well, I don't have to imagine very hard, it just came to me immediately — my mother.
Shorr: She is pushing you, you mean?
Lynne: The pressure.
Shorr: Pressuring you?
Lynne: Both pressures. They are sort of me and my mother combined. They are one in the same. I am my mother and my mother is me.
Shorr: And you are resisting as you said that.
Lynne: All of a sudden I'm not so much — I'm blending with it. I guess that would be the word — blending.
Shorr: You're just letting it happen to you, you mean?
Lynne: I'm accepting it, rather than trying to hold back from it.
Shorr: How do you feel about accepting it?
Lynne: Good! It feels like, well, to hell with it, you know. It's not a thing — it's something that I have imagined; therefore, I can release it. I can make it what I

On the part where I see the other telescope and I see the people that hate one another. It's rather strange that I say that people hate one another because perhaps at that point it was me hating myself and also me probably hating other people at their ability to communicate with one another.

On the part — I look through a mirror and I see a picture of my mother when she was about seventeen or twenty — uh, it's rather interesting that I see her looking gentle because most of the time, every time I can remember my mother, I see her looking annoyed and angry and displeased. So, well, I'm not too sure but I think that maybe the gentleness which I feel I have a lot of but I don't feel my mother is a very gentle person.

wanted to make it. I mean, it could be flowers falling or it could be anything, but it doesn't have to be dangerous.

Shorr: Now, what I want you to do is try to imagine something else. (IS) I want you to imagine that you are looking through a telescope and tell me what you see using your imagination as your guide.

Lynne: Oh, the first thing was the stars and the planets and then I see, well, maybe a never-never land.

Shorr: A never-never land? What does it look like?

Lynne: It's blue, a very beautiful blue and green and the people are happy and they are sort of tied into one another.

Shorr: You like that, huh?

Lynne: It makes me feel like crying. It's sad because it's like it's not going to happen. I've imagined that.

Shorr: (IS) Now what I want you to do is imagine turning around completely 180° and there you find another telescope that looks away from the one you just looked through.

Lynne: Oh, that's bad.

Shorr: What is it?

Lynne: Oh, it's like people are today. There's hate and dirty and dirty — the air is dirty and everything around it is nasty — there is no love maybe even worse than today — sort of at a time when there is no love at all, and people hate only — that's all they do is hate and destroy — they don't understand — they don't know anything. It's just black and gray and hateful.

Shorr: (IS) Now I want you to imagine — switching to another one — that you look into a mirror and instead of seeing yourself which you would of course see, try to imagine somebody else other than yourself. Whom do you see?

Lynne: I see another me.

Shorr: No, but if you were to see someone other than yourself — of course, you would normally see yourself, but to imagine someone other than yourself.

Lynne: Would it be someone I like or don't like?

Shorr: It could be anybody, see I don't have the answers.

Lynne: Well, the picture that comes to my mind is this picture of my mother when she was about sixteen and she posed for some kind of hair ad and she's got very long, long, black wavy hair and she's got very soft, dark eyes and she's smiling and she looks very gentle in that picture.

Shorr: And she was sixteen at the time?

Lynne: She looks (Pause) — and gentle in an appealing way.

Shorr: (IS) Now I want you to say something to your mother that you see in the mirror — the image you've just seen — say something to her.

On the part where I talk to my mother through the mirror and I hear her saying when I ask her what happened, I hear her saying I don't understand. It's rather reminiscing of my behavior when things get too much pressure for me and I can't handle them for me to say that I am mixed up or I don't understand — there's quite a great deal of similarity here that perhaps it is more me saying that I don't understand, or that I am mixed up, than my mother.

Lynne: I don't think I can.

Shorr: Try.

Lynne: This is very hard. Well, I could ask her what happened. You want me to talk to her?

Shorr: What does she say back?

Lynne: She doesn't know.

Shorr: What does she say, what is her statement to you back?

Lynne: I don't know. Or she could say in Italian, "*No capisco*" — I don't understand. I don't know why I am throwing in the Italian but that's coming to me.

Shorr: *No caprisco?*

Lynne: *No capisco* — I don't understand — it's a smile and everything but yea, I put this up — I don't understand, it's like I could say to her, why don't you accept me and she would still say I don't understand.

Shorr: No capisco.

Lynne: She threw another language in — Spanish — *non comprendo* — it wouldn't matter — it would always be confusion. It would be something that I — I try to reach but I can't because what I am reaching for — it's such confusion.

Shorr: That's the way she dealt with you, you mean, with confusion. And so when you talk to her now in the mirror — even though she is sixteen years old at the time — the image you got you feel a lot of confusion. Now I want you — we'll go back I'm sure to this again but now I want you for a moment to switch to another thing and that is — I want you to imagine two animals — any two at all — there is no right or wrong about any of these as you know.

Lynne: The same kind of animals?

Shorr: (IS) No, any two different kind of animals I should say. Just whatever comes to your mind.

Lynne: A cat.

Shorr: (IS) And another one. A different one.

Lynne: A parrot.

Shorr: A cat and a parrot. (IS) Now can you give me an adjective for each of the animals.

Lynne: Cat's love, loving.

Shorr: Loving.

Lynne: The parrot's bickering.

Shorr: Now here's what I want you to do. (IS) I want you to imagine a statement that would come from the parrot if it spoke first to the cat.

Lynne: Cat nasty, nasty, nasty.

Shorr: (IS) O.K. Now one from the cat back answering that.

Lynne: Oh, that's O.K., I don't care what you say.

On the part where I feel the confusion in my mother when I look at her through the mirror. It's rather strange again that the confusion actually was created by my mother but I create my own confusion, it appears to me, when I can't deal with something on an emotional level or I can't understand it. There's quite a great deal of similarity here.

Shorr: (IS) Now if the cat were to speak first to the parrot what would it say?

Lynne: I wonder if you are a friend or an enemy.

Shorr: (IS) And the parrot would say back?

Lynne: I don't like you, I don't like you.

Shorr: (IS) Now if the cat and the parrot were to fight, who would win?

Lynne: The parrot.

Shorr: Why is that?

Lynne: 'Cause it would punch out the eyes of the cat.

Shorr: The eyes.

Lynne: And the cat couldn't see.

Shorr: Now this thing between the cat and the parrot − does that remind you about anything in your own life perhaps?

Lynne: My childhood.

Shorr: Your childhood. How's that?

Lynne: Oh, my mother bought me a parrot and it was always getting into trouble and I picked out an alley cat and I loved the cat and she gave it away. You got any Kleenex's?

Shorr: Yes, right in front of you. Sorry . . . you had a very strong reaction to that, huh?

Lynne: It's like all my rights were taken away.

Shorr: (IS) I'd like you to imagine a house in another city − one perhaps you have never seen before, and then try to imagine two rooms in that house. And after you have done that, now try to put a person in each of these rooms that you have imagined. Can you do it?

Lynne: I'm trying, it's hard to imagine a house that I have never seen before.

Shorr: Take your time.

Lynne: O.K.

Shorr: (IS) Can you see the two rooms?

Lynne: There are two separate parts of the house. One is sort of white and peaceful with pretty music − soft. And the other is dark, dreary with no music − it's just empty, it's kind of creepy feeling. It's not horrifying, it's so empty in there, it's so dark.

Shorr: (IS) Can you think of a person in that room?

Lynne: My mother.

Shorr: (IS) Who is in the other room?

Lynne: I am.

Shorr: (IS) Now can − if you had a telephone connected, could you say something to her on the telephone?

On the part between the cat and the parrot, it's interesting that I say, well, the parrot would win because it would punch out the eyes of the cat. Uh, my mother is constantly talking about birds punching the eyes of cats and so forth, and I see this as the cat being nonthreatening and a loving figure and the parrot possibly doing a mother symbol or a bickering and angry symbol of some sort.

Lynne: No, I wouldn't want to talk to her.

Shorr: I see. Does she say anything to you?

Lynne: Well, if she did she would take away the white room. It's just like the telephone would wreck the whole.

Shorr: You mean, as long as you could keep them separate you could survive it?

Lynne: Uh huh.

Shorr: Can you finish the sentence? (FTS) My mother defined me as _____. What word comes to mind?

Lynne: My mother defined me as a *machine*.

Shorr: As masheen? What does that mean?

Lynne: A machine to fulfill . . .

Shorr: Oh, a machine, I'm sorry. I thought you were giving me another Italian word.

Lynne: A machine to fulfill her needs. Not a human being.

Shorr: Just an automaton, you mean. Just a functioning automaton to do as she, as she . . .

Lynne: A doll would be better.

Shorr: Even a doll, huh?

Lynne: A doll that, that can be dressed up, and fixed up and made to look pretty, that has no feelings. You can do anything you want with the doll.

Shorr: At twelve years old I would assume then that that's the way you defined yourself then? The way you just described.

Lynne: At twenty I did.

Shorr: Even at twenty. And how about today in your heart of hearts. Finish the sentence (FTS) I define myself as a _____.

When I imagined the two rooms and I imagined the dark room where my mother is and there is a telephone there and I feel she might call me or I might call her and I feel that she would take away the good feeling and the beautiful room I am in: I feel this is sort of a reflection of a fact, whenever I have done anything, even though my mother says that she is happy that I did it, she asks in such a manner as to make me feel that I didn't do anything very good or to bring about something or say something or insinuate something by the tone of her voice and by this tone of her voice and by this tone sort of take away everything I have gained. I don't think I buy this package anymore, however, oh, I think I'm a little afraid of it. Actually, in the part where I say I won't be allowed to grow even though it is in imagination, I still wouldn't be allowed to grow by my mother. Uh, in that I feel I have grown, however, if I let her get in the picture I wouldn't grow at all. I can feel it very strongly as a part of the saying that kept me back all of the time from really developing all of the time as a human being. I could function in the theatre as a doll, not as a full-fledged performer — it's pretty dull. I think at this point perhaps there is more of a freedom about me than there ever has been even though I still look at my mother in that particular relationship with a deep sorrow now because I don't ever think it will be a workable relationship. She will constantly see me as a little child or a doll and I just can't let it bother me. I have my own life to lead and that's about it.

Lynne: A growing human being.

Shorr: That sounds good.

Lynne: I'm not even frightened about growing. It was kind of interesting but I cannot tie up to that other because if I do it's going to — I've got to remain separated because if I tie up it's going to bring me down. I won't be allowed to grow. Even though I know this is imagination the threat in any way you look at it is there that if I accept anything she says I might as well vegetate. And I don't think I would accept it anymore anyway.

Shorr: Now, I want you to do something — (IS) go to another room completely away from the house you have just mentioned — you are just there by yourself and you walk into a room and in the center of the room is a hole — now I want you to look through the hole, again using your imagination of course as your guide, and tell me what you see with the imagination as you look through the hole in the floor.

Lynne: Well, the first thing that I imagined immediately was like a snake pit. The hole is full of rising snakes and it's slimy and it's — maybe the snakes turn into — into crazy women, maybe even men. They are all locked up down there.

Shorr: (IS) How would it feel if you went down into that pit?

Lynne: Part of me feels that I would be afraid and part of me feels that maybe there could be something I could give, but it's such a big test.

Shorr: It's more than you care to get into, huh?

Lynne: Well, not more than I care to, more than I'm ready to at the moment.

Shorr: (M/L) Who is the most giving person you have ever known?

Lynne: I'd really have to search for that.

Shorr: It's O.K.

Lynne: Maybe my grandmother. Yes — my grandmother.

Shorr: (M/L) Who is the least giving person you have ever known?

Lynne: My mother. Buts my grandmother would be my father's mother. My grandmother was just a delight to be with. She used to wrestle around with me and pretend she was asleep and then I'd go up to bite her nose and she'd come awake, she wasn't really asleep, and she'd wrestle around with me and she had a good mind and everything was pleasant around her.

Shorr: It sounds like a lot of fun, and happy times, huh?

Lynne: But my mother was there and she made things bad.

Shorr: (S&O) How did your grandmother define you as?

On the part where I remember my grandmother and I remember wrestling with her when she pretends she is asleep and she really isn't and so forth. As I go back now and think about it, I think that was really — I was about three at the time — when we went back to Germany I must have been about nine — but it seems to me with my grandmother I had a real deep human contact — a sense of touch and feeling and enjoyment. And about the only time I did have a sense of contact and being just close to someone for a long, long time. Since then, I hadn't had any and I'm just beginning to recapture that feeling of touching and being close to somebody, but just barely.

Lynne: Somebody she loved. Every time I say love, I think I'm going to cry. I do, as a matter of fact. Wait a minute.

Shorr: Good. (IS) Now if you had telepathic powers so that you could tell what a person in a foreign country was thinking or feeling using your imagination, tell me who the person would be plus what country it's in and what they are feeling or thinking.

Lynne: It would be Spain. And they would be very brave and a lot of fun.

Shorr: You are thinking of a particular person?

Lynne: Yes, a Spanish dancer and, come to think of it, she was also very giving.

Shorr: Someone you've known, I take it.

Lynne: When I was a little girl and she was full of fun. My mother didn't like her either.

Shorr: Your mother didn't seem to like anybody.

Lynne: No — anybody that likes me. That love me. There was a fight for possession there and if they loved me and then I like the, like the Spanish woman — she was a Spanish dancer and she had dogs and animals and I like animals, and I used to want to spend weeks up there and I asked to go there for weeks to stay and my mother would — well, one of the times I went that's when she gave my kitten away and then she kept saying that's no good for you, you shouldn't go there — and it was very happy, very happy. She was married to a Canadian and he was happy too and somehow or other they appeared to be my mother and father but friends too. It was fun there.

Shorr: (IS) Now if you were to imagine yourself on a balance scale — like they use in chemistry or weights — a balance scale and on one side you are standing and on the other side is your father. Tell me what you'd imagine you'd feel and do and so forth.

Lynne: He would weight me down. In other words, his weight would be so heavy that he would bring me down — I mean, I would be up but his weight would be so heavy that I couldn't balance it. He wouldn't do anything; he wouldn't try anything but the weight would be so heavy for me to try to keep those scales even. I couldn't do it.

Shorr: (IS) Could you say something to him?

Lynne: Oh yes. I like my father.

Shorr: (IS) What would you say to him? Can you give me the statement?

Lynne: Yea, I would say, why can't you help me?

Shorr: (IS) And what would he say back?

On looking back on the Spanish dancer and her husband the Canadian man, perhaps when I think of where some formative good feelings began besides my grandmother I think they would have been instrumental in giving me some healthy feeling versus the awful crappy feeling I was getting at home and I think possibly, oh, I can only feel kind of sorry for my mother that she could not give any love to me. She could give me things but never love, and therefore she constantly must have felt threatened when I found someone that could give love and I could give love in return. And I guess she did feel that I could not give her any real love or communicate with her too well.

Lynne: Well you know how your mother is.

Shorr: And how would you feel to that?

Lynne: Rejected.

Shorr: (IS) Now I want you to imagine you are on a train — perhaps in a foreign country — and you are sitting next to a stranger — whom you never see again and I want you to imagine that you tell him a secret — since you won't see him again that you tell him a secret — and tell me what that secret is, using your imagination again.

Lynne: I have to pick a secret first. It's very hard to reach that stranger. I have to make him warm first — approachable.

Shorr: You mean he is not responsive to you?

Lynne: He's a shadow.

Shorr: (IS) Well, how would you go about making him warm toward you then?

Lynne: I was thinking of sex. (Ha, Ha) That's my old hangup. I couldn't talk to him.

Shorr: (IS) How old do you imagine him to be, Lynne?

Lynne: He's about — oh, maybe fortyish. But he's not real defined. I can't make up a definition for him. That's where my problem comes. I . . .

Shorr: (IS) Now I want you to imagine holding his face in your hands and looking straight at his face. Could you get a better definition of him? Could you imagine doing that?

Lynne: He is a ballet dancer. He's all made up in sort of — oh, arched eyebrows and heavy makeup and sad lips — like a clown but not really a clown, he's really more like a satyr. His hair is all curled up and his ears are pointed, and I can't figure out whether he is wicked or evil or good or he is just teasing.

Shorr: You just can't figure him out at all, huh?

Lynne: No — he's . . .

Shorr: (IS) What happens when you hold his face in your hands though?

Lynne: Oh, he smiles. I guess the closest I can come to the stranger is somebody I know or used to know. He was a sculptor named Vito and he had that kind of a face. His eyes gleamed. There was a gleam in his eyes all of the time and he smiled, but you could never be sure whether he liked you or not. But that doesn't matter, I can like him — can't I?

It's interesting when I meet the stranger I'm sitting next to the stranger in the train and at first I see him only as a shadow and I can't reach him and then the fact that I should use sex as the only way in which I could reach him. In the past I used this — this is my only means of communication with anyone. Uh, and it was a bad hangup just trying to communicate with people or feel in touch with people through sex. Since then, I think that I am able to communicate with people through touch and complete warmth and giving but not necessarily calling it sex except perhaps with my husband where I think he's sort of hesitant of touching me in a friendly manner and I — although I used to approach him and hug him and so forth in a friendly manner, I freeze now when I'm close to him because I think I'm going to be rejected — now I don't know how much of this is my own feeling and how much of it is the actual rejection I may be getting from him — I have sort of half a mind to think right now it's probably fifty-fifty and that I'm not really opening up all that much myself.

Shorr: Yea.

Lynne: I'll try to like him.

Shorr: But what is it you want to say to him before you tell him the secret? I want you to say something to him. (M/L) What would be the most difficult thing to say to him? To speak to him?

Lynne: That's kind of hard to do.

Shorr: I know. It's not easy.

Lynne: The most difficult. Maybe that I would like to be a Bohemian like him.

Shorr: Why would that be so difficult to say?

Lynne: Because being a Bohemian then means you have no responsibilities and you sort of paint and draw and act or do whatever you want to do — but you sort of feel like I would be letting somebody down.

Shorr: (S&O) Who would you be letting down if you were a Bohemian? Or you felt free about things?

Lynne: My parents, I guess.

Shorr: So what is this secret you want to tell Vito in this case?

Lynne: That I want to be free like him. Sort of . . .

Shorr: (IS) Try saying that to him — like you are holding his face — and say it freely — don't be afraid — just let it out.

Lynne: Vito, I would like to be free like you.

Shorr: Do you have any feeling behind that? Or are you just saying it?

Lynne: It's sort of a strange feeling.

Shorr: Come on — go ahead — say it.

Lynne: It's good and it's sad.

Shorr: (Focus) Try to say it and mean it and not be afraid of any retaliation. Just say it — just be it.

Lynne: VITO — I WOULD LIKE TO BE FREE LIKE YOU.

Shorr: More feeling this time?

Lynne: And then I could — I COULD DO SOME GOOD THINGS, maybe.

Shorr: You like saying that, don't you? Gee, say it again.

Lynne: Hmmmm.

Shorr: Too much? How do you feel right now?

Lynne: Good!

Shorr: I'm glad.

Lynne: Just give me a minute to . . .

Shorr: Oh, sure.

Lynne: It feels very good, like I — I could really be something different.

It's interesting when I finally do hold the stranger's face in my hands I disguise it still further by making him or putting him in the wild ballet makeup which further confused my seeing anything in his face, and it looks to me as if I'm also seeing him as a clown, perhaps. Uh, I think this is a tool by which I keep myself from actually being in contact with a stranger.

Shorr: (Focus) Right now I'd like you to try, Lynne — I'd like you to try that again. And this time, you know, scream it out. Have your guts — give your guts.

Lynne: O.K., give me a minute.

Shorr: Sure — take your time. This is no rush. We may be on the tape but we're not — we're not interested in a performance — you know we just want your real feelings.

Lynne: I know.

Shorr: I know you know.

Lynne: This should get some interesting feelings this way. It surprised me.

Shorr: I'm glad.

Lynne: It really does. 'Cause I get a lot of insight when — it's very interesting. O.K., I'll try it again. I don't know . . .

Shorr: (Focus) But this time I want you to let it come from your guts and don't be afraid — like I'm here and no retaliation is going to happen. Just say that to Vito — let it out.

Lynne: VITO — I WOULD LIKE TO BE FREE AND JUST BE ABLE TO DO ANYTHING I WANTED TO DO. That's painful.

Shorr: (Focus) Could you get even louder — like more from your guts — like from — from your guts and . . .

Lynne: I'm trying just as hard as I . . .

My goodness, When I'm talking to Vito the sculpturer or thinking of him or holding his — the stranger's face and the hands and thinking of Vito — it just occurred to me that Vito was quite a giving person and he appeared to like me even though I couldn't at the time whether I like him or not or he likes me or not. Uh, he did an awful lot of things for me and he accepted me a hundred percent. I think the problem was I couldn't quite accept him a hundred percent, but he did quite a bit for me in many ways. I think because of Vito, that I finally went to see Shapiro — it was — it was a Doctor. . . . that was going to Vito's sculpturing class and I think it was him that I finally got Shapiro's number and started going there. So, actually Vito was the start of a brand new life for me and he was completely altruistic I think in his own Bohemian manner — he was quite a likable guy as a matter of fact. I remember him as great fun when I tell Vito that I would like to do some good things like he does and I felt like crying and I cried up a time even to this day I still feel that I would like to be much freer than I am now. I would like to be a completely giving person so that I could do something for other people. At the present moment I feel like I'm sort of on the borderline between being giving and not giving. Sort of on a seesaw, but I think I probably will get to the point where I am more giving. I did notice a thing in my voice that when I talk at any time and I am afraid or in connection with my mother or father in any way my voice is very much that of a little girl and that when I talk to Vito with understanding and emotion my voice is that of a mature woman. It's rather indicative of the feeling there. If I am my mother and father's daughter, then I must remain a little confused girl — if I am a grown-up outgoing woman — well, if I ever get there it is a feeling that is both likable and at the same time where the fear is fearsome because it would mean that whatever I decide or do I would have to take full responsibility for it.

Shorr: (Focus) I know it's very difficult — I'm just pushing you — like don't be afraid — let it out.

Lynne: VITO, I WOULD LIKE TO BE FREE — I WOULD LIKE TO DO ANYTHING I WANTED TO DO IN LIFE.

Shorr: That's good.

Lynne: That makes me feel like crying.

Shorr: That's all right. Cry all you want — feel free to cry — if you want to cry. But you felt it a lot more.

Lynne: It is so sad because being free is such a good thing why should it be so sad.

Shorr: You pose a very philosophical question. I couldn't agree with you more.

Lynne: If you were free you could — you could give. When you are not afraid, you can give of yourself.

Shorr: And when you are free you can also accept good things.

Lynne: True.

Shorr: Not only give, but accept that which is good.

Lynne: I think giving is important.

Shorr: Sure.

Lynne: I think you have to have plenty to give a great deal. I've never done so and it's sad that I haven't done it.

Shorr: Well, let me ask you this question, Lynne. (S&O) Who does your giving belong to? A strange question maybe.

Lynne: It's never belonged to me.

Shorr: Who does it belong to?

Lynne: Oh, it goes back to my mother I guess. I remember when I was five years old and there was a benefit for poor children who didn't have anything and so everybody had given these beautiful dolls — all kinds of things for these poor children and my mother and this other lady took me over to look at the toys and they asked me to pick something for myself and I said I didn't want anything for myself because it wasn't for me — it was for the poor children and somehow or other I wound up with this big doll and I hated it because I was depriving some poor kid. They were forcing me to take it instead of enjoying the giving.

Shorr: You mean, they were encouraging selfishness, I gather?

On the part about being free so that I could accept things and give — that's rather strange — I had a point to make here and I sort of blocked it out altogether. It must be meaningful but I had a very definite point to make and I just can't seem to remember what it was. I'll go back to the tape.

The part about the doll at the benefit that was supposed to be given to the poor children and instead my mother and my teacher actually, my first grade teacher that was what it was, wanted me to take it and I did take it even though I had said I didn't want to take it. It's quite vivid in my mind when I think back how I felt this was completely unfair and I could no longer feel that my favorite teacher, her name was Elema, or my mother could ever be fair about anything again. It was sort of a complete disenchantment at that time. I think it may have been a deepening of the feeling that I just could not trust anybody.

Lynne: I didn't want it. I realized at five years old that it was wrong and I knew that I didn't want to do it and that I didn't want that doll and what they were doing was wrong, but they were deciding − I had no choice. I felt rotten because it wasn't a very human thing to do It was worse than selfishness − it was cruel.

Shorr: (S&O) What were the rules in your family for owning things − what was the mother's rule for that or the father's?

Lynne: No rules.

Shorr: The unspoken rule, I mean.

Lynne: Oh I guess everything was my mother's. We did everything to please her − dad wouldn't make a move if my mother didn't approve and I guess we were all afraid of her wrath or more than the wrath was the silent disapproval of − we'd get − both my dad and I kept trying to manipulate ourselves around my mother so that we could not escape punishment because we get it one way or another anyway − to get the least possible. And then my dad depended on me so much that I had to do all of the protecting of him. Even at a young age I had to look out for him − and that was too much for a man. You don't do that to a child.

Shorr: (S&O) Let me switch for a moment and ask you what was your way of punishing your mother?

Lynne: I didn't want to punish her, but I could stop her and I would stop her by getting sick. 'Cause when I got sick then she couldn't touch me.

Shorr: That was your protection and you punished her − she had to take care of you?

Lynne: Yea, I guess it was a form of punishment. I never felt very revengeful towards her, it was more like I wanted her to get off my back − I was so busy protecting myself I didn't have time to get mad − which was later in life that I got mad at her. And then I just couldn't hold a grudge against her.

Shorr: (IS) Now I want you to imagine your mother looking at herself in the mirror − seeing herself. Now what I want you to imagine is the most difficult thing that she could say to herself. The most difficult thing for her to say to herself.

Lynne: You want me to be my mother?

Shorr: (IS) Yea − I want you to imagine you are her and tell me what you imagine if she were to look into the mirror and see herself − what the most difficult thing for her to say to herself would be.

On the part where my dad and I are trying to manipulate ourselves around my mother so we can at least get the least possible punishment. It's sort of, well, it brings to mind my own behavior in my life where I've sort of learned or being conditioned I suppose, to sense the other person's level of wrath or whatever and go by that. In other words, always do get a feeling of the other person and then react or behave accordingly. Not react the way I really wanted to react but react in the manner in which I hear or feel the other person will want me to react.

On the part where I could keep my mother from reacting towards me by getting sick. It's rather strange that even today when the pressures at work are too heavy or the pressures around me are too heavy I will invariably come down with a heavy, heavy cold and will have to stay home in bed with medicine and so forth. It's almost as if I have been conditioned to avoid pressure by getting sick.

Lynne: I'm ignorant.

Shorr: Now switching — (IS) what is the most difficult thing for you to say to yourself if you were to look in the mirror and see yourself?

Lynne: That I'm smart.

Shorr: That's the most difficult, huh? (IS) Now I want you to imagine that you are sleeping in a field overnight or something and then in the morning you were awakened and you saw footprints on your body. Now I want you to tell me on what part of your body you imagine the footprints to be on.

Lynne: Oh, on my belly.

Shorr: (IS) And whose footprints would they be?

Lynne: At first they were big — they became little all of a sudden. They were a baby's. baby's.

Shorr: A baby's, a baby's footprints?

Lynne: I feel sad because I've never been pregnant. Maybe that's what made me imagine that. That's sad.

Shorr: (IS) Now I want you to imagine again two large boxes, and using your imagination, I want you to . . .

Lynne: Wait a second!

Shorr: You want to take your time — sure.

Lynne: Well, I just want to wipe my nose, I . . .

Shorr: O.K.

Lynne: I seem to open all of this meaningful material — I choked up a little bit here. Can I have a cigarette while . . .

Shorr: Why, sure.

Lynne: This is just absolutely incredible —

Shorr: You like it, huh?

Lynne: But it's like having fast therapy. These things are many things I've never thought of for a long time. O.K.

Shorr: You ready?

Lynne: Uh huh.

Shorr: (IS) O.K. Now I want you to imagine two large boxes — now using your imagination again I want you to imagine two different men — one in each box.

It's amusing when I go over the part where my mother looks at herself in the mirror and says or I say she says she's ignorant and then I look at myself in the mirror and I say I'm smart. Even to this day I can't quite — even though I know it intellectually, I can't feel that I am smart. It's not so much a feeling of snobbery or feeling that being better than others, but a feeling that I would be able to perhaps do things for others or better than most people; therefore, I would be able to help others and help them help themselves because of my knowledge and ability to understand almost ahead of time how they are going to react or feel about things. That's almost as if I were saying on that part of the tape that I got smart by learning to side-step my mother or predict ahead of time what my mother's reactions to things were going to be, and I got pretty nimble-minded about reacting to other people's emotions or coming emotions or whatever.

Lynne: What kind of boxes are they?

Shorr: That's up to you again, Lynne, you can . . .

Lynne: Well, you know I think of hearse, or funeral boxes.

Shorr: Coffin.

Lynne: Coffins — I couldn't even think of the word.

Shorr: (IS) Now can you imagine a man in each one?

Lynne: My dad would be in one.

Shorr: And the other?

Lynne: Billy.

Shorr: I don't know who Billy is.

Lynne: Oh, he is somebody I loved many, many years ago. He died. And they are two people I basically liked. One is dead and the other isn't. The other is old. And I guess someday he is going to go. That's kind of sad but I guess he would be happier if he did.

Shorr: (IS) Now switching again. I want you to imagine you are in a room and there is a hole in the room looking into the next room over — now look through that hole and tell me what you see there.

Lynne: It's a Bacchanalian feast (Laughing).

Shorr: Well, that's nice.

Lynne: People are like the old Roman days, they are having a ball — they really are — they are having fun though — at first I thought it may be just a, a sexy Bacchanalian feast but really isn't. It's them drinking wine and dancing and — somebody is sculpturing and somebody is painting — oh, somebody may be reading fortunes, but everybody is doing their thing.

Shorr: (IS) How would you like to go through the wall and join them? Can you do that?

Lynne: I would, but I wouldn't belong.

Shorr: Why not?

Lynne: 'Cause I'm not all that happy.

Shorr: (IS) No, but I want you to imagine that you are a part of it. Can you try?

Lynne: O.K.

Shorr: Just let yourself be part of it.

Lynne: That's hard. O.K. I go in there and I dance.

Shorr: (IS) Good. Can you let yourself relax and enjoy it?

On the part where I imagined the footprints on my belly to be a baby's, uh, even to this day it has quite an emotional impact and I think that perhaps, well, my husband and I have been talking about it but perhaps maybe we ought to adopt some older children or something like that. I have a very big need to give to children and I rather enjoy them. At least I think I do. I, we would not have known how much until I try it.

The hearse or coffin, it's still painful to this day. I think maybe it was a deep meaningful relationship and I have not been able to have such a relationship since that time. Hearing the tape — it does make me very sad remembering.

Lynne: Uh huh.

Shorr: Are you a part of it? You belong there — stay there.

Lynne: I can't.

Shorr: (Focus) Now I want you to stay there.

Lynne: It's very hard.

Shorr: Why don't you belong there?

Lynne: Something drags me back.

Shorr: Who drags you back?

Lynne: Things I have to do I guess. My mother, duty . . . so many things.

Shorr: So how long do you think you could stay there?

Lynne: A minute.

Shorr: (Focus) Just a minute? Now I want you to try and stay there a couple of minutes. Come on — you imagine it. Stay with it.

Lynne: Oh, that is so hard.

Shorr: You allow two minutes — now go ahead — at least.

Lynne: O.K., I am dancing.

Shorr: Come on — you are free — let it happen.

Lynne: And I find some other dancers — a fellow, and we are dancing.

Shorr: Good.

Lynne: And he tosses me in the air and I go up and down and . . .

Shorr: Terrific!

Lynne: Like a ballet dancer. And I enjoy moving.

Shorr: That's good — stay with it.

Lynne: And then all of a sudden we are Shakespearean actors.

Shorr: That's nice.

Lynne: And I'm doing a wicked, wicked woman — Macbeth maybe — Lady Macbeth — I'm having a ball — the meaner the better. It's such fun to do bad people. I mean to pretend that you are doing bad people. And then, on the other hand, we could also be doing Romeo and Juliet and she is so naive and so nice. Or then I could be painting something — oh, I know — I'd be writing poetry and I'd be writing about older things that shouldn't be so.

Shorr: That shouldn't be what?

Lynne: So. Why? It would be very good poetry.

It's funny, but the memory of looking through the hole and seeing the Bacchanalian feast makes me feel like crying. Maybe it's because I've never been able to really enjoy myself at anything quite yet. Maybe someday I will.

The part where I imagine myself in that room and I'm writing poetry makes me feel like crying because when I was very little I wrote quite a bit and as the years went by I wrote from time to time and I like my poetry, but I just enjoyed doing it and as I got older it seems that I just, oh, just let it go by the side like I did everything else that was important to me. I just couldn't hang on to any good feelings, maybe I will someday.

Shorr: It sounds beautiful.

Lynne: It would have such — and on the other hand it would be critical — it would have to be. That it would be nice to be. Oh, and I'd have a cat there and it would be the most beautiful cat and I could write poetry and have the cat there. And that's nice.

Shorr: See, you stayed with that a long time, and you enjoyed it. And it wasn't so bad at that, because you allowed it.

Lynne: I haven't written poetry since I was — many, many years ago I wrote poetry when I was a kid. And — this is most enjoyable.

Shorr: Thank you. We can start again now.

Lynne: O.K. I imagine — when my cigarette starts to run out and you'll let me know. (Laughing)

Shorr: We'll have to get you some new ones. (Pause) Now I want you — you feel O.K.?

Lynne: Oh fine, this is great — I feel so much better — I feel like I could do things really.

Shorr: Good.

Lynne: You know it's — every time I think I could do things I start to feel like I'm going to cry.

Shorr: (IS) Well, now I want you to imagine sensing your body from your head to your toe — I want you to imagine . . .

Lynne: You want me to keep my eyes closed or . . . .

Shorr: Yea, you seem to do quite well that way, but . . .

Lynne: O.K.

Shorr: You can do that or you can focus on some distant object or something, but whatever you want.

Lynne: O.K. Well, we'll try it this way. (She closes her eyes)

Shorr: (IS) OK. Now sensing your body from your head to your toe, I want you to sense the body core part of your identity. The body part core of your identity — from your head to your toe. What do you sense?

Lynne: Oh, I sense it's . . . .

Shorr: (IS) Where is it though — what body part?

Lynne: It's — well, it's hard to pinpoint because it flows out. It could be my mind, my head. It started with my heart, my chest.

Shorr: Well, if you had to pick one part that was the body core part — body part core center of your identity?

Lynne: My eyes.

On the part where I'm centering on the body core and I center on the eyes, it appears as if the maturing in the voice keeps increasing as there is a feeling of security — having been an actress I am very conscious of the voice — and it is really amazing how when you think of the little girl your voice is like a little girl and as you, you grow or mature or become more reassured within yourself, you're more centered within yourself, your voice becomes much nicer really, much more like a, an instrument. As a vibrating instrument rather than a squeak.

Shorr: Your eyes.

Lynne: It's like a camera.

Shorr: Your eyes are, huh?

Lynne: Uh huh. It's like you are flowing out through your eyes. You're — the whole person flows out and it's good.

Shorr: You like it?

Lynne: Yes. Because you can contact — I mean I feel this or . . .

Shorr: Looking into somebody's eyes you can make the contact.

Lynne: Clear contact.

Shorr: But that's the center of you — I mean if you think of your body from head to toe that is the body part core center is your eyes. (IS) What would you say is the body part core center of your mother, for example?

Lynne: Her vagina.

Shorr: Unmistakably.

Lynne: Oh, yes.

Shorr: There was no hesitation on that.

Lynne: A demanding vagina. It would even try to suck me back into the womb.

Shorr: If she could. Are you ready for this? Closing your eyes this time.

Lynne: Sure.

Shorr: (IS) I want you to imagine what you just said.

Lynne: Being sucked in?

Shorr: (IS) Yes — into her vagina.

Lynne: I don't want to.

Shorr: (IS) I don't want you to either, but I want you to get out of it. I want you to imagine being in there and fighting your way out. Can you try that?

Lynne: No, if I get in there I get trapped.

Shorr: (Focus) Now I want you to get in there and this time I want you to focus getting out — for example, if you want any help of any kind — if you want a sword or if you want any kind of help at all — let me know and I'll let you have it so that you can come out — I want you to fight out of there.

Lynne: That's tough.

Shorr: It's not easy.

Lynne: If I get in there — I'll feel myself in there in a minute — and it's — I want to get out.

Shorr: (IS) O.K., what do you want to get out — do you want a big knife, or a . . .

The part where the body core of my mother's, the vagina, that would try to suck me back into the womb reminds me of an oil painting that I did, oh, in about my fourth or fifth year in therapy when I started to realize that I could be free, slightly free anyway at that point. I did an oil painting of this mother and child and the mother is a dark figure that encompasses the child and the child is trying to reach out of the darkness into the lighted area. Instead of a picture that I painted in, oh, I guess it was a couple of hours it went so fast it must be meaningful.

Lynne: No, no.

Shorr: (IS) What are you going to use to get out — anything, or do you just want to use your own power?

Lynne: My own power.

Shorr: (IS) O.K., now I want you to imagine getting out. Would you go through the motions and feeling of getting out of your mother's vagina.

Lynne: She's fighting me — she's tightening up.

Shorr: (Focus) I want you to get through. I want you to get out. Don't let her win.

Lynne: It's like I get my head out and she chokes me.

Shorr: (Focus) Now I want you to use your arms and flail and push and no matter what, get out of there. Don't let her win.

Lynne: I got it.

Shorr: Where are you now?

Lynne: Floating somewhere.

Shorr: You like where you are now? Stay with the feeling.

Lynne: It's like the feeling when I was writing poetry.

Shorr: It feels good?

Lynne: Uh huh.

Shorr: (IS) That's fine. Now I want you to imagine that you are standing on top of a dry well — then I want you to imagine another you which is identical to you but that you is in the bottom of the well and one at the top which is also you — equally — no difference at all — one is at the bottom of the dry well and one is at the top of the dry well, but the one at the top has a rope that is lowered to the bottom. Now tell me what happens — what would happen?

Lynne: The one at the top would try to get the rope to the one at the bottom. The one at the bottom wouldn't want to grab it. I wouldn't want to help her up.

Shorr: (IS) What would happen then?

Lynne: That's hard. I think I'd rather leave her down there.

Shorr: You don't like her?

Lynne: She's too much like my mother. The one on the top is the person I want to keep.

Shorr: (IS) Could you put a boulder over that hole?

Lynne: No, I wouldn't do that either.

Shorr: Just leave her there and go away you mean?

Lynne: Let her work her way out.

Shorr: But the one on top goes away happy?

Lynne: Ah huh. I don't want any part of the other one. She can work her way out

---

It is interesting that when I have the two me's — the one in the bottom of the well and the one on top with the rope — I try to get rid of the one part of me that is like my mother. It's interesting to me because consciously whenever I have acted or reacted in any manner at all there was similar to that of my mother. I would try to reject it and when I would give in and behave just like my mother, I would absolutely be thoroughly and completely disgusted with myself.

of it — and that feels good.

Shorr: Now finish the sentence (FTS) the only good woman is a _____.

Lynne: *Bright* woman.

Shorr: (FTS) And the only good man is a _____.

Lynne: *Good* man. That's free association.

Shorr: Whatever comes to your mind — that's fine. (IS) Suppose that you imagine that you went into a cage — well, I'll change it — a cave instead of a cage.

Lynne: Why not a cage?

Shorr: Why — did you have a thought on that? What was it?

Lynne: I was going to my own cage where my animals are.

Shorr: Oh, you have animals now?

Lynne: I raise Siamese Bluepoints — and I was going to go in there and . . .

Shorr: And have fun.

Lynne: Uh huh.

Shorr: Good.

Lynne: They are fun. I like animals — especially cats. Especially Siamese — they are so proud and beautiful. But maybe that doesn't fit with what you wanted.

Shorr: No that's fine. (IS) I want you to imagine that you go into a cave and when you walk into the cave at some distance you find a magician standing there — now tell me what you feel or do about the magician and your feelings.

Lynne; Well, I watch him.

Shorr: Yea . . .

Lynne: I want him to do something very special, but I don't know what.

Shorr: (IS) What do you imagine that might be?

Lynne: I don't know.

Shorr: (IS) Well, use your imagination — anything at all.

Lynne: Even if it is impossible?

Shorr: (IS) Sure. If you are using your imagination.

Lynne: Take me back to when I was twelve. No, no take me back when I was five. O.K.

Shorr: Sure.

Lynne: I could tell people what I think of them instead of keeping my mouth shut.

Shorr: You remember some incident, I gather.

On the part where I have to finish the sentence the only good woman is the bad woman and the only good man is the good man. It's very interesting in associating the bad women with good — I don't know at this point whether it's me that's supposed to be bad or my mother. There is a dichotomy here — on the other hand, the man part of course would be my father and my father would be good. Good mostly because he would stand my mother and he would not try to make waves and a person that tries to make waves in a way, as I do sometimes I guess, would be a, a bad person. Oh, no it doesn't make any sense because you have to make waves if you want anything done in this world.

Lynne: It's not just one, it's everything. It's when I — my mother came to me with some note some little boy had written to me about how crazy he was about me — I didn't even know who the little boy was — but I thought it was kinda nice — but she made somethin' dirty out of it. And she had the maid walk me to school every day from that day on. Like I was being guarded. And I'd say mother — ah shut up — mind your own business and let me go. And she'd stand there and she wouldn't know what to do.

Shorr: You could speak up to her then, huh?

Lynne: Uh huh. Because I wouldn't give a damn. Let her have a temper tantrum. I want to be a little girl.

Shorr: And you've done nothing wrong.

Lynne: I just want to be a little girl.

Shorr: You weren't a dirty little girl, were you?

Lynne: I'd be a happy little girl. In spite of her.

Shorr: Good. Now when you were twenty you say you still felt this kind of thing she put onto you. You said earlier, I believe, that at twenty you still felt that — that pressure she put onto you. She defined you as nothing, as an automaton, as a doll.

Lynne: That's why she wanted — she said she did not want me to be an actress but everything she did made me feel that I had to be an actress.

Shorr: You mean she defined you as an actress?

Lynne: I don't think I ever defined myself as a actress. Oh, I could.

Shorr: But that's what she wanted you to be?

Lynne: I defined myself more as a — oh, I guess writer or somebody that worked with — you know, I'm very bad with words but I still like it.

Shorr: So it was her that defined you as an actress, huh?_

Lynne: I'd rather write the plays and the books.

Shorr: If you were to speak to your mother right now — as you remember her — and you finish the sentence that "I am not." How would you finish the sentence? (FTS)

Lynne: I am not bad.

Shorr: Yea, and if you said I am to her, how would you finish that sentence? (FTS)

Lynne: I am very good.

Shorr: (Focus) Now, suppose you said that to her very loudly — like imagine she's in front of you. Can you close your eyes and imagine that she is right in front of you and I want you to say that "I am not . . . " and finish it and then say "I am . . . " and finish it.

On the part where I say that I like cats and I'd like to be in a cage with my studs. It's rather strange, you know, my liking cats because actually this is the only similarity I have to my mother — she loves cats.

On the part where I say to my mother I am good, very good and I am not bad, I formed a mental block again. This particular area seems to be conducive to mental blocks.

Lynne: MOTHER, I AM NOT BAD — IT'S ALL IN YOUR THOUGHTS — NOT MINE. BECAUSE I AM VERY GOOD.

Shorr: And "I am . . . "

Lynne: VERY GOOD.

Shorr: No, but I want you to say it without trying to convince her — just say it as you feel it — that's what you are and that's what you are, period. I am not . . .

Lynne: I would have to grow up for that.

Shorr: Well, I want you to do it right now. Where you are right now, but imagining your mother right in front of you, and I want you to say that as you are right now, Lynne.

Lynne: Me?

Shorr: You! "I am not . . . " to her. Now I want you to speak to her now. (IS) Can you imaginé her in front of you?

Lynne: Yea, we'd have an argument.

Shorr: (IS) No, but I want you to imagine her in front of you.

Lynne: O.K.

Shorr: And I want you to say nothing more than however you finish it. I am not — you finish it — I am . . .

Lynne: I am not bad.

Shorr: (FTS) I am _____ .

Lynne: I am very good.

Shorr: (Focus) Now I want you to say it with a lot more anger in it and a lot more conviction and not proving anything to her.

Lynne: I can't be angry with her. I feel sorry for her. I feel so sorry for her.

Shorr: But nevertheless I still want you to try that, Lynne.

Lynne: That would be cruel.

Shorr: It would be cruel? For you to say I'm not a bad person — I am a good person, is a cruel statement? Doesn't sound very cruel to me.

Lynne: No, it isn't.

Shorr: O.K., let's try it then. Don't protect her.

Lynne: I am protecting her.

Shorr: O.K., don't protect her.

Lynne: MOTHER, I AM NOT BAD. I AM VERY GOOD.

Shorr: Now, I want it more from your guts. I want it to come out with — with a little scream — with a . . .

On the part where I am telling my mother that I am not bad, I am very, very good, it's rather strange that any time I've ever been angry, not only at my mother, but at anyone, I most of the time have tried not to release that anger in order to what I thought, was protect the other person. Actually, what I think that it was, was avoiding rejection, possibly more fear of rejection, than consideration for the other person so much.

Lynne: I'm giving you as much as I can.

Shorr: I know, but I want to try it again. I want it from your guts out to her — don't protect her.

Lynne: MOTHER, I AM NOT BAD — I AM VERY, VERY GOOD.

Shorr: (Focus) O.K., let's try it again, and this time really more from your guts — don't be afraid to be — to let it out — don't protect her — she will not wither — now let it out!

Lynne: Oh, I'm trying as hard as I can.

Shorr: I know — it's not easy. But don't protect her. Yield that protection.

Lynne: MOTHER, I AM NOT BAD — I AM VERY VERY GOOD. (Screaming)

Shorr: How do you feel?

Lynne: That scares me.

Shorr: But how do you feel?

Lynne: Tired.

Shorr: Is there a good feeling, though?

Lynne: Yea, but being angry always wears me out.

Shorr: Yea. Also protecting the person to whom you are angry I think wears you out a little bit more. As a matter of fact, you'd feel very good if you didn't protect her and just let the thing out.

Lynne: Or anybody else.

Shorr: All you are saying is that I am a good person — I am not a bad person. Now one would think that you are saying the most horrible thing on earth — you were saying the most critical devastating remark on earth and obviously it isn't.

Lynne: Sure is silly, isn't it?

Shorr: Before you let up, how about trying it once more?

Lynne: Oh!

Shorr: With all the feeling. Yea, that's right, get comfortable and — but really get your guts into it — but don't protect her — liberate yourself from that definition of you that she put on you.

Lynne: It's hard to do.

Shorr: It's not easy.

Lynne: (Screaming) MOTHER, I AM NOT BAD — I AM VERY, VERY GOOD. That's as hard as I can do.

Shorr: Are you begging her to — are you begging her to acknowledge that you are good? Are you begging her?

Lynne: No.

Shorr: That you separated from her?

Lynne: Oh, I think I separated from her way back in the womb scene.

On the body — core center of my father when I mention it there it is his hands and how kind they were. It seems to me that any time that I have ever gone out with a man I have always noticed his hands and no matter what else he looked like, if his hands were gentle or looked gentle and they reminded me of my father, then I would immediately like the man. It was a ready connection there — the hands.

Shorr: Good, O.K., this is really a statement of you of your own identity. That's fine. (IS) I wanted to go back to asking you about the body core, you know, of your father — what would you pick up as that?

Lynne: I don't know — he's hard to pick out — 'cause there's sort of a definite — indefinite sort of a — hands.

Shorr: Hands.

Lynne: Gentle.

Shorr: (IS) That was the core of his identity?

Lynne: Gentle, gentle hands. Like you would expect a priest or Jesus Christ maybe or somebody like that.

Shorr: (IS) In other words, when he put his hands upon you, it felt very good.

Lynne: Well, it was really the way he used them. I used to as a little kid look at his hands and thought how kind they were but everything else about him was kind of — oh, I hate to say this — wishy-washy. He was afraid of my mother. Can I have a cigarette?

Shorr: Oh sure. It was just that screaming that was holding you back for a moment.

Lynne: That's hard, that screaming bit.

Shorr: Yea. (S&O) What is your responsibility to your father?

Lynne: Protecting him.

Shorr: (S&O) And what is your responsibility to men?

Lynne: You mean to all men?

Shorr: Well, those whom you have known, of course.

Lynne: Protecting them. Yea, I'm a big protector. Particularly men.

Shorr: (S&O) What is your sexual responsibility to men?

Lynne: None.

Shorr: (S&O) What is a man's responsibility to you?

Lynne: None.

Shorr: But how do you protect them exactly?

Lynne: Oh, first thing that comes to mind is being smarter and wiser and making things in life easier for them — like I did for my father.

Shorr: Now, do men do that in return for you? I mean, do they make things easier for you and protect you?

On the part where I relate to protecting my father and also protecting men in general, I can relate at this moment to the fact that I was making things so darn easy for my husband that I was practically making him into a vegetable and it wasn't until, oh, I guess November of the year before last that, oh, I would think it was right after this tape, uh, that uh, no, that was February of '72, anyway, about a year ago, I just decided that I wasn't going to protect my husband anymore. I was going to let him take the pension and just accept him for what he was. He could do what he wanted to, but I wasn't going to be responsible for him and amazingly enough he suddenly grew up and got a job and got himself all involved in growing up, so I guess actually by protecting them I was kind of doing the same thing that my mother was doing to me — making him helpless.

Lynne: Has anybody ever done that – I'm trying to think. I can't think who. No, anybody who had made anything easier for me has demanded something. So they haven't made things easier.

Shorr: And you have demanded very little? Were you protecting these men?

Lynne: No, I demanded.

Shorr: I don't quite understand what you are saying. You protected them, but you also demanded.

Lynne: I think I demanded that they behave according to my ideals of what a man should be.

Shorr: Which is?

Lynne: My father.

Shorr: Helpless, wishy-washy, and giving you the role protector – that gives you a purpose.

Lynne: Well, I think it's more the only pattern I ever learned.

Shorr: What would you like to be then? If you give up the protection – the protection racket – what would you do?

Lynne: Oh, I'd like to be free and just – just be free – I guess I don't like marriage very much.

Shorr: But could you have a man protect you? Could you have that?

Lynne: Not very well.

Shorr: You wouldn't know how to accept it you mean?

Lynne: This may sound funny, but I don't think a man lives that can protect me.

Shorr: Why not?

Lynne: Because that's the way I feel.

Shorr: But what is there in your life that's so difficult for a man not to protect?

Lynne: I can take care of myself.

Shorr: Yea. What would you want then from a man?

Lynne: I first thought of Ed's Stud Service. (Laughing) It's awful.

Shorr: Why is that awful?

Lynne: Well . . . .

On the part where I am talking about the helpless wishy-washy type of man that I protect it's – darn it, I blanked out again. Let's see if I can remember it now. Oh, yes, the helpless wishy-washy type of man, well, when my husband started to go out and be quite aggressive and work in the work place and do fairly well, uh, that's another scene that started to throw me out in the open – one of them was the fact that I got my masters degree – the other my husband became independent so he could go out and earn his living, and the third was that the library where I work was not – I had problems there and things weren't allowed to grow the way they should. So, therefore, I was completely surrounded and am at the present time by the problems where I have really no way out really and I can find no excuse for anything except to look within myself and find the answer within myself, within my own growth, and I think all of these situations have helped although by accepting a more agressive male now, I find myself feeling more insecure and more uncomfortable, but I think it has been a step in the right direction.

Shorr: Would you want something more though?

Lynne: Oh, I suppose I would want somebody I could talk to.

Shorr: Is that too much to ask for?

Lynne: Yes.

Shorr: You mean you have to give up your protection racket if you do that?

Lynne: I suppose.

Shorr: You can't protect somebody and start talking about yourself. You wouldn't be listening.

Lynne: I don't listen anyway.

Shorr: You don't?

Lynne: Not on a man/woman relationship, I don't think I do.

Shorr: You don't hear what the guy says, you mean?

Lynne: I don't think so. I feel very deeply that I don't think I hear. It's kind of kooky.

Shorr: It sounds a little contradictory. You say you are very protective of a man — at the same time you don't give to a man.

Lynne: I don't give to anybody.

Shorr: You mean your protection is a way of not giving?

Lynne: Probably.

Shorr: I want you to finish the sentence. (FTS) My whole life is based on proving that _____.

Lynne: That *I can take care of myself.* Very much so. Alone.

Shorr: So what do you need a man for?

Lynne: You know, a thought just struck me. Wouldn't it be marvelous if you were back in the cave days and women were the ones that drag men with their hair (Laughing) and they did everything and they drag the men and say "come on." Now it's your turn.

Shorr: I think the way you talked earlier your mother would be very good in that role.

Lynne: Yea, I think I've learned a lot. I haven't learned any other roles.

Shorr: What would happen if a man really took care of you? Thought about you, protected you?

Lynne: I wouldn't like it.

Shorr: What would happen?

Lynne: I would feel guilty.

Shorr: Why?

On the part right after I say I would like stud service from a man and then I go into saying that I don't listen in a man/woman relationship. This is very interesting that this is the first time that I, well, it's taken me completely by surprise because I didn't realize that I recognize the fact subconsciously that I wasn't listening in a man/woman relationship. I mean it comes like out of the blue, and when I come to think about it, it's terribly quite right in relationship to sex that there is no listening on my part, and it's something I didn't realize until just now.

Lynne: I don't know. I'm free associating — I would feel guilty.

Shorr: Yea, I believe what you are saying, it's just that the standard — what is the standard?

Lynne: It's not standard — it's just a feeling thing. I would feel I'd have to pay him back in kind. I couldn't owe him anything — if he did too much for me, I would owe him something and if I owed him something I would have to work so hard to repay him. Like I worked with my mother. We paid her all of the time and it was just too much — I mean . . .

Shorr: You mean she constantly obligated you to her.

Lynne: Uh huh.

Shorr: And you were constantly in bondage. It was always impossible to feel a man would not want to obligate you and put you into bondage.

Lynne: True.

Shorr: (S&O) They really take you over and engulf you — the closeness of a relationship.

Lynne: I never looked at it that way before, but it's true. So I couldn't unless I was able to take without feeling I had to return twofold.

Shorr: Now, in other words, if your husband came home one day and he found — and he said why aren't you doing my socks right.

Lynne: Oh well, I wouldn't bother with that.

Shorr: Oh, what kind . . .

Lynne: That's — that's a feminine — I resent feminine roles.

Shorr: (S&O) What kind of criticism you know that your husband might put upon you would you really feel bad about?

Lynne: Oh, maybe by not thinking intelligently. Or doing something dumb.

Shorr: Something relating to brain power, you mean?

Lynne: Uh huh.

Shorr: (IS) Suppose you imagine a penis on a balance scale on one side and a vagina on the other.

Lynne: Oh, the vagina would be way too heavy for the penis.

Shorr: (IS) If the vagina could speak — could make a statement to the penis — what would it be?

Lynne: I've got you under my power.

Shorr: (IS) What does the penis say?

Lynne: It would be helpless.

Shorr: And how would you feel?

Lynne: (Ha, ha) I feel like laughing.

It is so interesting that when I am talking about being protective towards men I bring out the fact that I don't like women that are overprotected or that maybe I am jealous of them. Uh, it's sort of a dichotomy I think in that as a child I was brought up to feel that the only role for a woman was to be the one protected and sheltered and so forth, at least that's what my mother told me. But then, on the other hand, she gave me boys' toys to play with and encouraged aggressiveness — so, I guess there is sort of a dichotomist picture right here.

Shorr: Why?

Lynne: I don't know. I don't seem to have much of a picture of men. It's like women are the amazons. The old accomplishers, the achievers.

Shorr: They are the strong ones?

Lynne: I don't like women that are all protected — maybe in general there are some of them — I don't know. I've never liked them. I wouldn't know how to act if I was protected.

Shorr: What do I do next then? Is that what you'd be saying?

Lynne: I would be suspicious — I know I would think there is something that he wants.

Shorr: And usually it's . . . ?

Lynne: Oh, usually it's sex or if it's not sex then it's something I can do — some kind of help he wants.

Shorr: (S&O) Nobody would like you for yourself alone, huh?

Lynne: That's a hard one, but that's the way I feel.

Shorr: What do you have to do for me so I'd like you — just like that when you don't know me very well but what would you have to do for me so I'd like you?

Lynne: Oh, I'm here so you'd have to like me.

Shorr: Because you're doing something I want you to do.

Lynne: Right.

Shorr: Now you've paid your obligation so you're all right.

Lynne: So I feel O.K.

Shorr: You're O.K.

Lynne: Yea.

Shorr: So each time you have to earn your position with . . .

Lynne: Right.

Shorr: You don't know where you are at any one time if you're not earning it, huh? What do I do next? It puts you in a real bind — constant. Incessant activity, huh?

Lynne: Pressure.

Shorr: The pressure.

Lynne: There's a lot to think of it there. I hope I don't forget it. That's like somebody that's kind of trained. That's the way I am. And they trained me to automatically react to anybody doing anything for me — I automatically repay him twice in kind. And so I'm conditioned.

Shorr: Well, what about the sexual part of it then? Do you have the obligation of going that way too? Who is sex for, the woman or the man?

It's interesting in the part where the father's brought out that I have to earn everything, that I can't just take anything for free, everything has to be earned, and that at work in particular lately I have gotten more and more to the point where I feel guilty if I am not rushing around always doing something. Actually, part of me is saying, well, what for, I'm not interested in helping the library, then why should I try to knock myself out which I hate. If I have this attitude at this point then, the attitude I had before, is always having to pay back for everything double.

Lynne: Uh, women use it to achieve a purpose. If sex could be right the way I'd imagine it to be, it would be a mutual thing, but it hardly ever is. As I can think of it.

Shorr: What do you mean?

Lynne: In the past somebody always has something to gain — maybe me — maybe demanded something and I paid him back — I'm talking about work — you know . . .

Shorr: Uh huh.

Lynne: And the days I was in show business. Or maybe that's why sex and marriage is kind of there's nothing to prove so there's no — I mean the women can do the conquering sometimes too but if you do it just for the sake of conquering or for the sake of proving a point — there was one guy I had sex with that wasn't proving anything.

Shorr: What was there about him that was different?

Lynne: He was strong. And yet he was weak. But he wasn't all that weak. He could top me intellectually and yet he was in my business — in show business at the time and I would say something with most of the time he would accept something I'd say. He could say something to top me and I had my mind about it, but he would do it in such a way that he wasn't humiliating me. He was conversing with me. I like him.

Shorr: (S&O) So what kind of a contest are you in with men?

Lynne: Oh, about the same contest I am with anything else.

Shorr: Uh huh. (IS) Using your imagination, how does it feel to have the semen of a man in your vagina?

Lynne: Not very much.

Shorr: Not very much?

Lynne: No.

Shorr: What do you mean by that?

Lynne: In the past I wanted to have a baby and I never did. So what is the purpose of the semen? You can't do something.

Shorr: Finish the sentence. (FTS) I hate men because _____.

Lynne; (Laughing) A crazy thought came through me — because *they masturbate.*

Shorr: You hate that because they masturbate — because they're not . . .

Lynne: That's crazy.

Shorr: What do you get out of that?

Lynne: I don't know, that's what came to my mind.

It's kind of interesting in the part where I am talking about the penis and the mechanism of the penis and how it operates and how I was telling this one ex about it. Actually, I think I got, I don't know why, but I've got my men mixed up. I think the one that I'm referring to, I think I'm referring to, who's a very interesting man, not mentally, but physically, and the man that I actually told him about, told about the physiological reaction of the penis and an erection and all that was actually another person for I'm — I don't know whether it's on purpose or not — I'm confusing two men and making two men one.

Shorr: Because they're not giving you their semen?

Lynne: No — I'm not all that semen crazy unless it comes to cats — when you get a breeding thing going. I don't know why it leaves me, uh.

Shorr: You hate men because they masturbate, you said.

Lynne: I mean that's the feeling I had at that moment — it was a free association type thing.

Shorr: Fine.

Lynne: I don't know where it came from.

Shorr: Fine. I mean have you seen men masturbate? Have you had some experience along that line?

Lynne: Yea, my — one of my ex's — my ex-husbands — I thought he was kind of a pig. There was nothing — he wasn't even very exciting — I'll tell you what it was. I could look at him with a clinical eye — detached — just figure out how the mechanism of the penis worked physiologically. That's what you can think of. (Laughing) I remember one time I told him that and how his mechanism worked just when he had an erection. It didn't bother him but I thought it was kind of stupid afterwards. He didn't much like it. But I was interested — in the physiological aspect of it.

Shorr: Like clinically and detached apart from the feeling part.

Lynne: Yes. That must — I must have been doing something there because it was so clinical.

Shorr: (FTS) I hate women because _____. How would you finish that?

Lynne: I don't — I — I can't finish that. *Maybe they are helpless.*

Shorr: You hate women who are helpless, you mean?

Lynne: Because they are helpless. Not me, though.

Shorr: Now I want you to use your imagination again for a moment. I want you to close your eyes again. (IS) I want you to imagine entering your father's body — using your imagination — where do you enter?

Lynne: His heart.

Shorr: And what happens?

Lynne: He gets frightened. I don't know.

Shorr: Why should he be frightened?

Lynne: I don't know. Maybe it's because every time I wanted him to do something for me he would have a heart attack or something and so I guess he got frightened.

Shorr: You felt responsible for the heart attack?

Lynne: I didn't hurt him much. I let mother work on him. You see, I'm a buffer. Sort of like a thing between two people.

Shorr: You mean when the real chips fell, you let your mother take over.

Lynne: Well, I acted as a shield for my father so if she wouldn't hit him too hard emotionally. I'd take the hurt and the pain and the brunt.

It is strange, but at the mention of my father and how he is the dummy or teach me to bear things. I suddenly get very tired, it's a weariness — almost as if I just wanted to lay down and go to sleep. I'm just exhausted.

Shorr: (IS) Now, if you could imagine the opposite now — again using your imagination — if your father were to enter your body . . .

Lynne: I can just see minds, heads, brains.

Shorr: But where does he enter?

Lynne: Brain.

Shorr: He's in your brain and what does he do there?

Lynne: He teaches maybe.

Shorr: What does he tell you?

Lynne: He tells me to bear things.

Shorr: To tolerate things, you mean?

Lynne: To be kind.

Shorr: And how do you feel about that?

Lynne: Well, it's all right — not all the time — but it's all right — it's not bad.

Shorr: You mean you like that — what your father told you to do when he enters your head?

Lynne: I mean it's not unpleasant. Except it's too altruistic. It's too . . .

Shorr: It denies you a lot — it denies you of your individuality you mean? So what would you tell your father?

Lynne: You can't be kind and good all of the time. And you've got to tell my mother to knock it off.

Shorr: Be strong. You bastard.

Lynne: I once told him this and he had a heart attack.

Shorr: The next day!

Lynne: The next week.

Shorr: And you were responsible. So you protect men rather than tell them to be strong because they will die on you — they will disappear — is that it?

Lynne: I suppose. That is so funny.

Shorr: If you were to stand with your right hand and your left hand like this, you know, outstretched . . .

Lynne: Uh huh.

Shorr: (IS) Who would you hold with your right hand and who would you hold with your left hand?

Lynne: A person?

Shorr: Uh huh.

Lynne: I don't think I'd want to hold anybody.

Shorr: But if you were to imagine that you did, who would you hold with your right hand and who would you hold with your left hand?

On this part about my father — it has been altruistic and all this must have some heavy emotional content because I feel rather upset about it. I remember him as, well, I remember from what my mother has said that when I was a young child he was sort of a playboy, but that's what my mother said, but anyway I think this has something to do with my feelings towards my father. I can't quite figure out how I am reacting to this, but it's sort of an upset feeling.

Lynne: It has to be a human being?

Shorr: Yea.

Lynne: Oh shucks. O.K., let me think. Oh, I guess it would have to be my mother and father.

Shorr: But you fight doing it, huh?

Lynne: What?

Shorr: You fight doing the whole thing?

Lynne: Yes.

Shorr: You don't want to imagine that. O.K. (IS) Put your hands down and I want you to imagine a blank piece of paper in front of you and using your imagination I want you to imagine on the left side there is a word and on the right side is a word. Now you tell me what the word you imagined is.

Lynne: Fuck-it.

Shorr: What do you think you are talking about really when you say that?

Lynne: Everything.

Shorr: The world, you mean?

Lynne: Uhmmm. I guess I must be bitter. But then I think it's a healthy word. It expresses a lot of — not dirty word — it expresses a lot of good, healthy emotions.

Shorr: When you say that it means you don't have to be what?

Lynne: You don't have to take a lot of crap.

Shorr: Which is what you do a lot of.

Lynne: Yea — my whole life.

Shorr: (M/L) What's the most difficult thing to say to anybody?

Lynne: I love you. Well, you can say it and not mean it. But to really feel it — this is very hard.

Shorr: Have you said it much in your life?

Lynne: Not with feelings. Not meaning it. I meant it sort of haphazardly — but not 100%.

Shorr: You never really felt that real love towards anyone — anybody.

Lynne: Yea, I guess I did towards Billy — it was so long ago and I was such a young thing I guess I must of meant it. And then I got punished — I mean he died.

Shorr: Billy is who? I don't know.

Lynne: He was somebody that I knew when I was twenty-five and he died of cancer two years later. My mother hated him. It's the only time I opposed her. I think that was the beginning of my starting to do thing, but it was so painful because it was painful that he died and it was painful that I had to accept her afterwards as a substitute. I had to fall back on her again. While he was alive I didn't have to. He was a little stronger than her, I think.

Shorr: That was the first time you were actually able to oppose your mother, huh?

Lynne: Uh huh. The first time.

It's interesting that when I talk about my father always getting a heart attack that I get upset, almost as if I were going to have some kind of a stroke or heart attack or something like that — almost as if I were he.

Shorr: (M/L) What is easiest for you to give: sex, money, intellect or feeling?

Lynne: Intellect.

Shorr: That is the easiest?

Lynne: Easy, very easy.

Shorr: And the most difficult?

Lynne: You mean good sex or any sex?

Shorr: Whatever you — you tell me.

Lynne: I mean any sex — that's no problem, but I mean really to give feelings in sex to give it . . .

Shorr: That would be the most difficult?

Lynne: Very.

Shorr: I take it then — you say it's never happened that much, huh?

Lynne: It only happened that one time because I could admire the guy. It wasn't Billy — it was this guy and we weren't in any way tied up — I mean it was the kind of thing that — like ships passing in the night. He didn't owe me anything. It's one of the few times that I could be half free, I think.

Shorr: No obligations.

Lynne: No. It was a strange incident.

Shorr: It didn't last very long I take it.

Lynne: About two months.

Shorr: What happened?

Lynne: We passed.

Shorr: In the night. (IS) Now, if you were to imagine your mother and father nude in the bed.

Lynne: That's a hard one.

Shorr: (IS) And then in addition to that you are in there — all three of you there in the bed in the nude.

Lynne: Oh, my mother would be looking at me.

Shorr: (IS) Now I want you to imagine that you look at your father — what would happen?

Lynne: Nothing.

Shorr: What would your mother do?

Lynne: Nothing.

Shorr: How would you feel?

Lynne: Nothing.

Shorr: Nothing at all? I mean the situation would just be completely without any feeling at all? You wouldn't be afraid, frightened, or waiting for your mother to

---

It's interesting that after I mention Billy's death and how painful it was that I had to have at that time some kind of a substitute — I couldn't just stand alone — I had to have somebody to lean on. I didn't realize how much I was leaning on my mother and she was letting me and I suppose I resented that, but it's an interesting point. This whole sequence about my father and Billy is quite painful.

criticize you or something?

Lynne: Yea, yea, I guess I would.

Shorr: I had to remind you — how come? That she might criticize you.

Lynne: Because I'm moving away from her, I think.

Shorr: (M/L) What was the single most undermining sentence that your mother would repeat to you?

Lynne: Sex is dirty — I guess.

Shorr: What about her?

Lynne: Oh, don't do it — I'll do it for you.

Shorr: Anything you mean. Not just the sex, of course.

Lynne: Anything, I mean.

Shorr: She took over, you mean?

Lynne: Yea, that was the worst part, I guess. It wasn't so much that sex is dirty. I think it was if I go in the kitchen to do something when I was a young girl — don't do it — you won't do it right — I'll do it. Or no matter what I wanted to do she did it.

Shorr: So how did she define you that way? As . . .

Lynne: As a doll.

Shorr: This helpless doll.

Lynne: The only thing/duty I had — I had to look pretty. I had to be admired by people — I didn't have to say anything — I had to just be admired by people. That made her very happy. But I had to be a nonentity, like a doll, I guess.

Shorr: Who demands that of you today — that you just be a doll or nonentity?

Lynne: Nobody — since I got out of show business.

Shorr: That was like being a doll, you mean? Of being . . .

Lynne: I had to be a doll — I had to be pretty and I had to be — look good — and now I don't have to look good.

Shorr: (M/L) What is your greatest concern when you are with a man?

Lynne: That's a hard one. Ridicule, I guess. I would be afraid of ridicule.

Shorr: Now, finish this sentence. (FTS) I have to prove that every man is

————.

Lynne: *Stupid.*

Shorr: (FTS) And every man has to prove that I am ———·mmmmmm

Lynne: *Smart* was the word, but I don't know why it came out.

Shorr: And who carries the greatest authority in the world for you today?

Lynne: I would say the two women premiers.

Shorr: You mean like Ghandi and Meir?

Lynne: Yea. They appear to be very good leaders. They don't do anything half-assed.

It is interesting that when I mention the part about my mother saying that she wouldn't let me go into the kitchen, she'd do it all for me and to tell me don't do it, I'll do it for you, that actually at that point I sound just like my mother or the way my mother used to sound when she was talking to me at the time.

Shorr: Like the men do.

Lynne: If they do something — they do it — if it's bad or good, they do it.

Shorr: Like the men do?

Lynne: Yea. Men always.

Shorr: Not to mention names.

Lynne: Well, men are always all over — take the American presidents — practically all of them have done things half-assed. I mean, they always find a way out.

Shorr: But these other, they have stood up and fought the war and done the things that are necessary.

Lynne: They have done things. They, they — bad or good — they have stood by their beliefs and done things.

Shorr: Finish the sentence. (FTS) Why can't a man be _____ .

Lynne: A leader.

Shorr: Now I want you to try something a little different — switching — (IS) I want you to imagine handing your heart into my palm.

Lynne: Oh, that's easy.

Shorr: Let's see.

Lynne: O.K.

Shorr: I have it now — it's in my palm.

Lynne: It's all right — I trust you.

Shorr: Why do you trust me?

Lynne: Because I like you.

Shorr: But I'm a man.

Lynne: No you're not!

Shorr: But I'm a . . .

Lynne: Psychologist.

Shorr: So I'm not the wishy-washy man.

Lynne: Yea, clinician or person that has a clinical approach. A psychologist is not a man or a woman.

Shorr: In other words, you cannot give me a sexual gender?

Lynne: No.

Shorr: But if you were.

Lynne: I couldn't give you a sexual gender.

Shorr: If you were to, it would be dangerous?

Lynne: Yea.

Shorr: Then I would have to be just an ordinary half-assed, indecisive man. As long as I have my title and all that I'm . . .

It's kind of interesting that since — in the part where I am mentioning about the American presidents and about the two women premiers — since then I have felt that Nixon, for example, is a very decisive person. Right or wrong he certainly did, does do decisive things and this may be a change in my attitude towards men — I don't know.

Lynne: No, not only your title — I have to approve of you.

Shorr: O.K., you approve of me.

Lynne: Like you and Shapiro, I sort of . . . O.K.

Shorr: A clinician.

Lynne: I mean, I've met psychologists I couldn't stand so they were men.

Shorr: (IS) Suppose though that I were to give you my heart into your palm.

Lynne: I don't want it.

Shorr: If I were to, what would you do?

Lynne: Give it right back to you.

Shorr: Why?

Lynne: Because you are not supposed to.

Shorr: The obligation is so great, or is it just the prohibition of such a thing?

Lynne: I wouldn't know what I'd do with it.

Shorr: (IS) Suppose it is just any man that gives you his heart — what would you do with it.

Lynne: I don't think I'd want it. It would be too embarrassing.

Shorr: (IS) And what about your heart — can you hand that to anybody?

Lynne: I suppose — half-assedly.

Shorr: Like a little bit but not really vulnerable feelings you want to have?

Lynne: Yea. Sort of.

Shorr: What is your idea of a good time?

Lynne: Doing something constructive.

Shorr: Like what?

Lynne: Oh, I guess creating something. Oh! When I directed the company show and I had all these people under me working for me and I did a good thing — it was very good — I had a good time — it was work but it was fun work.

Shorr: (IS) Can you imagine a bird on your head — what would it be?

Lynne: . . . bluebird.

Shorr: (IS) Can you imagine an animal coming out of your stomach.

Lynne: A cat. It's silly.

Shorr: You seem to have a lot going for cats. You like them.

Lynne: They are smart — nobody can fool them.

Shorr: Tell me — how smart are you, Lynne?

Lynne: When not panicky, I'm smart — when panicky, I'm dumb.

Shorr: (M/L) Who is the smartest woman you have ever known?

Lynne: My mother appears to be pretty smart in her own dumb way.

It's funny that my relating psychologist to a none sex type of . . . . Well, there's many walls up if we could — if we weren't role playing. If we were in a regular clinical picture let's say we would have a greater tendency to be more careful as to what we say, but in — by role playing and pretending we can be less guarded and therefore get into the actual therapy situation much faster and work through some problems a lot faster than you would through the old therapy methods.

Shorr: What do you mean by that?

Lynne: Cunning is the word. Not smart.

Shorr: (M/L) What was the most cunning thing she ever did?

Lynne: Oh, I guess trap me and my father and she is helpless — there is a dichotomy there. Maybe by being helpless she is being most cunning — my mom never does anything for nothing.

Shorr: She's really manipulative, huh?

Lynne: Yes. That's the word. I guess I learned that from her.

Shorr: You regard yourself as manipulative, huh?

Lynne: Something — I don't particularly like it very much but there it is.

Shorr: It's a living, huh — instead of anything else it's a living. What do you do for a living — I'm a manipulator. (Laughing) "If I don't manipulate well somebody is going to manipulate me."

Lynne: That's about the gist of it. I would be nice if everybody could exist by accepting — I would like to think that would be kinda nice but it's kind of hard to find. That kind of a thing.

Shorr: (S&O) If you aren't manipulating, do you turn into your father or something like that?

Lynne: Probably — altruistic, and a dreamer and sort of . . .

Shorr: Then you could be used or taken advantage of — but rather than that you want to revert back to . . .

Lynne: I'm many people. Under certain given circumstances I can be extremely giving at that moment 'cause I felt that that particular party was, well, like when I was taking psychology I helped a few people and I wasn't being manipulative then — but I could help them because I was playing a role and when I was being an actress I was being a manipulator. And now I'm a librarian and I can be kind of clinical about my work 'cause it's information and so forth — occasionally when I get involved in something where I want to gain a point I manipulate. Now with my husband, I don't know what I'd do. I really don't. It's a strange relationship — it's not bad — it's not great. But I think the cats keep us together because we have so much in common, with the cats.

Shorr: Do you have a lot of cats?

Lynne: Yes.

Shorr: It appears we have to stop our talk now. Thank you for coming.

Lynne: Thanks. I enjoyed it.

Extensive use of imagery, comingled with dialogue, suggests that it can be a valuable source of awareness of the person's neurotic conflicts. Patients tend to react to the integration of imagery with dialogue so that the naturalness of the interchange is not affected.

On the part where I am talking about the relationship with my husband is sort of interesting that as time goes by I can see both of us sort of growing — for greater give and take — as we go along. In other words, the more honest I become it appears to me the more honest he becomes — maybe it's just me. I don't know.

CHAPTER V

Imagery and Group Therapy

In the last decade group therapy has become an integral part of the treatment of emotionally disturbed individuals and while some therapists regard it as a secondary method, others believe in it as the approach *par excellence.* To my way of thinking, group and individual therapy should complement and enhance each other; ideally, a patient should experience both. This does not always occur, unfortunately. Beyond the financial considerations, some people are hesitant about confrontation with other patients, and others fear exposure. If a patient has an especially weakened sense of identity, or "core," his fears may be aggravated by the group situation; when feelings of rottenness have engulfed the self-image, the prospect of group therapy may become unbearable. In such cases, individual treatment must proceed until there is a change in self-definition; this change, combined with a trust in the therapist, will finally allow for direct contact with the group.

How a person has been defined by others during his formative years, the degree to which he feels "condemned" to his alien identity, his efforts to define himself in a manner more consistent with his true identity — these issues constitute the very kernel of Psycho-Imagination Therapy. Therapy — individual or group — is an invaluable catalyst in the patient's forging of a new identity. It must help him become aware of the conflicts between the alien identity and the true (albeit inchoate or emerging) identity; it must help him recognize the strategies that were used by significant others upon him and the counterreaction strategies he used to survive them.

As patient and therapist become aware of central conflicts — invariably between what the patient really feels and the way he feels he *should* feel — group therapy provides a place where the conflicts can be seen in neurotic solution. It provides expanded awareness of the conflicts and their neurotic conflict resolutions. Neurotic conflict resolutions are effectually a treadmill to nowhere, and the experience and interaction afforded by the group situation will open avenues to *healthy* conflict resolution, to a new (true) self-definition. It will, hopefully, permit the patient to be nothing less than *himself.*

It is Rollo May who best expresses the neurotic's struggle to maintain his centeredness and the fear of what interaction with others involves: " . . . he sat nervously smoking in my waiting room; he now looks at me with mingled suspicion and hope, an effort towards openness fighting in him against the life-old tendency to withdraw behind a stockade and hold me out. The struggle is understandable, for

135

participating always involves risk; if he or any organism goes out too far, he will lose his own centeredness, his identity." (May, 1964, p. 176.)

Laing and Buber have pointed out that man basically needs to feel a confirmation of his existence from the other and equally to feel that he makes a difference to an other. Too often in contemporary life does man desperately search for confirmation, with only the meagerest of results. As Arthur Miller said in discussing contemporary writers, "Society in effect is a deaf machine; and they feel themselves competing with machines which have stolen the imagination of men." (Miller, 1966, p. 16.)

In the contemporary world, success often bears little relationship to fulfillment. "Can I make a difference to someone?" poses an existential safari for modern man, one which often leads to loneliness, purposelessness and powerlessness. For, to quote Rollo May again, contemporary man is prone to ask, "Even if I know who I am, can I have an effect on the world?" (May, 1964, p. 176.)

Our age is one of conformity, of the "other"-directed man; one finds it difficult to project one's uniqueness, one's authentic feelings; one offers up his own identity for the sake of social belonging and acceptance. Ostracism is the ultimate terrible position and to guard against it, meanings and values are borrowed from somebody else's meanings and values. Direct and open interchange, direct experiencing of other human beings and the world have become increasingly infrequent. Max Frisch in *I'm Not Stiller,* comments brilliantly on the subject: "We live in an age of reproduction. Most of what makes up our personal picture of the world we have seen with our own eyes, but not on the spot: our knowledge comes to us from a distance, we are tele-viewers, tele-hearers, tele-knowers. One need never have left this little town to have Hitler's voice still ringing in one's ears, to have seen the Shah of Persia from a distance of three yards, and to know how the monsoon howls over the Himalayas or what it looks like six hundred fathoms beneath the sea. Anyone can know of these things nowadays. Does it mean I have never been to the bottom of the sea? Or even (like the Swiss) almost up Mount Everest?

"And it's just the same with the inner life of man. Anyone can know about it nowadays. How the devil am I to prove to my counsel that I don't know my murderous impulses through C. G. Jung, jealousy through Marcel Proust, Spain through Hemingway, Paris through Ernst Junger, Switzerland through Mark Twain, Mexico through Graham Greene, my fear of death through Bernanos and the inability ever to reach my destination through Kafka, and all sorts of other things through Thomas Mann? It's true, you need never have read these authorities, you can absorb them through your friends, who also live all their experiences second-hand." (Frisch, 1958, p. 151-152.)

Group therapy provides direct and open contact for people. They can say what they feel, whether it be "right" or "wrong." Each group member can confirm the existence of any other group member and they his. A patient can begin to feel he makes a difference to the group as a whole and to each member individually. He comes to realize that he need not sell his soul in order to belong.

With the increased emphasis on immediate solutions to problems and the growth of computerization, dehumanization has become the vogue; less fashionable are the concepts of intimacy and growth, shared experience. It is precisely this lack of prolonged and loving intimacy that invariably catapults a person into neurotic behavior. Instant intimacy, instant love, the substitution of sheer encounter for real conflict resolution — all of these may leave the patient in a state of confusion, opened and raw, but basically no more solid than before in his centeredness or ability to trust other human beings.

There has come to be extensive use of imagery techniques in encounter groups, marathons, T-groups, sensitivity training, and related approaches which, according to Jerome L. Singer "can only be described as a national craze rather than as a systematic new treatment method." (Singer, 1971, p. 24.) Bach (1954) used group fantasy early in his work, but by and large the explosive burgeoning of imagery in group therapy (adapted from Leuner and Desoille, with a heavy overlay of Moreno's psychodramatic approach) is rather recent — part of the games technique that pervades the encounter movement. Alexander (1969) strongly suggested that the nuclei of the most commonly employed methods are outgrowths of children's play, used to expedite the breaking down of formalities and evasions inherent in the regular verbal interchanges among adults.

I suppose that as a counterreaction to the rigidities and inflexibilities of the more traditionally psychotherapeutic approaches, imagery was a natural development. But as Singer (1971) says, "The almost wild, unsystematic application of these methods in unselected groups (often organized by relatively untrained persons with little background in psychopathology and no special clinical training) must ultimately be a subject of professional, if not national, concern." (Singer, 1971, p. 24.)

When a person lacks adequate means to develop new inner strengths, a massive attack on his defenses may lead to precipitous decisions or greater entrenchment into himself. His self-image, already negative, may be made worse. He may leave one of these modish encounter situations without the tools needed to provide awareness of his basic conflicts; he may find that such "instant" precepts as he has acquired have little application to his everyday life. The transitory sense of intimacy disappears, leaving him alone and unhappy, without a sense of belonging.

In an on-going group, the patient finds it difficult to get away with duplicity and inauthentic behavior; he also acquires a viable view of the therapist, seeing how he behaves with him both individually and in the group situation. Given a chance to observe him thus, there is the opportunity to dissociate him from significant parental figures. This in itself may strengthen a patient's desire to solve his conflicts and liberate himself from a false identity.

Psycho-Imagination group therapy emphasizes the patient's self-definition and the degree to which his self-concept permits or constricts his behavior vis-a-vis the other group members. His awareness of how others in the group define him becomes crystallized. He is encouraged to be as truly himself as possible. The therapist is open and receptive, the atmosphere nonjudgmental. Furthermore, the group can become the arena for reenactment of old family interactions which molded the patient's false positions and negative self-image. By the process of interaction, transference reactions are brought to the surface. "Transference prevents each member from being able to accept another by conferring traits upon him which originally stood in the way of a full relationship to a member of his original family." (Wolf and Schwartz 1968, p. 27.) A minimum of restriction is maintained on the group interaction so that each patient's indifference, detachment or other withdrawal tactics can be observed, as well as the more easily detected forms of hostility.

The modes and techniques of imagery in group and individual therapy are so numerous and diverse that they can hardly be exhausted. Though I have participated in group therapy for more than two and a half decades, the groups that I work with now would seem foreign to people who were in my groups even five years ago. Therapy has been an evolving, growing, joyous and painful process for me as well as for my patients. There is so much to know and experience. At times, my own mistakes, my own lack of awareness, have hindered the growth of the groups. But with the development of Psycho-Imagination theories, with the improvement in imagery techniques, my ability to help the group patients has grown considerably. I am constantly looking forward to learning, participating, giving to the growth of the group and its members.

Perhaps the key word in group therapy is "interaction" between the group members — amongst whom I include myself. Without the possibility for spontaneous and unrestricted interaction, group therapy would be of little benefit. Here are some of the forms of interaction possible in the group therapy situation:

1. Nonverbal interaction of feelings. Some silent members may be strongly affected by other members' reactions without reacting verbally.

2. Testing the expression of certain feelings in interaction. Such feelings may be the expression of the near-impossible for that person: he may just put his toes in the water to "love" and "anger."

3. Interaction of the inauthentic, competitive and controlling feelings used to sustain the stake in the neurotic interactions.

4. Those interactions from the core of the person, genuine and authentic, designed to define him as his true identity: "I am not to be defined this way; I am to be defined *this* way."

5. Interactions that relate to and are intended to affect the therapist — perhaps provoking him, or testing his trust and understanding.

6. Interactions that spark awareness which heretofore had been unconscious to that person.

7. Interactions of a more cognitive nature — to clarify concepts of values and meanings — or just plain information.

8. Interactions involving touching and holding or stroking.

The Internal Conflicts

The overall purpose of interaction within the group is to help each and every patient become aware of his or her conflicts and then take the risks inherent in focusing for change. While, broadly speaking, nearly all of the approaches suggested for individual therapy can be utilized in group therapy, there are several factors that must be taken into account. First, groups involve interaction between men and women together; some patients find it considerably easier to express feelings and imagery to members of the same sex and almost impossible to make the same statements to members of the opposite sex. This is especially true with problems of masculinity and femininity. Overcoming this kind of reluctance, permitting oneself the free flow of imagery and emotional expression without the feeling that one is bizarre or weird is a barometer of the patient's growth.

Second, the factor of peer competition, which, while not always evident in one-to-one therapy, may surface as a host of symptoms in group contact. But the disclosure of such feelings and the coping with their source can be attained. Too, basic trust of authority figures and basic trust of one's peers are areas which may be subjected to considerable emotion and conflict within the group setting. By example, by identification, by stimulating one another, by giving increasingly free play to their fantasies, dreams, imagination and unconscious productions, co-patients often afford the conflicted group member a chance to develop and nurture the courage for new alternatives.

The use of imagery in group therapy may take the following directions:

1. Imagery within the person subjectively experienced.
2. All the persons in the group engaging in imagery about a single member.
3. That member's reactions and imagery in response to the other's imagery.
4. One person engaging in imagery about every other person in rotation.
5. All of the other people, then, emerging in imagery about the one person in return-reaction imagery.
6. All of the persons engaging in imagery about the therapist at various points in his past or present life (or the future).
7. The therapist engaging in imagery about each of the group members at various points in their past or present lives (or the future).
8. All of the persons interacting in imagery without any directed consecutive-ness, but yet having its own internal consistency in the sequences of reactions, depending upon the emotions generated and depending upon the particular group.

While the main thrust of this discussion involves imagery, it would be unwise to assume that imagery is the sole method used in group therapy. I have found that the "Finish the Sentence" questions can also be of invaluable help as "group starters." Among these "FTS's" are:

1. The more I know you the more I _____ .
2. I cannot give you _____ .
3. The most difficult thing to tell you is _____ .
4. If only you would _____ .
5. I like you best for your _____ .
6. The adjective that describes you best is _____ .
7. Sooner or later you will find me _____ .
8. Never refer to me as _____ .
9. I will not allow you to define me as _____ .
10. My best defense against you is _____ .
11. I have to prove to every woman or man _____ .
12. Your strongest point is _____ .

There are countless other "Finish the Sentence" approaches that can be used. Not only are they useful group starters, but they can also be used at any time in the group interaction for the purpose of clarifying reactions and feelings. They may also very well serve as leads into imagery if they result in particularly strong reactions. There are times, especially in the focusing approaches, that certain imagery may lead *back* to an appropriate "Finish the Sentence" question, as in Cathartic Imagery. The possibilities are extremely varied and can be created effectively at almost any moment of feeling and interaction.

Dual Imagery

One way to utilize dual imagery is to pose to the group as a whole an imaginary situation, such as (IS): "Imagine something inside of you and something outside of you." Follow this up by going around the room, asking each person to state his imagery. Eventually, key in on one person, with the group free to interact, and develop the imagery further for him to enhance his awareness and encourage liberation from old archaic ways. Sometimes, as we go around, the imagery of one individual may be so strong and compelling that we may not get a chance to include everyone's in-depth reaction. There is no way of absolutely anticipating such strong imagery with certainty. I remember once asking the group to (IS) "Imagine, above you and behind you, there is a force." As I went around, one woman began to cry and seemed to be badly frightened. It was not her turn, but I switched to her as soon as possible. She then described a very panicky awareness of her mother's being "above" her. Her mother died when she was four years old and the imagery had reactivated a terrible sense of guilt and conflict over her imagined responsibility for her mother's death. The group's support and reassurance were very helpful, and she was slowly able to break through her responsibility, conflict and guilt.

A further use of dual imagery might be for each person in the group to react to a single patient, as in (IS): "Imagine standing on Steve's shoulders — how would it feel and what do you imagine will happen?" Bipolarization of feelings and conflicts may be indicated between the central person of the situation and each of the other members in the group. For example, John's response was, "I can't get on Steve's shoulders because my heels would dig into his shoulders and hurt him. I will be too much of a burden on him." I then asked Steve (IS) what he would feel if John were standing on *his* shoulders. "I'd be in competition with him," Steve said, "I'd have to show him I can carry him with ease and never flinch even for a second. I can never show another man I'm weak. That's unmasculine."

As the group members take turns giving their imagery to standing on Steve's shoulders, and as he responds to them, it will be quickly revealed with whom he is in greatest conflict among them. At any one point in time a sequence of intense interaction may occur between two persons, or among several. The emphasis, to reiterate, is on helping the individual to become aware of his internal conflicts, his negative self-image, has other self-definitions, and the difference between how he defines himself and how others define him. This awareness may serve to engender in him the strength to attempt behaving differently, more in line with his "true" identity. If, as a result of the reactions to an imaginary situation, anyone in the group is being defined falsely, he or she must of course be encouraged (by me as well as the other group members) to assert himself or herself and insist, "You cannot define me that way."

The possibilities for situations in which one person may be centrally imagined by the others are countless. The therapist may ask, for example (IS): "Imagine sitting on Mary, as if she were a chair, and describe the feelings." The answers may bring to light feelings and conflicts which might remain submerged and undetectable in the course of ordinary verbal interchange. The therapist expects, for example, that Mary's imagery reactions to each of the other person's imagery may clarify her conflicts with that individual. Transferred reactions may be made sharper. As one man said about Steve, "Sitting on you is like sitting on my father — it's really like sitting on Spartacus' spike."

Other examples along similar dual imagery lines would involve the following (IS):

1. Imagine lying on a person as if he were a mattress.
2. Imagine standing on each other's chest or back.
3. Then reverse positions and people. Ask John to imagine what he thinks another person, Bill, will imagine if Bill were to be involved with yet another person, Theresa.
4. Imagine kissing a group member. His or her reactions in return.
5. Imagine what the hands of one group member would say to the hands of another group member. His or her reactions in return.
6. Imagine staring at the back or chest of a group member and imagine something. His or her reaction in return.
7. Imagine the eyes of one person saying something to the eyes of another person. His or her reaction in return.
8. Imagine something in the lap of a group member. His or her reaction in return.

Such combinations are quite various and are often a rich source of hidden reactions, frequently unsuspected by the person who does the imagining.

An additional use of dual imagery would be to ask each person in the group (IS): "Silently imagine two different musical instruments and imagine each musical instrument saying something to Jack; imagine what Jack says back to each instrument." Then one can ask each person in turn to report his dual imagery, sharing it with the rest of the group. The individual's awareness of the meanings of his own imagery production become clearer as reactions and interactions proceed. Surprise at one's own imagery and the imagery of the others is common. The feedback of reaction and the comparison of imagery may help clarify meanings and awareness of conflicts within each individual.

In this kind of dual imagery the numbers of imaginary situations are legion (give or take a little). Samples mentioned in Chapter II can be utilized, plus many others. The creativity of the therapist may be drawn to develop new examples. I have used (IS): "Imagine walking down a road; somebody taps you on the shoulder." I then proceed around the room asking each person to report his imagery and allow for interaction from all the group members. Other examples would be (IS): "Imagine a word on your chest and a word on your back; or, (IS) Imagine two different rocking chairs with different people in each — now have each person say something to the other;" or, (IS) "Imagine the left side of your brain and then imagine the right side of your brain."

Additionally, it is possible to ask a group member to go around the group whispering a statement into the left ear of each person and then to whisper something in their right ear. Reverse the interaction among the members of the group, allowing for the meanings to develop as the interactions occur. The results may illustrate the conflicts over intimacy as well as the bipolarized feelings each may have towards a particular person and that person's reaction in return.

In a personal conversation, Marylin Lovell reported working with institutional psychotics and has been able to get some startling results when she combined dual imagery with psychodrama. For example, she reports asking one psychotic man who rarely spoke to imagine (IS) any two different animals. Apparently finding it easier to imagine two different animals than to respond to a directly personal question, he surprisingly responded readily and offered: "A large German shepherd dog and a small poodle dog." He was then asked to imagine that he was the larger dog and was asked to say something to the smaller dog. In the psychodrama he was able to very forcibly shout at the smaller dog although he was previously extremely quiet and taciturn. With him (and with numerous others) such use of the dual imagery combined with psychodrama seems to have a highly therapeutic effect and, indeed, staff observers agree that it had great catalytic value.

With neurotic people in group therapy it is also possible to combine imagery with some form of psychodrama to help increase patient awareness of internal conflicts. I asked one man to (IS) imagine two different animals and he visualized a

Koala bear and a panther. I then asked him to imagine that he was the Koala bear and then to make a statement as the Koala bear to each group member. When he had finished I asked him to imagine he *was* the panther and then to make a statement to each group member as the panther. Without going into the details of his responses, I can say that this experience was highly therapeutic and effective both for him as well as the other group members.

Needless to say, such combined use of imagery and psychodrama can be utilized with effectiveness in other imaginary situations, in addition to dual imagery, such as Task Imagery and the like. The group therapy setting helps focus and crystallize the reactions for greater awareness and therapeutic change.

Group Imagery

Group imagery, in which the entire group is simultaneously presented an imaginary situation, permits participation of each person's imagination for a time, and then the imagery is shared by all.

One of the imaginary situations that can be used is (IS): "Imagine you are all in prison and then imagine that we all find a way out." The responses are sometimes quite individualized, seeming to disregard the group nature of the imagery, as in "I didn't want to get out; it was dangerous to get out. The way I would get out was to become an honor prisoner and I would get a job in the workshop and make a bulletproof jacket. One night I would make a run for it and get out. Even though the guards shot at me, they couldn't hurt me and I get away." Another man said, "I'd make a deal with the warden through my lawyers and the court in order to get me free. It would be a deal. I would give them information they wanted in exchange for my freedom." Other patients visualize the entire group lining up as a single, powerful unit and killing the guards in order to escape together.

Occasionally, one person's imagery may trigger off an awareness of a particular characteristic of himself and his style of life. One overindulged patient said he realized he really didn't care about anybody else's being in prison. "I am only interested in myself, ' he said adding, "Boy, that's hard to say." He had exposed his excessive self-involvement and narcissism to the group and was waiting for the counterreaction. There was a negative reaction to his remarks, forcing him to face up to his self-involvement, his pseudo-caring of others. In a sense this imagery served to invite the other group members to force him to stand up to his conflict. Apparently, he didn't want to get away with such behavior in the future. In this case, his own need to expose himself forced him to cope with the conflict.

Imagery in which the entire group participates may start from an imaginary situation such as (IS): "We are all in a stagecoach and we are going on a journey. What do you imagine will happen to us as we go?" Again, this is a good starting point for interaction, especially designed to see how others view us and how we view them.

Other group imagery situations that can further sharpen interaction and awareness of conflicts are (IS): "Imagine the entire group is part of a circus – what part would each of you take?," or (IS) "We are all stuck on the elevator near the top of a very tall building?" or (IS) "We are all stuck on an island for an indefinite time – what would you do and feel?" or (IS) "We are all forced to spend a winter in the frozen north in a very large hut."

In addition, one can ask a person to go around the group and (IS) imagine a bird on the head of each group member and their reactions back to him. Or ask each group member (IS) to cast a fishing rod into a river and then to see what you come up with. This again serves as a vehicle for reactions, interactions and awareness of conflicts.

I must emphasize again that group sessions are not so structured that imagery is the only function involved. Anything may be brought up at any time: a particularly traumatic situation or decision a person is involved with; carryover reactions from previous sessions; thoughts and feelings people have had about some of the others in the days between group meetings. Also included may be such awareness and feelings as patients have gleaned from individual sessions and wish to bring up spontaneously in the group situations. Nothing, certainly, should deter spontaneous behavior unless the spontaneous behavior is used as a cover-up for some difficult internal conflict. To keep the structure and the spontaneity of the group unfettered is a fine goal for any group therapist.

For all its beneficial aspects, group therapy does not always offer the most expedient determination of a patient's readiness to deal with the focusing approaches or what conflicts he is ready to face. In group therapy, each person is in a "different place" – his own awareness and plateau of growth; certain patients may require a great deal of clinical intuition and readiness for the unexpected on the part of the therapist which might not be necessary in a dyadic situation. I believe that the therapist should offer support when patients are facing heightened awareness of conflicts, and in the focusing approaches, I discourage wherever possible the extended one-to-one involvement between myself and a patient without the group members being involved. I encourage group support and find it an invaluable aid in helping a specific person through a "tough" spot. But clearly there are instances in which this is not possible or advisable.

Utilizing the Creative Imagery of the Patient

With patients that have been experienced in the use of imagery, it is a natural bridge to have them be the originator of imagery with each other. In order to facilitate the process, I asked the first, third, fifth, seventh and ninth person in the room to ask the second, fourth, sixth, eighth and tenth person an imaginary situation in rotation and have each person respond with his or her imagery. The first person asks the second person to respond with his or her imagery, then the entire group participates. Then the third person asks the fourth person an imaginary

situation and as he or she responds again, the group participates. This continues
until the entire group is involved in a similar manner. Of course, one can reverse the
procedure by asking the second person to ask the first person an imaginary
situation with group participation, etc.

What follows is a portion of an audio tape of ten people in a group where this
creative procedure is developed. It is difficult in printed form alone to indicate all
of the nuances, voice sounds and the gestures that can be seen in visual and
auditory observation. The reader should realize that I am emphasizing the creative
use of the patient's imagery and it is beyond us to explore in depth the conflicts of
ten people. It is my judgment that this procedure serves to intensify the interaction
among the group members and that many images developed in this session were
referred to in many subsequent sessions.

Shorr: I want you to try something that's a little different. I want the first, third,
fifth, seventh and ninth person to think of an imaginary situation. I want you to
create one and ask the person next to you an imaginary situation.
Martha: Like the thing on each side?
   (All talking)
Shorr: Anything, but you have to use your own — I don't want you to use one I
would use. You would use any one you want to.
Larry: That's really wild. (Laughs)
Nancy: Use one of Shorr's old ones and ask Robert to imagine so-and-so, is that
right?
Shorr: You can use any, but not necessarily one of mine. You ask anything you
want to, using your own imagination.
   (Everyone laughs and talks)
Nora: Robert, imagine "your wife as two women. . . ."
Robert: That's tough.
Shorr: Well, you think about that, Robert.
Robert: Oh, oh, I'm supposed to think about it?
Shorr: And go back to it.
Nina: Ah, somebody commissions you to do a mural on a wall and what do you
paint on the wall?
Arly: Do I think about this now or do I . . . ?
Shorr: Think about it and then we'll go back to it.
Roberta: I'll give you what I have.
Shorr: Let me hear you. (Roberta was speaking very low)
Roberta: Ah, there is a large grizzly bear in your left hand and your other hand is
full of rice.
Nora: A hand full of what?
Larry: Rice (Laughing) Jesus.
Roberta: Dick, make up an imaginary situation with those two.
Dick: Wow!
Shorr: Well, you think about it, Dick.

Martha: Yes, Dick, good luck (Laughing).

Larry: Imagine that you're like the, remember, the woman you once imagined?

Yale: The flying woman? (Reference to a previous image in another session)

Larry: Imagine that you're in that group of eight bicyclists up on top of that (Various people — Oh dear and Oh shit) thing, and, and, and imagine who's with you and what you're doing.

Yale: Hum . . .

Shorr: (Chuckle) While you think of that one, Nancy, ask Martha one.

Nancy: Well, what comes to my mind is a wooden plank in the shape of a Y and you're walking along it — imagine yourself walking along the long part of the Y and you come to where it turns into the V, and what do you see at either end of that V and which way would you go?

Shorr: Well, we'll start with Martha.

(Mumbled talking)

Martha: I saw water. I saw the plank at the end of — of a ship or boat and I just saw water.

Shorr: Are you happy with that answer. Remember what you asked her. (This is directed to Nancy)

Nancy: No.

Shorr: What did you ask her?

Nancy: Ah, I wanted to know what, who was at either end of the V.

Martha: Oh, I thought you said what.

Nancy: Or what, or who.

Martha: Well, I just saw a vast ocean — I don't see anyone at the end of that, I see that vast huge sea.

Shorr: But you say that there's a separate road up . . .

Nancy: Yes and you have to . . .

Shorr: And you want her to see something different on each one?

Nancy: Yes, something different on each one and you have to decide which way you're going to go, because you have to go this way or that way.

Martha: Yeah, I'm not going off that plank. I have to take it off the boat which I'm obviously going to have to do because there's just water there and I'm not going, I'm not going in it that way. So if I have to take that Y and put it someplace else. . . . (Sigh) I'm in the woods with it and I don't know, it doesn't matter which way I go 'cause I don't know what's at the end of either one of those paths. What I'll have to do is try one and if I don't like that one, I'll go back to the beginning and try and try another one, try the other one.

Nancy: Well, if you can see the end of the paths and you see something at the end of one and you know that you have to decide which way to go and you cannot come back, what would you do, or see?

Martha: What would I see at the end . . . I see a house at the end of one . . . I don't know where that other one's going, I just don't know. I don't see where it's going, it's just going into the woods, and I don't know, I, I don't see it.

Shorr: You want to go into it?

Martha: I'm not afraid to go into it.

Shorr: Go. Why not try it?

Martha: Okay — okay, it's like I came out the end of the woods, and the woods are — huh — it's the woods I used to play in — and then there is an open field. I used to love that particular field, like when you come out from all the woods. I like being in the woods but I like coming out too. So there was a sense of openness and freedom.

Shorr: Why don't you go towards the house more?

Martha: The house is very, it's a very nice, it's a warm welcome kind of a feeling I get from the house — and there's very plain people in there — I don't know them, I don't think, but they're good people and, and they're very comfortable and I like that house too, I like the feeling I get from being in it. . . .

Shorr: Does it represent anything to you? Does it have meaning — this place, this childhood place and the house?

Martha: The childhood place was a place where I would go because I couldn't face what was happening in my own home and I'd go off and be alone there and feel all right. It's like the only place that I had a sense of peace because when I was back in the house with my family, it was just hell. So that was a good feeling, you know it was . . . nothing could touch me there.

Shorr: And the house — what did you feel about that?

Martha: And the house was, I don't know where this house came from. I don't recognize that as any house I've ever been in, it's just like a little old one-room house and the thing I, that kinda comes to my mind is, I used to wish that I had been a pioneer when — when it was cut and dried what you had to do, you had to work to survive and there wasn't time to, to worry about that — should your kids take dancing lessons or some insignificant thing — it was, it was a simple cut and dried life. I used to think, God, maybe I should have lived then — life would not be so complicated.

Shorr: So what do these images mean to you? What do you think about them? Does it relate to your life today in any way?

(Pause)

Martha: My life is so complicated right now that I would like to be in a real peaceful spot. Yeah, yeah. Where nobody can touch me, either this quiet, little. . . . Yeah, which is kinda what I do, see I turn to a physical thing. Always when I can't handle something, I always go into some sort of physical activity with great vigor.

Shorr: So it's pretty illustrative of you, this, these two things you saw, huh?

Martha: Probably.

Shorr: I'm going to pull a switch. I want Yale to ask Larry an imaginary situation and Larry will have to answer before yours.

Dick: Sneak.

Yale: Yeah, mine is sort of prejudiced by his question to me.

(Everyone laughs)

Yale: No. no. Larry, you're on the back of a seat of a motorcycle, who's driving it and what's happening?

Larry: Do I have to answer or anything?

(Everyone laughs)

Shorr: There are no policemen. (Larry has had bad experiences with motorcycles)

Larry: Oh, I didn't know. Well, I don't like motorcycles, as you know, and I think that I'm trying to see who's driving it. I get this picture of sort of a playgirl, you know with the long hair and all that, you know — but she's really just fucked in her head, 'cause we're just going like a son-of-a-bitch, you know, so all I can do is figure how to tail out of the god damn thing. (Robert laughs; Nora says, "Fall off gracefully.") Yeah, that's my whole concern. (Group laughs) How to get off and be cool (Everyone laughs) at 80 miles an hour, you know. I had an image of that guy they have at automobile shows where they slide for life, you know, or he slides along and the smoke pouring out but he's, but he does it just right. I was thinking, if I could pull that off?

Roberta: Are you holding onto her?

Larry: No, not any more. I'm . . . ah, no, I'm not holding onto her, huh, uh.

Martha: Who is this girl?

Larry: I don't know. . . . She's almost like a, like a pop art, you know, kind of with the big Hollywood smile. I mean (Robert: "Barbarella.") Raquel Welch. You know what I mean. It was, it got, that got me thinking about it, but she's like just really, just you know, what's her name, there was a movie that was put out about a spy girl, you know (Yale: "Barbarella, is that what you mean?") Is that who it is, yeah, that, that type of thing, you know it just really — Barbarella.

Nancy: But do you do everything with so much finesse, but can you just let reality in and know that you're going to die if you don't get the fuck off that thing, can't you. . . .

(Background talking during all of the previous)

Larry: I think I do everything, I would die with finesse.

Yale: Wait a second, Larry. (Everyone laughing)

Larry: That's very important to me.

Robert: It was important to Byron too — You really think that she's definitely bound for a crackup, huh, there's no two ways about it, there, if you stay on, she's going to crash.

Larry: Good chance, I wouldn't say definitely. I'd say there was a damn good chance.

Martha: You couldn't talk her out of it?

Larry: I don't think she's aware. She's not aware of the perils, you see. She's in for the image and everything and it's just not — it's, I, it just does not cross her mind.

Yale and Arly: Well, were you in the image?

Larry: What image?

Nora: Uh, huh.

Arly: Well, you can't tell her to stop the fucking motorcycle and let you get off?

Nancy: You have no control?

Arly: Do you have to "finesse" it with her?

Larry: No, I . . . (Pause)

Shorr: An awful lot of danger involved.

Nancy: Yeah.

Larry: Oh, I don't think that would change, that's what I said, I don't think that would change my picture of decorum. There are ways to get off a motorcycle, no matter what. (Laughs)

Shorr: The most important thing is . . .

Roberta: In a life or death situation, you'd still hang onto the control thing.

Larry: Well, I feel that emotionally I don't know if in truth you know that's something that may be really true, although everytime I cracked up on a motorcycle I did it really pretty good, I think . . .

Nancy: You were cool and cracked up.

Robert: With aplomb.

Larry: That's right!

Nancy: But would you rather get off, than reach over and just turn something off or grab her arms or feet?

(Miscellaneous talking and laughing)

Larry: Yeah, grab her arms — (Laughs)

Roberta: Grab her boobs.

Arly: She'll hit you with a tit.

Nancy: I mean, it's almost like you have no power to do anything except get off gracefully.

Larry: That's about the way I see it. I don't think I do have much power. I mean to do anything else. I could throttle her or something like that but these would be a . . . (Pause)

Arly: Could you, could you force yourself to say, "Stop this motorcycle, I want to get off," or is that uncouth?

(All speaking at once)

Martha: Stop and let me off.

Nancy: It's not cool.

Robert: I forgot something, I . . .

Yale: I've got a letter to mail, would you pull over to the next mailbox. (Laughs)

Shorr: Well, how does this relate to your life when you think of this image? Is it protective of anything in your life? (Pause)

Larry: I think it fairly well exemplifies how I handle situations of this type, not that I don't have day-to-day life and death situations too often, but situations that are tricky in, in a respect. I think this is about the way I handle them, I try and do it very, very coolly whether I feel it or not.

Shorr: That fact that you include a woman in this without Yale indicating that there's a woman or anybody else that I know of, right, Yale?

Larry: Well, no, no of course not.

(Everyone Laughing)

Shorr: You think that's important that you got the woman on the bike?

Larry: Well, I think — you see I have — I get a pretty positive feeling about the whole situation. I think that it, is (Sigh) at least it's resolved, it's my resolving a conflict with, with women, that kind of woman is the woman that I had for a long time as an idealized image — idealized woman.

Nancy: A problem we didn't know about.

(Everyone laughs)

Larry: Well, I'm a transvestite. (Offered in a humorous fashion) (Laughing) Anyway, it's a Hollywood broad, it's a swinging, you know, hip chick. All that shit and I guess after all this in (Laughingly) my mind, the best way out of it is just to get off the motorcycle —

Roberta: And let her go screaming into the wind?

Larry: Because, because there's no way, there's no way that I'm going to be able to, to, talk with her.

Roberta: Yeah, it's like you can't deal with it, there's just no level that you can communicate, or nothing you know.

Robert: She won't listen to reason. Oh, then I can just win with the big smile and, azzoom, you know, and this is the whole thing and she wants a guy who's going to go along and say, "Faster, faster," you know, but like I've fractured my asshole with this kind of cunt and those kind of motorcycles and that's it.

Shorr: You want no more part of that.

Larry: No more, no more (Background talking) and I want to get out as coolly as possible, you know, without any hassle.

Shorr: But you're not facing that in life today?

Larry: No, it's something that I think I've resolved pretty well.

Yale: What would happen if you got off the motorcycle without cool, you just reach over and turn off the ignition, and, ah.

Larry: Uh, huh, very hard for me to believe that I would do it, it's not impossible, but it's like eating left-handed. I mean, you know, I guess I could do it. I could imagine it — aah, but I think I'd have a lot of . . .

Roberta: Can you scream at her for jeopardizing your life, like, "God damn stupid bitch," you know — I mean can you, you know . . .

Larry: Can, but ah —

Yale: Why is it still . . .

Larry: She couldn't care less, I mean, you know.

Robert: Is that the feeling you . . .

Arly: Yeah, but can you care less?

Nancy: Yeah, but it makes you feel good, to get it out.

Yale: Yeah, that's the point, I think Arly has a point there. Can you, can you turn off the key and get off and to hell with what she thinks about you. I mean it's like you're still getting off, and getting off and, getting off her way.

Larry: No, I'm getting off my way, not her way. This is my way of getting off.

Yale: Well, I don't understand that.

Martha: I don't see anything wrong with the way he got off that, that he walked away from a situation. He just turned his back on it.

Roberta: He wasn't going to walk away. He was going at 80 miles an hour, going to try to go off gracefully, you know, without damaging . . .

(Everyone talking)

Martha: Did you get off safely in your picture? That was the impression I got.

Larry: Oh yeah.

Martha: You got off and left and I . . .

Larry: I got off safely, yeah, I got off.

Robert: The details were a little vague, I think they . . .

Nora: Yah, it was a little vague to me, Larry, because you said you would die for them.

Larry: Well, oh well, I hadn't exactly figured it out then I, I really . . .

Nora: But at least you would keep it cool?

Arly: Yeah, that's what you said.

Larry: Well, I don't expect to die.

Nora: That's different than getting off safely.

Larry: Uh huh, no, I will get off safely, but with finesse.

Shorr: Do you have a reaction to that, Nina? What Larry just said?

Yale: (Laughs)

Larry: Just a motorcycle problem (Group laughter) Harley-Davidson.

Yale: Who's riding in back of your motorcycle? (Laughs)

Larry: Yamaha hangup.

Martha: I think it's great.

    (Group laughter)

Nina: I'm so nervous with that fucking thing going, I can't follow anything. I'm just catching words here and there and blanking out. (Laughs)

Shorr: No, now — say something to the damn tape recorder, so it doesn't intimidate you. Why do you let that define you? (Roberta squeals, "more softly")

Nina: (Very quietly) Ah, I don't know.

Larry: Just because everybody's going to play it tomorrow night and laugh, (Everyone laughs) sit around and (Background talking and laughing) listen to it.

Nina: That's what I'm afraid of, I'm afraid of, of being foolish.

Shorr: Well, nobody will hear you but this group — on a replay, how do you like that, except myself. Is that fair?

Nina: Well, I still think that I'll come off foolish.

Shorr: Then you're always coming off foolish in group. I mean, after all, we can tape any session.

Nina: I hope nobody remembers. (Laughs)

    (Background talking)

Shorr: (M/L) What's the most difficult thing to say to the tape recorder? Since you're investing it with power.

Nina: Just to talk.

Shorr: (Focus) No, say something to it, so it doesn't define you.

Nina: (Loudly) FUCK OFF!

Shorr: Good, now what did you think of Larry and the motorcycle?

Nina: (Chuckle) I, I thought that what he did was fine. I, you know, I didn't think going 80 miles an hour was any different that going 20 miles an hour. I felt, you know, he had to just get off.

Larry: It calls for a little more agility. (Group laughter)

Nina: I thought — I thought you'd do it anyway, no matter what.

Roberta: We all have great faith in him.

Arly: There is a little pocket parachute.

Nora: I'd like to see it myself (Laughingly) at 80 miles an hour.

Roberta: I'd like to see you take a different type of control of the scene, you know, like confronting her.

Larry: If you were driving the motorcycle, I could and more. There's the difference. Any woman in this group I think I could handle.

Arly: But why, why?

Larry: Because these women in here I have communication with, and I realize that they know me. Yeah, I mean this broad is detached from me.

Arly: Yeah, but you're giving her power, because you said —

Larry: No, I'm not giving her power, man. I used to give her power when I was trying to fuck her, trying to make something out of her. I'm not giving her any power.

Arly: Then why do you have to give up?

Larry: She doesn't have any, I just bail off of the motorcycle.

Arly: But you said you had to do it with a sense of finesse. You wouldn't die.

Larry: But that's for me. I think I would do that, I think I would do that.

Arly: But if Roberta were driving the motorcycle, would you do the same thing?

Larry: I could do the same thing but I wouldn't have to do the same thing. I could reach over to Roberta and say, "Roberta, would you please slow down, we're going too fast."

Arly: If you couldn't say that to some of them or —

Larry: This particular girl, this is my fantasy. Arly is not going to listen to that.

(Everyone laughs)

Arly: Okay, that's different than what I heard you saying. I thought, what I was getting from you is that she wasn't going to listen. It's that you couldn't say, "Stop this motorcycle, you're jeopardizing my life."

Larry: Oh, I could, but it's not going to stop that motorcycle.

Arly: Oh, okay, but I mean, in other words, her presence couldn't stop you from saying what you want to say?

Larry: No, I just, in this particular situation, I'm going to have to do it the best way I can and that's, you know, in order to save my life is what it amounts to, and the only way I could save my life with her, with Roberta, with Nina or anybody or you, you know, it could be done differently but not with this girl.

Dick: You assumed or you stated all along that you're going to die, I mean, that this thing is doomed.

Martha: No.

Roberta: No, no he changed it, he changed it.

(Various no's)

Larry: I'm not going to die, I'm going to live forever. (Underlying conversations) If I stay on, there's a damn good possibility I will die, yes.

Dick: Then, she's going to kill herself, is what she's doing?

Larry: I don't know what she's going to do, I'm not really (Laughingly) concerned.

Dick: You're sure, sure that there's going to be a crackup?

Larry: Yeah, positive.

Robert: I notice that you're disguising your voice, by the way.

(Group laughing)

Larry: What!

(Everyone laughs and various talking)

Yale: Is that why you've got that pebble in your mouth?

Larry: (Mutters) Yeah, a pebble here.

   (Group laughing)

Dick: Is there also a way possibly that you won't die, that you could ride it out?

Larry: That's a very slim possibility, I feel. You see, motorcycles has got me in a very bad way. It's a tough subject 'cause I think I've used up my chances on a motorcycle. (Group laughter) I don't have too many "freebies" left. (Group laughter)

Shorr: Dick, why don't you ask Roberta an imaginary situation?

Roberta: (In a quiet voice) I tried to get missed.

Shorr: I know.

Larry: Buried all the rice.

Roberta: I am ready for it.

Shorr: She still has hers.

Dick: O.K., there are three birds flying. Can you imagine that?

Roberta: Three birds flying?

Shorr: Will you say it louder, Dick? I didn't hear you.

Dick: (Loudly) There are three birds flying and you're one of them. Which one are you? And what's it about?

Roberta: All right! Yeah, I saw the three of them and I was in the middle, you know, like a V-type situation. I like them this way. Feels great. (Laughing) I've never flown before — fantastic! Then we get a little closer and we kind of huddle (Laughs) as we fly. What do we think? Who are they?

Dick: Who's in front of you?

Roberta: I was kind of like — in that — those birds were back there, those, those beautiful birds. Aaah, who are they? I immediately thought of the children, you know, Jimmy and Carol — great day, it's beautiful, I didn't see the tornado.

Yale: (Laughs)

Shorr: Dick, you had it with one in front, one in the middle, something like that and one in the back. You mean, you had it in a direct line?

Martha: In a line.

Dick: Yeah, I, I set it up as a line, yeah.

Shorr: Where there's one, two, three right in front of each other?

Dick: I wanted to know which one you were, and you said you were in the middle.

Roberta: Ooooooohhhhhhh — I did, didn't I, you see I was seeing it different. That's why. Okay. If I would be in the middle, then it would be different. Then there would be a man in front and — someone else, or you know.

Yale: A spare.

   (Laughter)

Roberta: You know more about me than you need to know.

Larry: A spare (Laugh) — a back-up stud.

Roberta: No, I saw it, you know, like children instead, in the back.

Larry: Children in the back?

Roberta: Well, you know if that, that's the direction. If I'm not in front, then the man's in front. Okay. The first impression I had was that I was flying and I had both kids on the side, okay, that's going like flying, okay but the situation he wants is someone in the front, me in the middle and someone in the back, well then I feel like I'd be — well with other people, if I'm in the middle in this particular situation, I'm comfortable, you know, the man's in front and the children in back.

Shorr: You have sort of a family scene there.

Roberta: Yeah — yeah, there's something to that.

Nancy: Are there any conflicts between you wanting to go up front with the fellow? I like the V-shape better myself, because it shows you do or are having some sort of a problem with your children as far as responsibility and guilt and all this sort of thing, but if you are in the other line with a man in front and the children in back, do you have any conflict in trying to get forward or do you feel a pull of any kind?

Roberta: I didn't, no, no, it was kind of like nice and I was wondering why I was there. It feels so good. No, no I love the unity, I love that effect, you know, like I want to gather it in.

Nancy: So, in other words, it's more comfortable. It's more comfortable being in the center of — the man in front and the children behind, then you in the front and the children behind?

Roberta: Oh no, no, no, they're comparable see, you know, parallel feeling.

Nancy: But in reality, they are totally opposite. They're not comparable, in reality you're not either. Right?

Roberta: Okay, let me, you know, get a feel on that I — (Pause) — Okay, if there's a tornado and I'm (Laughter) you know, in front with the kids, I tend to get a little nervous. Yeah, I do tend to get a little nervous and I really feel a lot more comfortable, you know, with a man in front, you know, and the kids in back, but will fly the tornado. When there's trouble, you know, where the hell are they? I need the man, and I do feel like, you know, that kind of feels good to be able to rely on him.

Nancy: Yeah, but if there is no tornado — the feeling, the feeling that I'm having is sometime, I might be inflicting a lot of my own problems and my own feelings of remarriage and stuff. Do you feel that if there is no tornado, is there a definite difference in your feeling?

Roberta: A bit incomplete with the kids — you know it feels good and, and it's comfortable, but again, it's like in case of trouble — like I'm all alone.

Nancy: It would be easy to give up your place in the front with the children and let a man take over. There's no problem.

Roberta: Welllll, you know, I'm going to make sure it's a good strong bird. You know, I know that. I mean, he'd have to be a goose instead. (Group laughter)

Shorr: So what does that mean to your life?

Roberta: Well, I'd, I'd be willing to give up, you know, the leader, sole responsibility for, you know, a nice relationship.

Shorr: Sounds like it's coming off good. Martha, how about asking one of Nancy.

Martha: Aaah, okay. Let's see. Picture a scale of justice. What do you see on either side and how does it relate to you? In other words, which one's heavier and what is it?

Yale: I think we've got justice sitting here right there, very proper as you. (Points to Shorr)

Nancy: Hey, I'm just like the statue (Laughter) now that you mention it. I was getting very regal up there, wasn't I. Aaah, I'm looking down instead of up. That's funny. Okay, I'm really having a problem here with authority, uumm. Now I'm looking at eye level to a statue that is holding a scale in either hand, but it is not the statue of justice that has a blindfold over its eyes and it should, ummmm. It is of a very — human, soft person, that is holding out these two dishes or plates or trays or whatever, with a lot of compassion and understanding and in the right hand, there is — all kinds of real pretty, shiny things — extremely brilliant, radiating, fantastic amounts of energy — and in the left hand — is a pile of rusty keys — and — it's sort of like I'm afraid of both of them in reality.

Martha: Which one were you the most, between them?

Nancy: They weigh totally the same. They weigh equally the same. Aah, the keys are frightening, because I know it's like confinement, imprisonment, aah hardship, slavery, which is from my slavery days. Oh no, I was a slave. It's a comfortable feeling with the keys, although it's, it's something that I know that's over and I don't want to have anything more to do with it. It's sad — lethargic. It's a feeling about it that's sad, but it's over with, and of thing and the sparkly things I really am moving towards, but I'm very afraid of them because I don't know what's there. I don't if that's really, really what belongs to me or not.

Martha: Who is that woman who's holding this stuff so compassionately?

Nancy: Oh, it has to be me, I'm sure. I'm sure. I'm sure that it's probably me.

Nora: Nancy, explain the keys to me a little better.

Nancy: The keys?

Nora: Yea.

Nancy: Well, they're old rusty keys, with round loops on them and —

Nora: Fantastic, but what do they represent, that's what I'm losing.

Nancy: Well, they represent a lot of years, I would say, that were spent imprisoned, just years that I have spent in imprisonment and now that I'm not in prison anymore. They're old and rusty — I feel like I'm looking back on my life and I see it in blocks, like a child's box of toys and you see building blocks in it and like they're numbered or lettered according to the phase of life that I went through and like the life that I have today I feel is just like a bunch of these blocks that are, that are built and this block I was imprisoned in, this situation or this feeling or this ignorance which is, whatever you want to call it. As I grew out of that into another stage of life or another aspect, each block that I passed through is like a prison with a key on it.

Nina: You're in possession of all of these keys, nobody else has them?

Nancy: No, they're there, I have them.

Dick: Can you throw them away?

Nancy: Oh yes, they're thrown away, they are old and rusty already, and I don't feel like I would ever be imprisoned again. Aaah, I don't feel restricted now like I was before, like I had no choice up until lately.

Shorr: What about that other side, can you luxuriate in the other side?

Nancy: Yeah, it seems like it would be.

Shorr: Experience the joy of it.

Nancy: Well this is it. There really hasn't been much joy up until recently and I don't know if I could really accept it or not right now or do you want me to go home and think about it?

(Laughter)

Shorr: Right now.

Nancy: (Laughs) Oh rats, I hate this spur-of-the-moment decision. Aaah.

Shorr: I'll take joy anytime I could get it.

Nancy: What's her last name? — It's, it's strange, I want to go to it and I know damn well I deserve everything that's there, I know it's mine, I earned it by physical labor. In reality, it's not just because I'm me, which is enough.

Shorr: Stop explaining and start experiencing it.

Nancy: Oh, I know, my body starts shaking, as I go towards it, it just starts vibrating so terribly much that the plates start shaking and all the little things start tingling —

Yale: Will you let some of that joy show in your face?

Nancy: You mean it hasn't?

Yale: It wasn't.

Nancy: Well, I'm too worried about the job — I feel out of place, I, totally feel out of place. If I could change those shiny thing to earth things, I would feel comfortable.

Shorr: (Focus) (IS) Change them.

Nancy: Aaah that, see that. I'm really fooling myself. I keep thinking I want all the shiny luxury things. I don't, I really don't, I would feel out of place with them and now that they're earth things, like dirt and plants and things like that and flowers — and trees and butterflies.

Shorr: Seems more natural.

Nancy: Yes, yes, then I can really luxuriate in that, I can just fall down and let it cover me up and it feels satiny and smooth and it smells just heavenly — Yeah, that's much better.

Shorr: The gold sounds like it's a false position of some sort.

Nancy: Yeah, I think it was, well I don't think it was, I know it was. You're right — realistically I'm much more comfortable here.

Nora: If they're earth things, do they still weigh the same?

Nancy: Oh yes, I think of them as higher though than the keys, but I don't understand how that is except that they're higher up — aah — the weights are —

Robert: They're not as hard to carry.

Nancy: Yeah, maybe that's it, they're much, they're higher up on the scale. Although I'm sure they weigh physically as much or more but it's not, it's not the burden, the keys are sort of dead and heavy, whereas this is strong but higher.

Shorr: You like that?

Nancy: Oh yeah, yeah, yeah. Now I have to go home and clean my mental closet out and get rid of all those diamonds and satins (Laughs) and jewels. (Group laughter) I want a pair of satin sheets (Laughingly). Okay, I'll go home and play in the grass. That's probably better. You know, really to put a little tag line on it, where I work. You know, it's all man-made structure and all and everytime the gardeners mow the lawn I have a horrible urge. I pick up handfuls of grass and stick them in my pocket and I take it in and put it on my desk, and the smell of cut grass, it's so delicious. Have you ever smelled fresh cut grass?

Shorr: I believe so.

Roberta: Live in California!

Nancy: Oh, it smells so good. I wish they would get that into a perfume of some kind, you know.

Robert: "Eau de Grasse."

(Group laughter)

Yale: "Newly Mown."

Shorr: Robert, ask an imaginary situation of Nora.

Robert: Of Nora?

Shorr: Un huh.

Robert: Hoo — Ummmm — (IS) You're in the, on the observation deck on the top of the Empire State Building and a man is coming towards you —

Nora: I'm standing by one of those telescopes — and I'm looking out at the city that I've never seen before and it's all so different and it's very exciting and I'm urging him to come on to see it with me and to look out and see what I've found, and it's chilly — I don't see myself in a coat but I see him in a topcoat which is unusual here — and it's a good place to be, that would be a nice place to be.

Nina: Are you sharing it with him?

Nora: Yes, I, I'm hurrying him on to see what I see and to share it 'cause it's going to be something new and awfully nice.

Shorr: What do you see?

Nora: Oh, I see these huge tall buildings and, oh, just a skyline I've never seen before — and the busiest harbor I've ever seen. My goodness, except for looking through it, the ships are going in like this, like cars on a freeway. (Laughingly) Of course, they can't do, but it's very busy and it's — seems very different and extremely exciting to me.

Nancy: After you look through the telescope and you turn away, what do you do?

Nora: We get in the elevator to go down and go somewhere else to see something in the city.

Robert: What does he say to you?

Nora: What does he say? (Quietly) "That was marvelous, what shall we do now?" It just seems, it's a very nice image, I really like it. I really like that.

Nancy: Would you feel that as out — between the two of you, which one would take charge and take the lead?

Nora: I can't see a leader, I can see two people just so anxious to go see what there is to see and one is urging this way and one is urging that way and so you go both. There's no leader.

Robert: Spontaneous interaction type.

Nora: Yeah, I love that scene — thanks, Robert, write me another. I love it.

Shorr: Self-explanatory. Yale, how about that imaginary situation you got before.

Yale: Yeah, riding a bicycle on the high-wire. I can only get the troupe up to three people at any one time. (Group laughter) Yeah, well it's like, I had to put it in a situation. At first I was out at one of the ends of the poles, sort of hanging on, and then I was sort of imagining who I would feel comfortable with on the other side. Can I be comfortable riding the bicycle and basically in control of the situation? And I can think of a number of people, like Helen or Nora, who I'd feel comfortable with out at the other end of the pole. Aaah, it's not a real dynamic situation. I don't imagine moving. It's just sort of a balancing act, you know, like who do I feel comfortable with in what situations. I put Harriet (woman friend) out on the end of one of the poles and boy it was just hard work to get her balanced. In fact, it was almost impossible. You know it was like she let go and I sort of poke her with the pole and it was, I guess, physically impossible. If you try to pull her up, why she'd go down a little bit further on the pole. Something of that sort, no one really at the moment. I was just about to say if I started to drive along, funny, well then I imagine seeing another bicycle coming in from the opposite (Laughs) direction.

(Group laughter)

Robert: (Laughing) Who's driving that "son-of-a-bitch?"

(Group laughter and talking)

Yale: I don't know — it's probably a woman.

Nora: Lousy women drivers. (Sarcastically)

Yale: Right, always going the wrong way on a one-way street.

Nina: Would you try to see how much you could do on a bicycle, like handstands or on one hand or two hands or —

Yale: Aaah, I don't think I would have thought of that, I can imagine it now that you asked me, but I don't think that I could have conceived of that myself.

Nancy: It seems like the one coming towards you is obviously not a woman driver as you said. You're really wound up in conflict or combat with women. There's nothing else but the combat?

(Laughs)

Yale: (Laughs) Yes.

Nancy: Yes, there is, or no, there isn't?

Yale: Yeah, I think you're right there. I think of it as meeting someone not necessarily as being combative.

Nancy: Well, if it was a woman driver coming towards you, when you met, what would the result be? What would you do?

Yale: (Laughs) That's your woman (to Larry) driver. I mean you just pedal faster.

Nancy: I want to see you jump out of her way, Yale.

(Group laughter and background talking)

Yale: I don't go for these Hollywood tricks. No, I see us sort of getting off our bicycles and holding the bicycle on one side as a counterbalance and just balancing there, facing each other for awhile, aaah —

Nancy: It would be like a partnership act?

Yale: I, I haven't gotten that far.

Nancy: Oh!

Robert: Are there spectators, Yale?

Yale: Aaah!

Robert: Is there a crowd?

Yale: Sort of phantom crowds. I don't see the crowd, but I feel their presence.

Nina: Is there a net below just in case?

Robert: No.

Yale: I hope so. (Laughs) (Group laughs) I don't see one.

Yale: Me and the woman, though I imagine in some cases, it's easier to – for each of us to go by each other and continue in the directions we were going. It is to turn one of the bicycles around and sort of have a bicycle built for two, in the middle of the high-wire and then go off in the same direction.

Roberta: Do you still see yourself meeting, exchanging, able to work it out and still continue?

Yale: Well, I'm not sure, it's like I got two solutions or two pictures.

Roberta: It's obvious – I don't like that.

Robert: Well, suppose that the person on the bike coming toward you were Harriet?

Yale: . . . We don't get that close – I'd back up aways and then she backs up aways – bikes are always ten feet apart.

Shorr: What does it say about you?

Yale: Ah – says I got to go down the path and when I do meet someone, I've got to risk trying to put the bicycles together and do a bicycle built for two. I see the whole thing as being trust. Whom do I trust and how does the trust balance out?

Nancy: And where your responsibility is?

Yale: Yes and no.

Nancy: Well, like when you were on one side and you had Harriet or somebody else on the other and you said it's hard for her to stay on there. If you were the one who was responsible to pick her up and put her back – if you got to give that up –

Yale: Yeah, but if I saw her falling off, I didn't feel "AAAAAAAGH," you know, calamity. I should jump after her, you know, that's something I should get to make an effort at. I guess there is some responsibility in it but I don't, I don't feel that it's a calamity.

Shorr: You're exercising trust more now in this thing?

Yale: Yeah.

Shorr: More than the responsibility?

Yale: Yeah, I certainly see it as something in regards to trust.

Roberta: I don't see you as terribly nervous up there either. I see you able to deal with it.

Shorr: How high up was it, Larry, that imaginary situation you gave to Yale?

Larry: Oh, waaaay up.

(Group laughing and talking)

Yale: I was high up too. I wouldn't want to fall off that thing. I'm not sure that there's a safety net down below.

Larry: No, no.

Nancy: It wasn't the fear of falling. It was the fear of encounter?

Yale: It was encounter and it would stretch between the Empire State Building. Well one, I think, Nina brought up something which I would like to emphasize. I wish I had been flamboyant up there. I seem to be confident to certainly go by someone else on the high wire, but whether I trust enough to make a bicycle built for two and then go wheeling off with the woman up front, or whether I'd be confident enough to be flamboyant, while I'm doing my own thing by standing on my head on the seat of the bicycle or whatever.

(Group laughter)

Nora: Thank you for explaining your image.

Body Routes to Conflict

One of the most powerful means to group interaction involves imagery in sensing one's body or a body part and then imagining handing that part to different persons in the group. As an example, I might suggest (IS): "Imagine your heart, imagine handing it to Bill." My patients' responses to this imaginary act, the myriad of comments, hesitations, false starts and facial reactions have been too numerous and varied to catalogue; the degrees of difficulty or simplicity they have encountered encompass an immeasurable spectrum.

My experience verifies that people relate the heart to love and feelings of tenderness. Noting the relative ease or difficulty with which the patient performs the task is an indication of his sense of his own love feelings (or lack of them); it also reveals how "safe" or "fearful" he feels about the person to whom he hands his heart.

I remember an experience in group therapy in which I asked Theresa, a detached young woman, to imagine (IS) placing her heart on the ground, next to Gerald's heart. I then asked Gerald, who was also prone to detachment, to (IS) imagine placing his heart next to Theresa's. With most detached persons, the giving and taking of love feelings is extremely difficult, implying, as it does, an inherent commitment.

Both Theresa and Gerald closed their eyes for a long time. Then Theresa slowly put her imagined heart on the floor, Gerald following suit a moment later. Both people then appeared to reflect for a time, saying and doing nothing. (They both told me at later times that they didn't want to "act out" the feelings they had had, but rather to allow themselves to really *feel*.) At least Theresa was about to "join" her heart with Gerald's and spoke of warm feelings for his heart. Gerald, despite prolonged concentration, was unable to join his heart to Theresa's heart. Theresa at this point expressed feelings of betrayal; Gerald became defensive. So it is that powerful feelings of interaction can occur through "body routes." (I must add that in a subsequent session Gerald finally did hand his heart to Theresa, and despite extreme caution was finally able to trust it to her.)

Other body imagery can be elicited by asking each person in the group (IS): "Imagine something inside Ned's guts." As the group goes around with each person describing his or her imagery, Ned's reactions — and the resultant interactions — reveal the interpersonal conflicts that exist and may also provide a vehicle for focusing for change. (IS) "Say something from your head to the head of another person in group." (IS) "From your heart to someone else's heart." (IS) "From your guts to someone else's guts." (IS) "From your vagina to Al's penis." — The interactions which result in the group sessions from such imaginary situations are immensely valuable in the revealing of conflicts and their resolutions.

One patient, Fred, seemed to be so intellectually bound that he could express virtually no emotion. At one point I asked the other members in his group (IS): "Imagine entering Fred's head and share your imagery." One response: "I see a giant computer inside, with thousands of levers and pulleys. On the other side are rows and rows of buttons, and a mechanical lever is pushing them in computer order." This from Clara. And each of the other people reported similar mechanical gadgetry and computer-like hardware in Fred's head. Fred was visibly shaken by their reports, and in time was able to allow himself to express feelings instead of mere description.

One of the most compelling body routes I've used in group therapy involves asking Hank (IS): "Imagine entering Jason's body." That body part through which Hank would imagine entering Jason may reveal conflicts and defenses present in both of them. While Hank is "moving about" inside of Jason, he experiences surprising imagery and many heretofore unsuspected feelings. And what he *avoids* as he travels around in there may be equally as revealing. Jason, listening in his imagination to Hank's inside-the-body travel, may express a whole host of defensive reactions, conflict awareness, and other unanticipated reactions which, at some time, may lead to the possibility of focusing approaches.

Focusing Approaches

The focusing approaches in group therapy are quite similar to those used in individual sessions, the main difference of course being that they occur in front of other people — the group members — in open view. It may happen that the focusing of an individual to be defined in a manner consistent with his true self-image may bring him in direct opposition to another group member or even the group as a whole.

Cathartic expression of feeling towards other group members is of course quite direct and utilizes little imagery; but one of the values of interaction imagery is precisely that it can lead to cathartic expression. Additionally, imagery can be used to make the patient aware of tender, warm feelings; it may involve imagining his parents or other nongroup members.

Interaction Imagery/Cathartic Imagery

Imagery that relates to intimacy can be elicited in the group by having each member (IS) "Imagine holding one particular group member in your arms — Chuck, for example — as you would hold a baby." When the group has gone around, each person reporting his imagery and associated feelings, Chuck will express his reactions to those reports. As a variation, it is possible to imagine the adult's being a baby. The responses to this particular imaginary situation are invariably strong ones and usually involve extensive interaction. A further variation involves (IS): "Imagine pushing so-and-so in a baby carriage." Or (IS) "Imagine pushing *me* in a baby carriage." Transference reactions and the abrupt exposure of conflicting feelings often surface during such an exercise.

To ask each person in the group to imagine holding *himself* in his arms as a baby is useful in eliciting conflict areas that relate to historical self-concepts or self-images which contrast with present ones. People whose early lives were highly traumatic and accompanied by frequent and powerful feelings of terror often cannot allow themselves to "go" with this imagery at all and flatly refuse to attempt it. Others, who find no difficulty with the imagery and find it accompanied by tender, soft feelings, demonstrate by example that such positive emotion is not beyond reach.

It is helpful for certain individuals who were badly neglected as children to (IS) imagine holding their mother or father − as an infant − in their arms. Or, the imaginary roles may be reversed.

Jane, a thirty-eight-year-old woman, found this kind of imagery very difficult to allow herself within the group situation. Her mother had totally neglected her deprived her of love, and competed fiercely with her when Jane was only a child What follows below is an excerpt from an audiotape of a particular session in which Jane experienced the imagery of holding her "infant" mother in her arms. She then reversed the roles and imagined being held by her mother. Although she was very bright and quite accomplished, Jane had introjected severe feelings of inferiority and self-doubt; she had often expressed a fear of retaliation on the part of her strong, controlling mother. The imaginary situation served, in this case, as a focusing experience of the cathartic/imagery type. It resulted in a changed self-concept, verified by her own reports of her feelings and by the judgment of her group in this session and subsequent ones.

Jane: . . . I like both ways, but, I'm imagining holding my mother. Once I said, you know, she was probably a squalling, angry baby and that she was hurt before I got her, which is kind of a weird thing − I mean, if I had her as a baby, I think it'd take all the psychiatrists in the world to find out what was wrong with her − (Long silence) and turning it around the other way, I feel that, you know, like if she poked at me and − she didn't really hold me like a baby and she never held me as if I was responsive − that − she was never responsive to me and never, made me feel like a baby. I feel hopeless. I feel that, you can talk about a lot of things in therapy, but like this happened before I even remembered. Like before I could even − talk about things − how is it ever possible? You know, I must have been so angry and a nothing from the way she treated me that I don't know how I'll ever get over it.

Shorr: Over what?

Jane: The anger I feel about that is so − so unverbal. I think that's what the world is like.

Shorr: (Focus) (IS) Well, what do you want to say to her or scream at her to liberate yourself from her?

Jane: But you see, I guess that's the point. I could. I could think about having myself if I could scream at her.

Ned: You could scream.

Shorr: It's still there.

Ned: You don't have to say anything.

Andy: Sometimes the words aren't necessary.

Shorr: What did you say you were?

Jane: (Tries to talk, but no words come.)

Shorr: Implicit or explicit.

Jane: I wasn't a person. I wasn't anything.

Shorr: So, you do know. (Focus) (IS) O.K., now how about screaming that. (FTS) "I am not ... "

Jane: I am not a piece of bread. I'm – I'm a person. (Not very loud)

Shorr: Try that again – 'cause there's a lot more pain in it – than that.
    (Said very softly)

Jane: I'M NOT A – I'M NOT A ROCK. I'M NOT DEAD. I'M A LIVING – BABY THAT NEEDS THINGS. (Sobs) I'M SO MUCH – FROM THE VERY BEGINNING.

Shorr: But you don't need her.

Jane: What?

Shorr: But you don't need her. She's never going to give it to you. She never did. She never will. You can't hold back on all that anger lest she might turn away from you someday. You have to ...

Jane: (SCREAMS VERY LOUDLY) (Pause) I guess I need to have cried from the very beginning and yelled and screamed.

Shorr: Uh huh.

Jane: I think I feel how my sister did, now. But – my – but she could never give it to me. Like, and – and never would, you know. I mean ...

Shorr: That's why it happened in the first place, because there wasn't anyone else around that could be for you but right now, and since then, there are many that could be there for you. And then you can liberate yourself. Otherwise you stand there waiting forever for her to come through to you and she never will.

Jane: She hates to – she hates ...

Shorr: And all your anger and your ...

Jane: She hates. That's all she can probably do – is to hate.

Shorr: Yeah.

Jane: She makes me – I guess maybe I'm afraid that if I get angry too, then that's all I know how to do is to be angry.

Shorr: I don't think so. That's just a way of keeping yourself immobilized.

Jane: (SCREAMS AND CRIES LOUDLY) You know, I feel like as if babies have a right to scream like that.

Andy: You do have the right to scream. Go on. Go on. Go on.

Min: Don't muffle it, Jane. Let it go.

Andy: Don't cover it up.

Jane: (SCREAMS) I – I – I – set it off to go. Like I screamed at three weeks of age.

Shorr: At three weeks?

Jane: (SCREAMS AND SOBS LOUDLY)

Shorr: Kinda like a baby. Not like an adult. You were thirty before you're born.

Jane: (SCREAMS) I'M A BABY, I HAVE THE RIGHT TO BE ANGRY.

Shorr: Sure. Damn right.

Andy: Good.

Jane: (Pause) It doesn't feel like — it doesn't, it doesn't. I mean, you know. What is it now about being angry?.

Shorr: What does it do now?

Jane: Oh boy!

Shorr: You have never heard a baby get angry? You never saw a baby angry? Or cry?

Jane: (Pause) Yeah, because I never was.

Andy: You don't have to. You don't have to scream either.

Shorr: (IS) How about feeling like you're hungry, and you want a bottle, and what are you going to do? Go through the feeling of it. Like you're a baby — not 30 years old, remember.

Jane: But . . .

Shorr: You're hungry. Now, come on. Don't intellectualize it. You're allowed. You are *allowed* to feel hungry.

Jane: But . . .

Shorr: (Focus) SCREAM AT HER

Jane: It — you know, like — boy! Did I have it rotten when I was a real baby, you know?

Shorr: I know.

Jane: Yeah, you can do it now, Jane.

Shorr: You better! Now!

Jane: All right. I . . .

Shorr: Selfish!

Ned: Take your glasses off. 'Cause you keep touching your face and don't express yourself.

Jane: They didn't let me do that when I was a real baby, yeah. Boy, that's a good way not to get fed all right.

Andy: Just go on and scream. Now just start screaming.

Jane: (SCREAMS AND CRIES LOUDLY)

Shorr: (IS) Here's a bottle, Jane. Try it. A bottle of good milk. Try it. Take it. It's yours. (Jane is sobbing) Sorry you had to cry for it. (Jane cries) Take it. (Jane sobs) Can you drink it, Jane? Can you let yourself drink it?

Jane: Oh, no, no.

Shorr: Huh?

Jane: I'm afraid I'd throw it up.

Shorr: You're allowed.

Jane: (Sobs) I don't know whether I can drink it.

Shorr: (IS) If I put you in a straitjacket, could you take the — the bottle?

Jane: Not if I'm still angry.

Shorr: (IS) But things are better in a straitjacket. I mean, just break out of it and just drink — and enjoy it.

Jane: Oohh.

Hank: You deserve it. It's yours.

Shorr: That's what you wanted is a straitjacket.

Jane: Yeah.

Shorr: (Focus) (IS) So break out of the straitjacket and just accept that bottle.

Jane: Hooohhh! (GASPING)

Shorr: (IS) Just drink it and enjoy it. Let it be yours.

Jane: Oohh.

Shorr: Relax. (Jane is breathing hard. Shorr hums a lullaby) Let it be.

Jane: Oh!

Shorr: You don't need that straitjacket anymore. Straitjacket says you can't be human. Live by schedules, minutes, seconds. Never cry. Never feel. Never want.

Jane: I don't know where I am. I got a tingle all over. You know I don't know what's happened.

Shorr: Let it be. Just be. It's O.K. You don't have to know anything. Just — just let yourself relax and . . .

Hank: That's true.

Shorr: No one's going to hurt you. No — no schedules to meet. No requirements. No nothing. No straitjackets. (Jane is breathing hard) You're all right. (Pause) What would you like right now, Jane?

Jane: What would I like?

Shorr: Hmmm? (Jane laughs) Huh? What would you like?

Jane: Well, I don't know — I don't know where I am.

Shorr: You're O.K. You're here, and you're comfortable and, you know, among friends. Everybody loves you. (Jane sobs) That's where you are.

Hank: That's right.

Shorr: And what do you like? What would you like to have? (Jane cries) Ask for something. You'll get it.

Jane: (Sobs) I don't care.

Shorr: Come on.

Min: Come on, Jane.

Shorr: Ask for something.

Jane: Oh. (Pause) I'm ashamed.

Shorr: You are? Come on. (Jane cries) You have rights. Ask for whatever you want. Come on.

Jane: (Sobs) I don't know. I — I'm really ashamed to show all this feeling. I really am.

Hank: What do you want?

Shorr: (IS) What do you imagine a baby shows?

Jane: I don't know what a baby shows.

Shorr: O,K., what do you want? You're allowed. You hear me? You're allowed. You hear me? You're allowed.

Jane: I'm a poor baby. (Pause) I feel terrible.

Shorr: No, you're not. It doesn't feel guilty for wanting.

Jane: I don't know where I am.

Shorr: There's no guilt for wanting. It's O.K. just to be and want.

Theresa: What do you want, Jane?

Hank: (Pause) Jane, nothing has disappeared. (Jane sobs) We're right here.

Jane: (Sobbing) I am being so much of a baby, nobody will love me.

    (Pause)

Min: A real baby, Jane.

Shorr: It's normal not to be a robot, you know. You deserve everything you want. You're not a robot. You're a human being. Do you feel guilty of being human? Or needing and wanting?

Jane: That makes me feel so good.

Shorr: You're not a robot anymore. That's what she wanted.

Jane: (Sobs) That's exactly what she wanted.

Shorr: You're not that anymore.

Hank; No, that's the real you, and you have a right to have everything you want.

Jane: (Sobs and cries) I don't see why I was a robot. (Cries)

Hank: But you're not.

Shorr: Don't — don't give her that power.

Hank: No.

Shorr: How 'bout — How 'bout smiling.

Hank: You can be real. You . . .

    (Several people talk at once and Jane sobs)

Shorr: How 'bout some smiles and, uh, laughter?

Hank: Let it in.

Jane: I WANT TO BE LOVED AND CARED FOR. (Sobs)

Theresa: Don't be ashamed of it.

Jane: I'm ashamed of it. (Sobs)

Theresa: There's nobody to be ashamed of.

Jane: I'm ashamed of it. (Sobs) I am really ashamed to be. I — I sort of tingle all over. I'm afraid I'll go out of control.

Shorr: No, you won't.

Hank and Andy: No. No, you won't. (Jane sobs)

Ned: That's your circulation coming back.

Shorr: Here's the real Jane. (Jane laughs)

Jane: I'm afraid the real Jane would get killed for doing this.

Shorr: Nooo.

Jane: Oh yeah.

Shorr: No.

Jane: (Sobs) I don't know where I am. I — (Cries) I want a friend.

Hank: We all do. I do. Everybody does.

Jane: (Sobbing and crying) I went too far.

Hank: You only did what comes naturally.

Shorr: Don't be afraid to let it in, Jane. Let it happen.

Hank: Yeah.

Shorr: It's true.

Shorr: Laugh, coo, laugh — anything. (Jane laughs)

Hank: Come on. Let it in. It's great. I know it. It shows. I can feel it.

Jane: (She breaks into a beautiful smile)

    (Group laughs and talks)

Jane: (Laughing) Goo, like 'a baby. I won't act like a baby. My mother said I was so serious all the time.

    (Group laughs and talks)

Hank: Yeah, I know that's bullshit.

Shorr: Can't always think about what — follow the robot on, you know? You wanted to be a robot. She had you wired to be a robot. You had to think of your next move. How could you be anything but serious?

Jane: Yeah. I wanted that robot dead.

Shorr: Right.

Hank: You have a happiness and a joy really that, when it first came through, that — that was the first time I ever saw you that way. It came through from you.

Shorr: No more crying — (Hank talks at same time) only laughing.

Jane: It might turn into a better world, but I don't know if I really feel that.

Hank: You're in a better one now.

Jane: Yeah, I know.

Shorr: It's called "After laughing." (Group laughter)

Jane: Oh, I don't know if I can believe it. I can try. I can look at it.

Shorr: Come on. (Focus) I don't _____. (FTS) I don't want to hear the robot _____.

Jane: NO, I DON'T WANT TO HEAR THAT ROBOT AGAIN. Ah, no, I – I –

(Group: Very serious and then laughter)

Jane: . . . I HATE THAT ROBOT.

Shorr: Feel free.

Jane: Oh, God! I can't believe it. (Laughs) (Laughs) (Laughs) It might be nice. The world would really be something.

Shorr: Uh, huh.

Jane: Yeah.

Shorr: You don't need all that compulsive behavior anymore.

    (Jane sighs, then laughs. Group laughs and talks)

Hank: Oh God! You're too much — that's beautiful.

    (Group laughter)

Jane: What is the point. Oh, no. (Laughs)

Shorr: If you don't have to be compulsive, then you're free. Compulsion is a robot. You don't need that.

Jane: I don't know how to be anything else, but, gee, I can try.

Shorr: I think you've done it already.

Min: Yeah.

Hank: You're doing it right now.

Min: . . . Natural. It's there.

Shorr: You don't need the robot anymore.

Jane: WOW! IT'S REAL.

(Group laughter and talk)

Jim: You're real.

Hank: You're real.

Jane: (Laughing) I — I might ask my mother if she's real. I don't know what she'd say. (Laughs)

Shorr: She'd say, "This is a recording."

Jane: " . . . a recording."

Jim: Push the button and . . . (Jane laughs)

Jane: She's the one who isn't real — not me.

Hank: That's right! Right!

Shorr: I think we got it.

Jim: Hey, that's nice. It's kind of a nice circle here. Jesus Christ!

Shorr: My mother, the robot.

Jane: (Laughs) That's for sure.

Hank: That's right.

Andy: I think you act real.

Jane: I'm real. (Laughs)

(Group laughter and talk)

Jane: She wasn't there ever. (Laughs) She wasn't there.

Shorr: That's right. She never was. Call the robot nevermore. (Jane sighs) Now's your chance.

Hank: She was an automated mind — with a bad plug-on.

Min: Wired. (Jane laughs)

Shorr: That's right.

Jane: With a bad plug-in! (Laughs)

Shorr: That's right. She was programmed.

(Laughter)

Jane: She was. She really was sick. She got sick a long time ago and she never recovered.

Shorr: That's right.

Jane: She died, and she didn't know it.

Shorr: That's right.

(Group laughter)

Jane: God damn! That's what comes of freedom.

(Laughter)

Shorr: I can feel the coils and springs coming out of your mother now.

(Jane laughs)

Hank: Boing! Tisssh!

Jane: Now that my mother's problem is straightened out . . .

    (Laughter)

Hank: They had to put her tog — they had to screw her to put her together.

    (Laughter)

Jane: My mother's a robot.

Shorr: That's what I say!

Hank: Be glad you're human.

Jane: To have a real live baby. She had one, but I — but she didn't ever know it.

Shorr: No, she would never know it.

Jane: Oh!

Andy: You ought to teach something like that.

Hank: Yeah, this was something.

Min: (Jane is laughing) Back to your seat.

Hank: It's incredible. Something tonight. I'll tell you that.

Jane: Oh! (Laughs)

Shorr: You finally found out who your mother was.

Jane: Hah! She never had real deep problems — she just — she never was.

Shorr: That's right. She never existed.

Estelle: What's — what kind? — What's wrong.

Ned: No problems.

Andy: She never had any, because she never existed.

Jane: And I've been trying to find out a long time what happened to her.

    (Laughs)

    (Group laughter)

Hank: Mmmm. This is different, Jane. I'll let you.

Shorr: I'll tell you what really happened. She changed her oil every 5,000 miles.

Andy: She got lubed.

Jane: She squeaks, but she never gets anything. (Laughs)

Shorr: Exactly right.

Hank: And ruins every man.

Jane: Oh, really?

Hank: Really got a man.

Shorr: Terrific. Hey, there! That's great.

Hank: Oh, that's too much, Joe.

Shorr: That's right.

Jane: Oh, that's wonderful.

Shorr: You got a heart — you got a heart and your mother doesn't have one.

Jane: Really.

Shorr: Your mother doesn't have one.

Jane: Really.

Shorr: Your mother doesn't have one.

Jane: She knows. People are all around me.

Shorr: Right, Right.

Jim: That's good.

Shorr: Can't tell your mother without a program card.

Jane: (Laughs) I don't know if I can look at her again.

(Group laughter)

(Group laughter and talk)

Jane: How — how can you analyze my mother? How can you — (Laughs) I can't think of anything that can analyze her.

Shorr: I'd need — I'd need a vernier scale.

Jane: (Laughs) Yeah. That's my problem. (Laughs) I took my problems to a computer.

Shorr: My mother, the robot.

Jane: The machine shop.

Shorr: That's right. And in terms of ecology I think we know where to dump her.

(Group talk and noises)

Shorr: All right.

Jane: GOO! GOO! GOO! GOO! WAH! WAH! WAH!

Hank: Where does . . . ?

Jane: Now you've got me wondering. What did you say, dump her?

Shorr: Hmm?

Hank: Do you know where to dump her?

Jane: Oh dump — oh, yes.

Shorr: You see . . .

Jane: In a field, I guess.

Shorr: Any kind of behavior's all right. That's what you misunderstand. Not prescribed, rigid, programmed behavior.

Jane: Yeah, but why — so I can act?

Shorr: Of course. You can let go.

Jane: I was trying to be a robot all my life. (Laughs) (Group talk) She bore me, so I thought I must be a robot.

Shorr: Right, Right. Get her a pouch.

Jane: Never mind, walk into a robot.

(Group talk)

Shorr: What's that?

Ned: It's just like the shell just fell off of that . . .

(Group laughter and talk)

Andy: . . fantastic . . .

Shorr: I'm allowed to be a person. (Group talk) I'm allowed to be a person. I have to be compulsive against just being anything I want to be. That's more real than all the programmed shit in the world.

Jim: It's really nice to have you here, Jane.

(Group talk and laughter)

Hank: Welcome. Welcome to the world. (Laughter and then quiet)

Shorr: Yea. Terrific!

Hank: Boy! (Laughter) Change yourself.

Shorr: You can't — your mother won't allow you to be a baby. Like with you. How the hell could she allow you to be anything? As you grow older, there's nothing allowable ever. You're wondering whether it's allowable to cry, to — to scream, to laugh, to hold your arms — do anything.

Hank: That's right.

Shorr: It's all there. Let it be.

Hank: That's right. That's right. If a mother can't even let a baby be, for Christ's sake! What — what the hell's going to happen?

Ned: Everything, because that got beyond all her intellectual shit.

(Group talk and laughter)

Shorr: That was certainly totally non-intellectual.

Min: Yeah.

Jane: Heard myself cry like a baby, 'cause it just . . .

Min: It really did.

(Group talk)

Hank: Yeah, it sounded like a baby . . .

Min: Sounded like a baby . . .

Hank: That was a very demanding bottle. That's the truth.

Min: Undoubtedly.

Hank: Yeah.

Min: That was a baby crying.

Shorr: That was like, preverbal. Wasn't even words that could do that.

Jane: Right. (Chuckles) That was — that wasn't me, was it? (Laughter)

(Group laughter)

Shorr: That's right.

Jane: Me.

Hank: Well, it wasn't any robot. I'll tell you that.

Jane: I'm me — a real — a live person — all right. (Group laughter) I feel a lot better.

Min: So do I. (Group laughter)

(Several people talk at once)

Min: . . . Jane be?

Jane: (Laughs) I'm just going to be. I really am.

Min: Great!

Shorr: You really felt a lot. Tremendous!

Hank: You felt right back to your source of it. Incredible!

Jane: Yeah.

Shorr: I don't see anybody ever say, "Gee, I think you're too intellectual, Jane." Anyone . . . (Group chuckles) Yeah. It's 'cause It's real.

Jim: That's the way you started out, too. You said it was before the — before you could talk.

Hank: That's right.

Jim: Didn't you?

Shorr: You knew right where it was.

Hank: You really knew where it was.

Ned: Yeah, 'cause you saw her with some other baby, and you started — I saw you — it really got to you.

Jane: Right. I guess I felt it's real. Like it's really — how could you talk about something that happened. I didn't even know you could feel it.

(Laughs)

Jim: Sometimes you say some of the greatest things, Jane.

Jane: That's really good. You know, like uh — yeah — I was stopped, because I couldn't talk about. (Laughs) Oh, but I — I really thought that I can't talk about it and express it. How could I, you know, do it?

Shorr: That's — that was the robot.

Jane: It — it must be all around me. I must be helpless about it. But — I — all the time I could have held and expressed the feeling.

Shorr: Right.

Jane: But I didn't know that. (Laughs)

Shorr: See, the robot demanded the intellectual explanation.

Jane: Yeah.

Shorr: But you don't need that.

Ned: That's right.

Shorr: To hell with the explanation. Let it happen.

Jane: I would be angry again like that.

Min: Let the laughter come through, Jane. It's terrific — physically. It's beautiful. It's wonderful.

Jane: Yeah, but that's — but I can be angry too.

Min: Yeah, you can be that too.

Hank: You can do anything you want to do.

Jim: But now you can laugh too. It's just like . . .

(Group talk)

Ned: You know that your feelings are smarter than your head now.

Jane: Yeah.

(Group laughter)

Hank: That's right.

Jane: (Laughs) Yeah.

Hank: Smarter, stronger . . .

Jane: Yeah.

Hank: . . . more alive — and the whole thing.

Jane: Yeah.

Estelle: You see what happened when you let out the anger and then the laughter comes out.

Jane: Yeah.

Jim: Your feelings are smarter than your head. That's . . .
 (Group talk)
Min: Write that down, Jane.
Jim: Yeah, I just did. (Laughter)
Shorr: What was that?
Min: Feelings are . . .
Jim: Your feelings are smarter than your head. That's really neat.
Jane: WHEW! (Laughs)
Shorr: That's what you're reacting to.
Hank: No more robot.
Jane: Down with robots. Down . . . (Loudly, but with laughter)
Jim: Going to picket your mother's house tomorrow. "Down with robots!"
Jane: Bumper stickers and do a whole campaign.
Shorr: Very good. Go tell Frankenstein about this.
Hank: Yeah.
Shorr: Don't build robots.
Jane: I could have told him his mistake before he experimented.
 (Group laughter)
Min: You certainly could, Jane.
Hank: I'll never forget when − when the first laughter came through − Wow!
Jane: I really did it, didn't I?
Hank: Uh! Pretty wild. Wow!
Jim: Finally! I got my money's worth tonight.
Hank: Yeah. (Group laughter) You can't say this was boring.
 (Group laughter)
Jane: WHEW! (Sighs)

Task Imagery

 Task imagery is an additional tool for focusing, useful in the recognition of conflicts and for the possibility of change. The group as a whole is asked, for example, the task imagery (IS): "Imagine you are a fetus about to birth." Each person closes his eyes and imagines himself going through the process. The reactions, as one would expect, are enormously different. Some persons don't want to leave the warmth of the womb. Here is one man's report:

 "I find myself in a womb. It is comfortable, warm and secure. I began to feel an ever mounting pressure pushing me down towards the vagina. I resist. I prop my hands and feet against the lower wall so as not to be pushed out. The pressure mounts ever increasingly and I find myself inexorably being forced out. Great fear overwhelms me as I realize that I didn't have the strength to resist.

 "As my head exits, the fear diminishes quite a bit. All of a sudden I plop out. Fear has left me and I feel angry at those handling me so roughly, but I no longer feel afraid. In fact, I am amused at my previous fears.

"I feel that I am always afraid of transitions. I fear the event most before it happens rather than when it does actually come about. I frequently feel joy after having survived through such emotions."

I may "force" the person to make the attempt to birth, supportively urging him on. Other group members may urge him on as well. For some people, this represents the choice they must make in order to establish a new self-concept. Facing their feelings of "rottenness" and now deserving is an important element of this task imagery. Others recreate their own actual birth scene, experiencing pain or pleasure and recounting imaginary dialogues with their mothers and fathers. Feelings forgotten early in life and reminiscent imagery may erupt, clarifying some heretofore hidden self-concept. It serves as a wonderful vehicle of feeling reaction in those who observe them and may, in turn, trigger reminiscent imagery in them.

Another example of task imagery that I have used requires asking the group (IS): "Imagine a lock attached to something, and then imagine a series of keys; choose one to open the lock." The imagery develops as the person finds the right key and proceeds further as he reports what the opened lock has revealed. What has been unlocked may be deep feelings, perhaps the very most secret feelings he possesses. At some point in the sequence of the imagery he may need to redo some aspect of it or be urged on.

Ned, a forty-year-old man, reports his experience with this particular task imagery in group therapy. He is struggling with a "double bind": torn between living his own life or living the other person's life, leaving him in limbo. Here is his own report:

"The situation in group was to imagine a lock. The following is what I first saw and wished to communicate to the group. I instantly saw a large, very old-style lock on a large steel door in a steel wall — all of it colored gun-metal. It was dark, but I could see the wall and door. It's surface was very smooth and cold and covered with moisture, like dew drops. This was all apprehended immediately, and just as quickly I saw in my hand a ring of keys, all of which, save one, were old, rusted and unused. The exception, which I felt without hesitation, would open the lock — was made of gold and had brilliant rubies, emeralds encrusting it. I put it in the lock and immediately the door opened and I beheld a brilliantly colored world. It contained everything our ordinary world has, but the colors were so intense, I was caught breathless and became afraid. I, immediately, felt it the world I could have if I just would reach out and take it. I fearfully ventured out and saw the intense color lessen but remain naturally strong.

"I looked back at the door and saw it still against the rear of the door. I saw that part of this new world that would exist if the door were closed. I knew that if I closed it, that I would be forever in this new delightful world and that I could never even, if I tried, get back to that dark limbo-like tomb.

"At this time, I stopped momentarily and got no response from the group, and the imaginary situation passed to others. While others were talking, I saw a further scene in this sequence which I reported after several minutes.

"Looking back at 'limbo,' the dark side of the door, I saw a woman — she may have been my mother, my wife or as I said at the time, a Brand X female. My mother beckoned me back into limbo and pointed to another world. She seemed to deny my right to be in my world and imply that either I should live in limbo or her world.

"My world was full of intense colors; many things were irridescent and when things, birds, people, etc., moved, they left trails of color behind them for several feet. In my mother's world, the colors were almost of sunset or dawn: reds, yellows, purples, blacks, but not somber. I didn't like it, because of the limited range of color. I knew that given a choice, I would prefer limbo to living in her world and that I could reject her world without worrying about her feelings.

"My wife also beckoned me in a like manner and while my mother had beckoned me, I have not even gone into limbo or her world but had seen it from afar and had rejected it. But when my wife beckoned me, I crossed limbo and went into her world which was colored in all colors of pastel. The contours were soft. No mountains, canyons or places of danger existed in her world.

"She seemed to indicate without words that in order to have her love, not only must I accept her world as valid for her, but that I must live in it wholly, make it my own and renounce my own world. To me, this was merely a soft prison and if I were to accept it, its lack of surprise and excitement would bore me. Again, I would choose 'limbo' to this if forced to. I would prefer to live in my own world.

"I got no group response from this and it passed on again. Later I got pissed off at the group for their lack of response — this provoked some reaction. They seemed to believe my world was exclusive. However, when I visualized a woman in my world, she seemed to be in it but not constrained by it. I did not feel that she had rejected or accepted it or her own vision of life. We simply talked. I didn't withhold my appreciation of her nor she of me. It was very pleasant.

"About this time, Joe asked me to close the door back into limbo. Since I had repeatedly indicated that I felt that if I could, it would be closed forever. I felt that all that it required was an exercise of will to close the door, but when asked to do this, I felt a great reluctance to do it. I felt that the woman in limbo would be intensely hurt or injured and at the same time, I felt if I didn't close it, I'd be back in limbo soon myself. Trying very hard, the most I could do, was to shut it to the point that just its outline appeared. In order to make it easier, I imagined a vision of me as I might be. I saw beautiful scenes and places, all of these to the point of closing the door. When in interaction with the group, they called these scenes lollipops or goodies, to make it easy.

"I then allowed just any scene to come up, and I saw a volcano in violent eruption. But in all these circumstances, the almost invisible outline of the door persisted over them. At this point, however, I realized that even if I ever returned to limbo, I would never close the door which I was in limbo and that sooner or later I'd leave limbo for good and live in my own world.

"I feel the above shows my perpetual double bind about living. If I live in my world, I'll hurt those with whom I live and if I give into them, I won't be able to live except in some kind of limbo. Living in limbo denies me to them and them to me. I feel it is an expression of anger at not being allowed to be myself which punished the significant other and also myself."

Here is another report of a man in group to Task Imagery: "Imagine trying to herd a group of horses into a corral a mile away."

"I'm in the country with rolling hills all around. I can see my destination ahead and it really looks far away. I'm a little unsure as how to begin so I mounted one of the horses thinking that the rest would follow. It's not working at all. I'll try to herd them from behind. I'm riding around the back perimeter of the group, hoping to push them as a group forward. This doesn't even begin to work. I'm getting frustrated. I feel like someone has trusted me to complete this job, and I can't even get started. It's an easy job, it seems, but I can't do it. I again ride around the back of them all, trying to move them forward, but nothing. They won't budge. I can see them eating and not even noticing my presence. I'm really frustrated now. It's now like a mental block. There is no fuckin' way those horses are going to move for me.

"What started out to be a seemingly simple request is now totally impossible. I can't even force my mind to see them walking or running forward. They just won't move. I feel terrible. Joe asked me to imagine this and I can't even begin to do it. 'I can't do it, Joe; they won't move.'

Shorr: "Take charge of the situation."

"That very second Joe said 'take charge,' I ran up to the horse with confidence to move mountains, and started to slap them on the ass saying. 'Come on you sons-of-bitches, get going.' I'm running around slapping them in the butt and they are all going. I'm really in charge of the total situation. I can feel the confidence with every slap. 'Come on you sons-of-bitches, let's get going.'

"I can see the group of horses all paying close attention to what I want them to do. I've got them all running together towards the pen a mile away. I remount my horse and ride alongside of them, occasionally slapping one that gets out of the main group.

"Now I can see them all running into the pen and I close the gate behind them feeling good. I put my horse in a separate stable and give him a pat of appreciation as I walk away."

Other examples of task imagery may be utilized. Here are a few additional ones:

1. Imagine descending or ascending 1,000 steps.
2. Imagine you are caught in a blizzard and it appears that you may not be able to survive.
3. Imagine you are invisible and cannot get anyone to recognize you.

There are countless other task imageries that one can utilize as part of a focusing approach. An important part of task imagery is to ask the person to face the part of the imagery that is difficult for him. Often one must ask a person to redo the imagery in a way consistent with an attempt to change his self-image.

Body Focusing

The body focusing technique in group therapy has already been mentioned in the chapter on Imagery and the Focusing Approaches. In the section entitled, "Imagine in What Part of Your Body Your Mother Resides," the question was raised in the course of intensive group interaction. In group therapy this area can be approached by asking the entire group (IS): "In what part of your body does your anger reside?" Each person senses his or her response and, in turn, shares it with the group. Invariably, it provides the opportunity for various persons in the group to deal with unexpressed anger and to find a way of directing it towards others who have defined them falsely.

One man had his anger "buried" in his chest, and after repeated urging "to get it out," found himself imagining the experience of vomiting it out — "in a black stench." While it was done solely in his imagination it nevertheless gripped him with the reality and intensity of an anger buried for a lifetime. It was focused against his father, who had been a crushing force in his life.

It is possible to ask (IS): "In what part of your body does your joy (or revenge, or self-doubt or misery) reside?"

Here is a report by Fred, a thirty-five-year-old man, in which the Finish-the-Sentence approach led to Body Focusing imagery in a group therapy session:

" 'I must not allow myself to be' . . . was the Finish-the-Sentence question that was asked of all the members in the group. When it came my turn, I responded with, 'I must not allow myself to be *judged.*' Then I was asked to expand my statement. I began to get images of something inside of me.

"At that time I felt that there was a whole part of me inside that I had never explored. It came in the form and shape of a pie inside of me and I knew that if I could take a slice of that pie and see exactly what I really am, what my ingredients are, it would be the best thing I could do for myself. Joe then asked me to 'imagine getting inside myself to have a piece of that pie.' I closed my eyes to imagine that. I then announced that I had a knife in my right hand, and became fearful of the find. I felt I would be unable to deal with the unknown, good or bad. Immediately, I thought of my relationship with music. What if I spent most of my thirty-five years in the wrong direction? What if I didn't want to be a musician? The truth would be too painful to see. The group urged me to take a chance. At first, I balked, but suddenly I said, 'O.K.' I don't even recall why it was as easy to say, 'I'll take a piece of pie,' as it was to resist through my fear. But I did agree.

"As I closed my eyes, I remember feeling only a slight self-consciousness. I was having great difficulty getting the knife near my body. I started squirming uncontrollably. My face contorted as the resistance grew stronger. Then I said to myself, 'There is a beautiful part of me in that pie that I should see.' Yet, I still hesitated.

"Somebody made a joke about something. I didn't hear it, but in the background, I did hear the laughter. I felt judged. Maybe the joke was the amount of time I was taking. I was getting colder and more frightened. Time rolled on. As the frustration of the moment mounted, it was like holding your nose and jumping into a swimming pool for an early morning dip, suddenly I made the incision. I cut from the upper hip bone on my left side down through the base of my pelvic bone. And I sliced again to form a piece of pie. I guess I was crying. I know I was.

"I opened my eyes to examine what I held in my hand. I had good feelings about what had just transpired. Christ! It was exactly what I did not want to see! Pie that was filled with the alphabet, emerged in a black, sticky substance, a filler like one would find in a blueberry pie. The letters of the alphabet all seemed to spell out the word 'judgment' hundreds of times. I put the pie down on the floor and looked away from it disheartened that I found what I knew was there somewhere inside me. It was in the way of something perhaps beautiful.

"Joe asked, could I change pies. I agreed to change fillings, but I felt the crust was good. I wished to leave it alone. I made the filler switch. Its ingredients were woven into space. Letters spelled out self-discovery, creativity, energy, vitality, essence. All floating around in my new pie filling. I felt much better. Really peaceful. Slowing down. The moments were longer. No pressure. No demands. I was floating around in space somewhere, at my own pace. I didn't know who I was. I expressed to the group my desire to savor things. 'I would like to be able to dissect things and follow them through to their essence.' I guess a long time went by.

"I heard Joe ask me if I'd like a drink of clear spring water. His voice sounded barely audible. I felt I was in a trance of some kind.

"I said, 'Why not. Sounds as good as anything.' I bent over and took in a mouthful of water from a brook. Sitting back in my chair and closing my eyes, I swallowed the water very slowly following it down my throat and into my stomach. I drank more. It tasted so good and I was in tune with my experience. Peace.

"Joe suggested that I get up and say something to each member of the group. I remember floating over to Jane and telling her how sad I was for her putting herself in an impossible bind during Christmas holiday.

" 'Liza, you are beautiful!' I said.

"I don't recall what I said to Hank.

" 'Richard, I wish I could really get to know you, because I like your sense of being human.' Richard expressed that he would like that, someday.

" 'Lynne, I wish you really knew me. I don't show too much of myself to you.' She responded with her lovely smile.

"On to Jim. 'You're still a little too heavy for me. I respect your growth, but you're too down and weighty. I can't handle that yet.' I don't remember how Jim responded to that.

"I told Angie that she should slow her movements down. She agreed completely.

" 'Helen, you really, show me somebody in this group, but I don't know who it really is, because it sure as hell isn't you. I haven't the foggiest who you really are.' She stared at me like a poor, wounded animal.

" 'Eloise, I respect your contributions to the people in the group. You have fine insight. But I don't know who *you* are. You are very quiet about yourself.'

" 'Hale, whatever I have done to help you get your new job is purely an act of friendship and nothing more. I have no other interests invested. I also feel that at this moment in your life, you are walking a tightrope without a net.'

"I don't remember what I said to Joe, but I remember remaining peaceful.

"I realized I had to start to know Dennis sooner or later, so I shook his hand slowly drawled, 'Hey!' My eyes got teary.

"I didn't feel nervous throughout the group experience, and the few times I started to feel slightly self-conscious, I quickly nipped the feeling in the bud. I wasn't afraid of anybody or anything. It was a beautiful feeling.

"I can call myself a 'judgaholic.' I have to deal with it from day to day. And I am. Soon it will be easier to deal with. It will be an enemy for awhile. But not forever."

Debra had tried to develop changes in her attitude towards her father, who had rejected her. That relationship had influenced all her relationships with men. Using the Body Focusing approach, she (IS) imagined entering her father's body. Other approaches had been attempted previously with no change in her attitude. This Body Focusing experience was able to make a change in her self-image and her attitude towards men:

"He is sitting rigidly, as usual, and stiffly in the chair in the living room, listening to some dreary and heavy music. I close my eyes and climb up his arm which is warm and hairy and enter through his mouth, because he ate delicious corned beef and lots of dill pickles and it smells good — indeed it is warm and smooth and dark but not a bit scary — I climb up and down, onto his ribs and play like it is a ladder. I come towards the front and pat his heart — it is beating softly and evenly and I touch it — I put my ear next to it. I climb down into his legs and they are crossed so it is annoying. I'd like to uncross them and slide up and down. So I go up again past the delicious smells in his stomach and up into his throat where he is humming softly, and then up into his head — the brain in his head is moaning softly and I am impatient — I see the images of dark, poverty-stricken farms and I put my fingers softly in the brain tissues and will good and happy images to appear — I hear and feel some movement. I climb down towards his legs again and see a ghastly sight. He is having trouble walking and I can see why. The entrance to his penis is blocked and sore, like a lump of clay has hardened and the tissue is irritated all around it. I am enraged and sick and angry and can't wait to dislodge it — tenderly and most carefully I try to loosen it without making too much noise, but it soon comes loose and I am so angry I just pull it out and climb up and out of his mouth very quickly and throw it a mile away. Then just as quickly I climb back up into his mouth and back down into his penis and softly touch it to see if it isn't sore anymore — and I climb down into his legs and I feel his muscles tensing up as if he would like to run, and I climb back into his brain and will another part of it to play great early jazz, and I can hear him laughing and I hear him calling, 'Debra, Debra, where are you? Let's go for a walk. Come on now. I'll carry you on my shoulders and we can walk around the block. Listen to that music — isn't it wonderful? Come on, Debra, it's time for daddy and his little girl to have fun!!!!!!!!!!' "

Some Concluding Observations

The use of imagery in individual therapy and group therapy is ever increasing. In order to study imagery in a systematic way, one must be concerned with:

1. The use of imagery to make the patient aware of his internal conflicts between historical negative self-concepts and his potentially positive contemporary self-concepts. This involves the use of Dual Imagery, Body Route Imagery, Nonsymbolic Imagery, as well as Symbolic Imagery.

2. The use of imagery to help the person focus for a change in his self-definition against the archaic forces and self-defeating defenses. This involves the use of Cathartic Imagery, Task Imagery, and many Body Focusing Imageries.

3. The use of imagery when combined with dialogue to heighten awareness and focus for change. The use of listening to one's own Imagery and Dialogue audiotape at a later point as a further possibility of awareness and change.

4. The use of imagery in group therapy for the awareness of internal conflicts which involves Dual Imagery, Group Imagery and Body Route Imagery. Additionally, the use of imagery as Cathartic Imagery, Task Imagery and the various Body Focusing Imageries in the focusing approaches for change.

5. The infinite possibilities of creativity on the part of the therapist and his patients to utilize therapy more effectively in order to help resolve their conflicts.

CHAPTER VI

Summary

A person's imagery, more than any other mental function, indicates how he organizes his world. The central importance of imagery in man has been eloquently stated by Sylvia Ashton Warner, who has taught children of Moiri tribesmen in New Zealand and children in Colorado. She states: "The pictures in (man's) mind are part of his mind as an organ is part of his body, are indispensable to the life of the mind as the heart to the body." (Warner, 1972, p.14)

Only in the last decade has the function of imagination regained respectability among psychological investigators. In addition, the use of visual imagery as a therapeutic agent in individual and group therapy from the Behaviorists, Gestaltists and the Psychosynthesis group has mushroomed and is gaining momentum. But, while the experimental investigation of imagination and imagery has increased enormously in the work of Singer (1965), Segal (1971), Pavio (1971), Richardson (1969), Sheehan (1972), Klinger, et al. (1971), the systematic investigation of imagery in psychotherapy has not been attempted within a large scope of dimensions. The experimentalist engaged in the investigation of imagery, invariably, does not carry a *full* work load of psychotherapy with his patients. Likewise, the psychotherapist engaged in the full time psychotherapeutic experience with patients would be hard put to set up experimental designs. In this book I have been aware of this schism since my own emphasis has been almost exclusively in the practice of psychotherapy. However, whenever and wherever possible, I have attempted to incorporate what the experimentalist has made known to us into the psychotherapeutic experience. From this book one hopes the researcher will gain insights to incorporate into his experimental designs. Both the researcher and the clinician should complement each other's work.

Allow me to point out at least one example of how research and clinical experience can complement each other. Goldberger and Holt (1958) studied fourteen subjects who spent eight hours lying in isolation in a soundproof room under conditions of uniform stimulation. Diffused light let in through halved ping pong balls covering the eyes, were used in combination with a steady input of monotonous white noise through earphones. While the visual imagery of some subjects became quite bizarre in their isolation, they did not necessarily mistake these images, however bizarre, for hallucinatory perceptions. Goldberger and Holt concluded that reality testing remained relatively unimpaired while the sensory functions were involved in the experience of imagery. The subjects' capacity for judging the plausability and implausability of such experiences was also unimpaired.

Patients deeply immersed in their own imagery with powerful reactions and feelings even for prolonged periods in a therapeutic session do not lose their power of reality testing however bizarre and weird the imagery may be. Neurotic patients will emerge with no impairment in their judgment of the plausability or implausability of their imagery. I have observed it with hundreds of patients over thousands of hours in deep imagery involvement. This conclusion then, can be reached from both vantage points of experience, experimental or clinical.

I do not know of any psychotherapeutic procedures that do not depend in one manner or another on the presence of imagery. Is there a psychotherapeutic procedure that does not depend on the patient's ability to recall and to recreate situations and persons, real or imagined, which are a central part of a person's inner world regardless of whether they are verbalized in a therapy session? Sheehan accurately states, "Only through the image can they be actualized and 'animated' and so brought into relationship with each other, with the person of the therapist and with the here-and-now of the patient's actual life circumstances." (Sheehan, 1972, p. 73.)

Perhaps the most important factor about imagery as it is used in psychotherapy is its ability to bypass the usual censorship of the person. Lowenstein (1956) makes the point that the patient through hearing himself vocalize may control his own reactions to his thoughts. In short, he is "editing" and in so doing attempts to control the reactions of the analyst. Because we cannot usually tell in advance what effect or meaning the imagery will have, we may reveal in imagery what we would not ordinarily reveal in verbal conversation. The use of imagery has a prime value in that it can help break resistances usually found in verbal transactions. Indeed, we reach a near ultimate of the elimination of verbal insights and analysis by the exclusive use of symbolic imagery.

Another function of imagery that has special relevance to psychotherapy is the fact that images can be transformed, reexperienced and reshaped in line with a healthier self-concept. Gardner Murphy anticipated the concept of transformation of imagery when he stated: "But images . . . are manipulated just as are muscular acts, and they may be rearranged, freshly reconstituted, to give new and better satisfactions." (Murphy, 1947, p. 550.) In this book the development of the concept of transformation of images is demonstrated by use of Task Imagery, Cathartic Imagery and Body Focusing.

The patient's awareness of his internal conflicts should be one of the most important functions of imagery. This complementary opposition within experience results in a bipolarization of imagery. Dual Imagery is an impressive means of demonstrating this phenomenon. Other methods that help define conflicts involve concrete Nonsymbolic Imagery, Symbolic Imagery, Imagery in Dreams as well as Depth Imagery. The implication is that the patient in becoming aware of his internal conflicts can hopefully do something to resolve them.

In this book, I have tried to emphasize that imagery can be comingled with dialogue to develop meanings and awareness during therapeutic sessions. There are others who work exclusively with Symbolic Imagery who would prefer a hypnoidal state that tends to minimize dialogue. My own opinion is that both procedures should be utilized so long as it serves the best interest of the patient. Moreover, the possibility of greater awareness in the patient is increased by listening to audiotapes of his sessions with special reference to his own imagery.

Insofar as group therapy is concerned, the systematic use of imagery is presented covering a wide range of areas. These include Cathartic Imagery, Dual Imagery; the use of the patient's own imagination in interaction with the other members; the Transformation of imagery; Group Imagery; the use of Task Imagery and Body Focusing.

It is all but impossible to imagine a therapist that had poor knowledge and experience of his own images. Again, Sheehan graphically clarifies this point: "Where his capacity to image is limited, there he fails to comprehend with ease the experience of his patient; in fact he may be tempted to disregard, disbelieve or dismiss those experiences of his patients which his own imaginal disposition does not allow him to share." (Sheehan, 1972, p. 73.) It appears sound to assume that the greater the range of imagery the therapist possesses, the greater his effectiveness.

A practical application of the active use of imagery for the patient when not in a therapy session is for him to receive greater awareness and increased meaning from the stream of images in his waking existence. One patient reported that when he was in a state of anxiety, he asked himself to imagine something different in each hand and then proceeded to speak to each image in turn. From his images, he began to clarify the conflicts beneath his anxiety, developed increased meaning and then set a course of behavior that he felt would resolve the conflict. Certainly, when one can learn to transform negative images into positive images, greater control over the anticipation of events and pessimism may be secured. It is possible for the patient to develop this skill independent of the therapist following a certain therapeutic experience using imagery.

The creative use of imagery in psychotherapy whether it be by the patient or therapist is a goal not to be achieved for its own sake. The range of the dimensions inherent in helping a patient make a basic change within himself are so vast that creativity becomes mandatory if we are to meet the formidable problems therapy presents.

BIBLIOGRAPHY

Alexander, Eugene D. In-the-Body-Travel: A Growth Experience with Fantasy. *Psychotherapy.* Vol. 8, No. 4, Winter 1971 (319-324).

Assagioli, Roberto. *Psycho-Synthesis: A Manual of Principles and Techniques.* New York: Hobbs, Dorman, 1965.

Bach, G. R. *Intensive Group Therapy.* New York: Ronald Press, 1954.

Bachelard, Gaston. *The Psychoanalysis of Fire.* Boston, Beacon Press, 1964.

Barron, Frank. *Creativity and Personal Freedom.* New York: D. Van Nostrand, 1968.

Bartlett, Francis. Significance of Patients' Work on the Therapeutic Process. *Contemporary Psychoanalysis.* Vol. 9, No. 4, August, 1973 (405-416).

Battegay, R. Individual Psychotherapy and Group Psychotherapy as Single Treatment Methods and in Combination. *Acta Psychiatricia Scandinavica.* 48: 1972 (43-48).

Berdach, Elsie and Backan, Paul. Body Position and the Free Recall of Early Memories. *Psychotherapy Theory, Research and Practice* Vol. 4, No. 3 1967 (101-102).

Binswanger, L. *Being-In-The-World: Selected Papers of Ludwig Binswanger.* J. Needleman (Trans.). New York:Basic Books, 1963.

Binswanger, Ludwig, *Grundformen und Erkenntnis menschlichen Daseins.* 2nd Edition, Zurich: Niehans Verlag, 1953.

Binswanger, Ludwig. *Sigmund Freud: Reminscences of a Friendship.* New York: Grune & Stratton, 1957.

Boss, Medard. *The Analysis of Dreams.* New York: Philosophical Library, 1958.

Brenman, M., Gill, M., and Knight, R. Spontaneous Fluctations in the Depth of Hypnosis. In *Psychoanalytic Psychiatry and Psychology,* edited by R. K. Knight. Austin Riggs Monograph Series, Vol. 1. New York: International Universities Press, 1954.

Breuer, J. and Freud, S. *Studies in Hysteria.* (1895) Standard Edition, 2. London: Hogarth Press, 1953.

Bugental, J. F. T. *Challenge of Humanistic Psychology.* New York:McGraw-Hill, 1967.

Buhler, C. and Massarik, F. *The Course of Human Life. A Study of Goals in Humanistic Perspective.* New York: Springer, 1968.

Burnham. D., Gladston, A., Gibson, R. *Schizophrenia and the Need-Fear Dilemna.* New York: International Universities Press, 1969.

Caslant, E. *Method of Development of the Supernormal Faculties.* Paris: Meyer, 1927.

Clynes, Manfred. Sentics: Biocybernetics of Emotion Communication. *Annals of the New York Academy of Sciences.* Vol. 200, No. 3, 1973 (57-131).

Dellas, Marie and Gaier, E. M. Identifications of Creativity. *Psychological Bulletin.* 73-55-73, 1970.

Demille, R. *Put Your Mother on the Ceiling.* New York: Viking Press, 1973.

Desoille, R. *The Directed Daydream.* Monograph No. 8. New York: The Psychosynthesis Research Foundation, 1965.

Ellenberger, Henri, F. *The Discovery of the Unconscious.* New York: Basic Books, 1970.

Fingarette, H. *The Self in Transformation.* New York: Basic Books, 1963.

Fisher, C. A. A Study of the Preliminary Stages of the Construction of Dreams and Images. *Journal of the American Psychoanalytic Association.* Vol. 5, 1967 (5-60).

Fisher, Seynour. *Body Experience in Fantasy and Behavior*. New York: Appleton Century Crofts, 1970.

Fisher, Seymour. *Body Consciousness*. Englewood Cliffs, New Jersey: Prentice Hall, 1973.

Forenczi, Sandor. *Final Contributions to the Problems and Methods of Psychoanalysis*. New York: Basic Books, 1955.

Forenczi, Sandor. *Further Contributions to the Theory and Technique of Psychanalysis*. London: The Hogarth Press, 1950.

Frankl, Victor. *Man's Search for Meaning*. Boston: Beacon Press, 1966.

Freud, Anna. *The Ego and the Mechanisms of Defense*. New York: International Universities Press, 1946.

Freud, Sigmund. *The Ego and the Id*. New York: Norton, 1923.

Freud, Sigmund. *An Autobiographical Study*. (1925) Standard Edition. 12: 3-70. London: Hogarth Press, 1959.

Freud, Sigmund. *Character and Culture*. New York: Collier Books, 1963.

Freud, Sigmund. *On Creativity and the Unconscious*. New York: Basic Books, 1970.

Freytag, Fredericka F. *Hypnosis and the Body Image*. New York: Julian Press, 1961.

Frisch, Max. *I'm Not Stiller*. New York: Vantage Books. 1958.

Fromm, Erich. Remarks on the Problem of Free Association. *Psychiatric Research Reports 2*. American Psychiatric Association, 1955.

Gary, Romain. *The Roots of Heaven*. New York: Simon & Schuster, 1958.

Gendlin, E. *Experiencing and the Creation of Meaning*. New York: The Free Press of Glencoe, 1962.

Goldberger, L. and Holt, R. Experimental Interference with Reality Contact (Perceptual Isolation): Method and Group Results. *Journal of Nervous and Mental Disease Disorders*. Vol. 127,(99-112).

Gorman, Warren. *Body Image and the Image of the Brain*. St. Louis: Warren Green, 1969.

Gruenwald, D. Hypnotic Technique without Hypnosis in the Treatment of Dual Personality. *The Journal of Nervous and Mental Disease*. Vol. 153, No. 1, 1971. (41-46).

Hammer, Max. The Directed Daydream Technique. *Psychotherapy*. Vol. 4, No. 4, November 1967. (173-181).

Hammer, Max. *The Theory and Practice of Psychotherapy with Specific Disorders*. Springfield, Illinois: Charles C Thomas, 1972.

Healy, William, Bronner, Augusta, and Bowers, Anna. *The Structure and Meaning of Psychoanalysis*. New York: Alfred A. Knopf, 1930.

Hilgard, E. R. and Tart, C. T. Responsiveness to Suggestion Following Induction of Hypnosis, *Journal of Abnormal Psychology*. Vol. 71, 1966 (196-208).

Hilgard, Josephine R. *Personality and Hypnosis*. Chicago. University of Chicago Press, 1970.

Holt, R. R. Imagery: The Return of the Ostracised. *American Psychologist*. Vol. 19, 1964. (254-264).

Horney, Karen. *Neurosis and Human Growth*. New York: W. W. Norton, 1950.

Horney, Karen. *Our Inner Conflicts*. New York: W. W. Norton, 1945.

Horowitz, Mardi. *Image Formation and Cognition*. New York: Appleton Century Crofts, 1970.

Horowitz, M. and Becker, Stephanie S. The Compulsion to Repeat Trauma: Experimental Study of Intrusive Thinking after Stress. *Journal of Nervous and Mental Disease*. Vol. 153, No. 1, July 1971. (32-40).

Jellinek, Augusta. Spontaneous Imagery: A New Psychotherapeutic Approach. *American Journal of Psychotherapy*. Vol. 3, No. 3, July 1949. (372-391).

Jones, E. *Papers on Psychoanalysis* (Fourth Edition). London: Bailliere, Tindall and Cox, 1948.

Jung, C. and G. *Memories, Dreams, Reflections*. Edited by Arriela Jaffe. New York: Pantheon Books, 1961.

Jung, Carl, G. *Contributions to Analytical Psychology*. New York: Harcourt Brace, 1928.

Kanzer, M. Image Formation during Free Association. *Psychoanalytic Quarterly*. Vol. 27, 1958. (475-485).

Klein, George. *Perception, Motives and Personality*. New York: Alfred A. Knopf, 1970.

Klinger, Eric. *Structure and Functions of Fantasy*. New York: Wiley Interscience, 1971.

Kubie, L. The Induced Hypnotic Reverie in the Recovery of Regressed Amnesic Data. *Bulletin of the Meninger Clinic*. 7, 1943.

Laing, R. D. Violence and Love. *Journal of Existentialism*. Vol. V, No. 20, Summer 1965. (411-422).

Laing, R. D., Phillipson, H., and Lee, A. R. *Interpersonal Perception*. New York: Springer, 1966.

Laing, R. D. *The Divided Self*. Chicago: Quadrangle Books, 1962.

Laing, R. D. *The Self and Others*. Chicago: Quadrangle Books, 1962.

Leuner, Hanscarl. Guided Affective Imagery, (GAI) A Method of Intensive Psychotherapy. *American Journal of Psychotherapy* Vol. 23, No. 1, January 1969. (4-22).

Lowenstein, R. M. Some Remarks on the Role of Speech in Psychoanalytic Technique. *International Journal of Psychoanalysis*. Vol. 37, 1956 (460-467).

Maddi, Salvatore, The Search for Meaning. *Nebraska Symposium on Motivation*. Lincoln: University of Nebraska Press, 1970.

Maslow, A. H. *Toward a Psychology of Being*. Van Nostrand. Princeton, New Jersey, 1962.

May, Rollo. Passion for Form. *Review of Existential Psychology and Psychiatry*. Vol. VII, No. 1, Winter 1967. (6-12).

May, Rollo. On the Phenomenological Bases of Psychotherapy. *Review of Existential Psychology and Psychiatry*. Vol. 4, No. 1, Winter, 1964. (22-36).

May, Rollo, Angell, E., and Ellenberger, H. F. *Existence: A New Dimension of Psychiatry and Psychology*. New York: Basic Books, 1958.

Miller, Arthur. "The Role of P. E. N." *Saturday Review*. Vol. 4, June 1966.

Murphy, Gardner, *Personality. A Biosocial Approach to Origins and Structure*. New York: Harper, 1947.

Nye, Robert D. *Conflict Among Humans*. New York: Springer, 1973.

Paivio, Allan. Imagery and Synchronic Ideation. *Abstract Guide*. XXth International Congress of Psychology. Tokyo, Japan. 1972. (127-128).

Paivio, Allan. *Imagery and Verbal Processes*. New York: Holt, Rinehart and Winston, 1971.

Perls, F., Hefferline, R. F., and Goodman, P. *Gestalt Therapy*. New York: Dell, 1951.

Reiff and Scheerer. *Memory and Hypnotic Age Regression*. New York: International Universities Press, 1959.

Reyher, J. Free Imagery. *Journal of Clinical Psychology*. Vol. 19, 1963 (454-459).

Richardson, Alan. *Mental Imagery*. New York: Springer, 1969.

Rossi, Ernest Lawrence. *Dreams and the Growth of Personality*. New York: Pergamon Press, 1972.

Sadler, William A. *Existence and Love. A New Approach to Existential Phenomenology*. New York: Charles Scribner Sons, 1969.

Schacter, S. and Singer, J. E. Cognitive, Social and Physiological Determinants of Emotional States. *Psychological Revue* Vol. 69, 1962. (379-399).

Schutz, W. C. *Joy. Expanding Human Awareness*. New York: Grove Press, 1967.

Segal, Sydney and Glicksman, Michael. Relaxation and the Perky Effect; The Influence of Body Position on Judgement of Imagery. *American Journal of Psychology*. Vol. 60, 1967. (257-262).

Segal, Sydney J. (Editor) *Imagery: Current Cognitive Processes*. New York: Academic Press, 1971.

Seidenberg, R. Who Owns the Body? *Existential Psychiatry.* Summer-Fall 1969. (93-105).

Shahn, Ben. Imagination and Intention. *Review of Existential Psychiatry.* Vol. VII, No. 1, Winter 1967. (13-17).

Shapiro, David L. The Significance of the Visual Image in Psychotherapy. *Psychotherapy: Theory, Research and Practice.* Vol. 7, No. 4, Winter 1970. (209-212).

Sheehan, Peter W. *The Function and Nature of Imagery.* New York: Academic Press, 1972.

Sheehan, P. W. Functional Similarity of Imagining to Perceiving. *Perceptual and Motor Skills.* Vol. 23, 1966. (1011-1013).

Shorr, Joseph E. *Psycho-Imagination Therapy: The Integration of Phenomenology and Imagination.* New York: Intercontinental Medical Book Corp., 1972.

Shorr, Joseph E. The Existential Question and the Imaginary Situation as Therapy. *Existential Psychiatry.* Vol. 6, No. 24, Winter 1967. (443-462).

Shorr, Joseph, E. In What Part of Your Body Does Your Mother Reside? *Psychotherapy: Theory, Research and Practice.* Volume 10, No. 2, Summer 1973. (31-34).

Shorr, Joseph E. The Use of Task Imagery as Therapy. *Psychotherapy: Theory, Research and Practice.* (In press).

Silberer, H. Report on a Method of Eliciting and Observing Certain Symbolic Hallucinations Phenomena. In Rapaport (Ed.). *Organization and Pathology of Thought.* New York: Columbia University Press, 1951.

Singer, Jerome L. Imagery and Daydream Techniques Employed in Psychotherapy: Some Practical and Theoretical Implications. In Spielberger, C. (Ed.). *Current Topics in Clinical and Community Psychology.* Vol. 3. New York: Academic Press, 1971.

Singer, Jerome, L. *Daydreaming: An Introduction to the Experimental Study of Inner Experience.* New York: Random House, 1966.

Singer, Jerome L. *The Child's World of Make-Believe.* New York: Academic Press, 1973.

Smith, Barbara Hernstein. The New Imagism. *Midway.* Vol. 9, No. 3, Winter 1969. (27-44).

Spiegel, Rose. Specific Problems of Communication in Psychiatric Conditions. *American Handbook of Psychiatry.* Vol. I. Silvano Arieti. (Ed.). New York: Basic Books. New York, 1959.

Stampfl, T. G. and Leavis, D. J. Essentials of Implosive Therapy; A Learning Theory Based on Psycho-Dynamic Behavioral Therapy. *Journal of Abnormal Psychology.* Vol. 72, 1967. (496-503).

Straus, Erwin W. (Ed.) *Phenomenology, Pure and Applied.* Pittsburgh: Duquesne University Press, 1964.

Szalita, A. B. Renalysis. *Contemporary Psychoanalysis.* Vol. 4, No. 2, Spring 1968. (83-102).

Szalita, A. B. Regression and Perception in Psychotic States. *Psychiatry.* Vol. 12, 1958. (53).

Tart, Charles T. (Ed.) *Altered States of Consciousness.* New York: John Wiley, 1969.

Tillich, Paul. *The Courage To Be.* New Haven: Yale University Press, 1952.

Ullman, Montague. Dreams and the Therapeutic Process. *Psychiatry.* Vol. 21, No. 2, May 1958. (123-131).

Van Den Berg, J. An Existential Explanation of the Guided Daydream in Psychotherapy. *Review of Existential Psychiatry.* Vol. II, No. 1, Winter 1962. (5-35).

Vernon, J. A. *Inside the Black Room.* New York: Clarkson N. Potter, Inc., 1963.

Vespe, Raymond, Ontological Analysis and Synthesis in Existential Psychotherapy. *Existential Psychiatry.* Summer-Fall 1967. (26-27), 83-92.

Wann, T. W. *Behaviorism and Phenomenology.* Chicago: University of Chicago Press, 1964.

Warner, Sylvia A. *Spearpoint.* New York: Alfred Knopf, 1972.

Warren, M. Significance of Visual Images during the Analytic Session. *Journal of the American Psychoanalytic Association.* Vol. 9, 1961. (504-518).

Weisman, Avery D. *The Existential Core of Psychoanalysis.* Boston: Little Brown & Co. 1965.

Weisskopf-Joelson, E. Experimental Studies of "Meaning" through Integration. *Annals of the New York Academy of Sciences.* Patterns of Integration from Biochemical to Behavioral Process. Vol. 193 (260-272).

Werner, H. and Kaplan, B. *Symbol Formation: An Organismic Developmental Approach to Language and the Expression of* Thought. New York: Wiley, 1962.

Wilson, Colin. *New Pathways in Psychology. Maslow and the Post Freudian Revolution.* New York: Taplinger Publishing Co., 1972.

Wolf, Alexander and Schwartz, Emanuel K. *Psychoanalysis in Groups.* New York: Grune & Stratton, 1962.

Wolpe, J. *The Practice of Behavior Therapy.* New York: Pergamon Press, 1969.

Zubek, John P. (Ed.) *Sensory Deprivation: Fifteen Years of Research.* New York: Appleton Century Crofts, 1969.

INDEX

Adler, Alfred, 7, 19
Alexander, Eugene, D., 137
Assagioli, Roberto, 7, 18, 50, 51, 68
Autochthonous, 69
Aversive conditioning, 5

Bach, George, 137
Bachelard, Gaston, 7, 8
Barron, Frank, 15, 22
Becker, S. S., 49
Behaviorists, 6, 181
Bernanos, 136
Binswanger, L., 26
Body focusing, 61, 75, 176, 177, 179, 180, 182, 183
Body routes to conflict, 43, 160, 180
Body touching and holding, 61, 74, 75
Brenman, M., 18
Breuer, J., 2, 26
Buber, Martin, 136
Burnham, D., 16, 17

Caslant, E., 7, 8, 50
Cathartic Imagery, 141, 162, 180, 182, 183
Clynes, Manfred, 14
Concentration technique, 2
Conditioning, aversive, 5
Countertransference resistance, 17
Creativity of patient, utilizing, 144

Daydream, 13, 50
Delusions, 1
Depth imagery, 58, 59, 60, 182
Desoille, R., 7, 8, 18, 50, 69, 137
Despised image, 10, 11
Directed imagery, 48
Diversionary imagery, 67
Dreams, 1, 11, 13, 17, 54, 55, 56, 57
Dual imagery, 22-32, 37, 140, 180, 182, 183

Fantasies, 2
    forced, 4

Feeding, principle of, 69
Finish-the-Sentence, 22, 31, 49, 139, 140
Fischer, C. A., 18
Forenczi, Sandor, 2, 4
Forethought and imagination, 15
Four walls, 41
Fragmented images, 17
Frankl, Victor, 11
Franklin, Benjamin, 1
Free association, 2, 19
Free imagery, 4, 19
Fretigny, 7
Freud, Anna, 5
Freud, Sigmund, 2, 3, 4, 7, 8, 17, 18, 26, 50, 54
"Frightening events, fascination for," 21
Frisch, Max, 136
From the universal to the specific, 47
Fromm, Erich, 5

Gary, Romain, 11, 12
Gendlin, Eugene, 50
Gerard, Robert, 51
Gestalt therapists, 6, 181
Gibson, R., 18
Gill, M., 18
Gladstone, A., 16, 17
Goldberger, L., 181
Good guts vs. bad guts, 87
Greene, Graham, 136
Group imagery, 143, 183
Guided affective imagery, 8, 50

Hallucination, 13
Hammer, Max, 18, 19, 69, 70
Happich, Carl, 7
Hartman, Heinz, 5
Hemingway, Ernest, 136
Hitler, A., 136
Hold, R. R., 181
Horney, Karen, 7, 10, 11
Horowitz, Mardi, 5, 49
Hypnosis, 2

189